THREE WEEKS EIGHT SECONDS

THE EPIC TOUR DE FRANCE OF 1989

NIGE TASSELL

POLARIS PUBLISHING

First published in 2017 by

POLARIS PUBLISHING LTD
c/o Turcan Connell
Princes Exchange
1 Earl Grey Street
Edinburgh
EH3 9EE

in association with

ARENA SPORT
An imprint of Birlinn Limited
West Newington House
10 Newington Road
Edinburgh
EH9 1QS

www.polarispublishing.com
www.arenasportbooks.co.uk

ISBN: 978-1-909715-53-0
eBook ISBN: 978-0-85790-344-0

British Library Cataloguing-in-Publication Data
A catalogue record for this book is available on request from the British Library.

Designed and typeset by Polaris Publishing, Edinburgh

Printed in Great Britain by Clays, St Ives

CONTENTS

To the memory of Pat Williamson

'Tis best to weigh the enemy more mighty than he seems

Henry V, Act II, Scene IV

PRELUDE

YOU COULD HEAR the helicopter before you could see it.

It was getting louder, getting closer, with each second. The chop of its blades was cutting right through the peace of the early morning, across the rolling hills and perfect-blue California skies. For those on the ground, it was the best sound of all. It was the sound of hope.

Usually on highway patrol duty, monitoring the rush-hour traffic on the roads feeding into Sacramento, the helicopter's crew had had a quiet morning. Easter Monday. A day for commuters to leave their cars on the driveway, to kick back, to relax.

Quiet until a few minutes ago.

Rather than attend a minor auto accident, the crew diverted to a more pressing assignment, one they just happened to overhear on the emergency radio. An early-morning, three-man hunting expedition had gone very wrong here in the western foothills of the Sierra Nevada mountains. One of the hunters, dressed in battle fatigues and crouching in a berry bush, had slowly risen up to assess the positions of his party. A second hunter mistakenly interpreted the upward movement as being that of a wild turkey. His trigger response, from around 30 yards away, inundated the victim's back and side with around 60 buckshot pellets. The victim was the shooter's brother-in-law.

The flashing lights of various emergency vehicles on the ground guided the helicopter pilot to the correct location. As the chopper came in to land, the victim could be seen on a stretcher, his shirt cut open, an intravenous drip attached. He was conscious but, because of a collapsed lung, was finding it difficult to both breathe and talk. He was also bleeding heavily and in need of urgent surgery, but an uncomfortable ambulance ride to the nearest hospital would have very much lowered his chances of survival. Not only would getting airborne speed up the victim's rescue, but it would also mean that he could be taken to a different medical unit, one that, while further away, was more appropriate for his needs. It specialised in gunshot wounds and trauma, boasting a permanent on-call team employed to stymie Sacramento's high murder count.

With the severely wounded patient carefully placed on board, eleven minutes later the chopper landed on the helipad on the roof of the University of California Davis Medical Center. By this time, the hospital had called the victim's wife. She was at home making breakfast pancakes for the couple's two-year-old son. 'Is he dead?' she asked. 'No, at this moment he's alive.' Eight months pregnant, she was soon on her way, with toddler in the back, driving the 20 or so miles into Sacramento along thankfully quiet roads.

The surgeons' diagnosis confirmed the gravity of the situation – and the vital, life-saving intervention of the highway patrol crew. Another 20 minutes and the victim would have bled to death. He had already lost four pints of blood, half the capacity of the human body.

The next few hours were taken up by surgery as the team repaired his collapsed lung and removed pellets from his liver, kidneys and intestines. But it was too dangerous to get them all out. Those in the lining of his heart couldn't be removed without open-heart surgery and were left in situ.

The victim wouldn't come out of the heavy anaesthesia for the best part of another ten hours, but his wife was allowed to visit him in the recovery room. She was shocked by what she saw. Her husband was suspended above the bed while the staff changed the sheets, blood still dripping from the 60 holes in his back, blotting red onto the crisp, white linen. 'He was like a colander,' she later confided.

But she couldn't stay with him for long. The shock of the incident had sent her into premature labour; she was having contractions every two minutes. Her destination was a maternity hospital a couple of miles across town.

The baby, the couple's second son, didn't actually arrive for another three weeks. By then, the shooting victim had been discharged and was home, albeit only able to slowly – painfully – move from bed to chair and back again. While the initial pace of recovery would be infuriating for a patient who was anything but patient, his resolve did accelerate the healing process. Just six weeks on from Easter Monday, six weeks after his body was decimated by that buckshot blast, he carefully climbed onto a bike and gently rode for five kilometres.

At this point, he was still the reigning champion of the Tour de France.

ACT I
THE FIRST WEEK

ONE

THE CONTENDERS

'I'd again become salesworthy in the eyes of the press. Pictures of the likely winner shift a newspaper or two' – Laurent Fignon

TWO YEARS, TWO months and eleven days after Greg LeMond's gurney crashed through the doors of that emergency room in Sacramento, the American was back in competition in the world's greatest bike race. It was 1 July 1989 and the occasion was the Prologue time trial of the Tour de France, the opening encounter of that year's race. It was also LeMond's first appearance since his victory three years earlier. Back then, he was radiating in the golden glow of the fêted yellow jersey as the Tour's first North American winner. By 1989, however, he was wearing the lime green and indigo colours of the Belgian ADR squad, a wildcard outfit who'd only been accepted into the race after LeMond himself organised an additional, half-past-the-eleventh-hour sponsor who could cover the team's entrance fee.

Here in Luxembourg, the city around which the Prologue was to kick off the Tour, LeMond's presence was somewhat remarkable. Following the near-death experience of the hunting accident, he had missed the two subsequent Tours, back under the surgeon's knife for appendicitis and tendinitis respectively. By now, LeMond was a pale shadow of his former formidable self – a man rebuilding his career, learning his craft again, all the while battling demons both physical and psychological.

Were he signed to a more prestigious, more reliable and better-funded team than ADR, one or two more observers might have taken his participation a little more seriously. But the team's raggle-taggle roster, allied to his lack of form over the previous 18 months, meant the collective verdict on LeMond was that he was an also-ran. A spent force. Yesterday's man.

While the eyes of the Luxembourg crowd were fixed on him, it was more out of morbid curiosity than viewing him as the man most likely to succeed both that afternoon and over the following three weeks. While he didn't exactly represent a freak show, the talk that day was more about him actually competing than indulging him with talk of possibly being crowned champion ever again. It was LeMond's bravery that was being admired. This was, after all, a man who still had more than 30 shotgun pellets lodged in various muscles and organs, including that pair in the lining of his heart. By the time he arrived in Luxembourg, he viewed the pellets as 'part of my body now, part of my character'.

Nowhere – not on the lips of fans, pundits or bookmakers, nor among the tactical plans of various team *directeurs sportif* – was the name of Greg LeMond being touted as a serious contender for the title come the peloton's arrival in Paris three weeks hence.

Instead, the sensible eyes and the safe money were on reigning champion Pedro Delgado – the clear favourite. An exhilarating climber whose riding style became more explosive the steeper the gradient, the Spaniard's triumph on the Champs-Élysées the previous July had been more than comfortable, his seven-minute margin of victory indisputably made easier by the absence of both LeMond and the 1987 champion, Ireland's Stephen Roche. Delgado's elevation into the Tour's history books, though, was a tarnished one.

After the 17th stage of the '88 Tour, the French TV channel Antenne2 reported that Delgado had failed a doping test. The next morning, the substance he had been tested positive for was revealed to be probenecid, a drug used to either assist the kidneys or mask the use of anabolic steroids. However, while it was banned by the International Olympic Committee, cycling's governing body – the Union Cycliste Internationale – had yet to declare it an illegal substance. And the Tour marched to the UCI's tune. Legally, Delgado had no case to answer.

'I took probenecid just after the Alpe d'Huez stage,' he explained to the Spanish newspaper *AS*. 'We used it to assist draining from the kidneys. If I'd wanted to hide something, I would have had to have used it every day and it only appeared on that one [test].'

No matter his protestations, suspicions lingered and opinions were aired. A huge question mark floated over the legitimacy of Delgado's title. The Irish rider Paul Kimmage – who doubled as a correspondent for the Dublin-based *Sunday Tribune* – likened Delgado to 'the politician caught leaving the brothel who claims he is only canvassing'. The Spaniard had his supporters too, though. The affair led to a mini international incident when loyal fans stormed the French Embassy in Madrid to protest at their hero's treatment by the race authorities.

Nonetheless, controversy had followed Delgado into 1989 when rumours of skulduggery abounded after his victory at the Vuelta a España in mid-May. Having seen off the challenge of Colombia's Fabio Parra – the pair were separated by just two seconds going into the final days – a Colombian TV crew alleged that they had filmed Delgado giving an envelope to the young Russian rider Ivan Ivanov. Ivanov's pursuit of Parra on one particular stage had effectively assured Delgado of the race-winner's crown. The TV crew, armed with little hard evidence, claimed the envelope contained cash; Delgado responded with the counterclaim that, having become friendly with the Russian over the course of the race, he had been merely giving him his address in nearby Segovia.

While anxious to put in another dominant display in the general classification to shush – or to even silence – the doubters, Delgado's shoulders were heavy with expectation and pressure as the Tour entourage gathered in Luxembourg. Being a serious contender was one thing; being the even-money favourite was another. 'The difference was enormous,' he nods, nearly 30 years later. That said, Delgado – starting his sixth Tour after podium finishes in both the previous two years – was also buoyed by an assuredness and confidence when it came to his fitness. 'My physical condition was at its peak,' he smiles. 'I won the Vuelta a España. I finished fourth at, and nearly won, Liège-Bastogne-Liège. I spent two months in a training camp at altitude and I arrived at the Tour very focused. I felt very, very well. Until the first day…'

It ended up being a first day to forget, a day to erase from the career history. For now, though, prior to the Prologue's start, controlled optimism was the dominant mood in the ranks of Delgado's Reynolds team. He was certainly the rider in the peloton whose good form had been sustained over the longest time. With him installed as the clear – if not nailed-on – favourite, the next two most-fancied riders were both on the comeback trail, both former Tour champions wishing to retrace their tyre tracks to glory.

Like Greg LeMond, Stephen Roche never had the chance to defend his Tour title, absent from the start line in 1988 because of an ongoing knee problem sustained two years previously, an injury that would make reappearances throughout the rest of his riding days. But the first half of 1989 showed signs that Roche might be able to taste again the form that had propelled him to the top of the pro cycling tree. He won the Tour of the Basque Country, placed second overall in the eight-day Paris-Nice (the evocatively nicknamed 'Race to the Sun') and, less than three weeks before the Tour, enjoyed a top-ten finish at the Giro d'Italia. While these performances weren't suggestive of Roche's scintillating form of 1987 when he achieved cycling's Triple Crown, scooping the Giro, Tour and World Championship titles, there was at least a sunny belief that a high finish in Paris was more than possible.

'After what I'd gone through, I would have definitely been grateful for a top five or podium,' he says. 'They always say, "One month out is two months to get back", so one year out takes two years to get back. And that's very hard to cope with.' There was also the unknown quantity of his Fagor team. Having lost key men at the end of the previous season – hardy perennials like the climber Robert Millar and the uber-domestique Sean Yates – the squad was in a state of flux and chaos, the source of which was a power struggle among the team bosses. Not that, incidentally, this internal civil war had prevented Fagor from becoming the highest-placed team at the Giro less than a month before.

If Roche was moderately encouraged by his form in Italy, Laurent Fignon surfed into Luxembourg on a wave of unstoppable confidence – a confidence that, Fignon being Fignon, blurred the distinction between self-belief and God-given arrogance. A double Tour winner as a young professional, his first victory, in 1983, had come in his very first Tour at the age of 22. He repeated the feat a year later. He had endured several *anni miserabilis* in the years since, thanks to long-term injuries. 1989, though, was shaping up to be something of a renaissance. Fignon followed up success in March's one-day Milan-San Remo with an even more impressive Italian victory; the Parisian returned home from the Giro with the winner's *maglia rosa* jersey in his luggage. These successes stoked the internal fire of an athlete written off as a busted flush. 'I was still going strong after being given up for dead at least a hundred times,' he later wrote.

The notion of a French victory at the 1989 Tour was showing itself to be irresistible – even if the tempestuous, temperamental Fignon had earned himself a love-hate relationship with both the press and the public in his home country. 'Before and after the Prologue, the photographers were going berserk around me. I was still radiant with the reflected glory of the Giro's pink jersey, so I'd again become salesworthy in the eyes of the press. Pictures of the likely winner shift a newspaper or two, as we all know.' Short on confidence Monsieur Fignon was not.

And the leader's confidence trickled down into the ranks of his ambitious Super U team. This was a squad stuffed to the gills with tried, tested and proven French talent: the eight-Tour veteran Pascal Simon; former yellow jersey-wearer Thierry Marie; and Vincent Barteau, who'd led the Tour for 12 days in 1984, the year of Fignon's last triumph.

The Super U ranks also contained a rookie Danish rider who, while 'gulping the wind' as a determined domestique for Fignon in the Giro, helped himself to a stage win there too. Seven years later, he would end up being a Tour winner in his own right. His name was Bjarne Riis.

And controlling this powerful team – or, at least, pulling the strings as much as a headstrong team leader like Fignon would allow – was the wily Cyrille Guimard, cycling's true starmaker. As a rider, Guimard had won seven stages in the Tour during the 1970s. As a *directeur sportif*, he claimed overall Tour titles through several of his decorated charges – Fignon, Bernard Hinault and Lucien Van Impe. Seven Tour victories in his first nine years as a team boss was a statistic envied by every other *directeur sportif*.

French hopes weren't exclusively pinned on Fignon, though. At the same time that he was slipping on the leader's jersey at the Giro, his compatriot

Charly Mottet was winning the Critérium du Dauphiné Libéré in and around his native Alps, the eight-stage race often studied as a measure of form ahead of the Tour. It was the second of what would be three Dauphiné titles for Mottet, earning this modest rider the ranking of world number one following other victories earlier in the season, including the prestigious Four Days of Dunkirk.

Mottet's modesty, cast into the deepest shadow by the force of Fignon's ebullience, certainly allowed him to operate comparatively unnoticed, despite topping the world rankings. A fourth-place finisher behind Roche, Delgado and Jean-François Bernard in 1987, he had left Super U – or Système U as it was still then known – at the end of 1988, graduating to team leader by signing for RMO, the squad managed by former rider Bernard Vallet.

A one-time King of the Mountains, the recently retired Vallet had history with Mottet. Good history. They had been victorious partners in the Six Days of Grenoble series two years previously. Now, as *directeur sportif* and team leader respectively, they made a great potential pairing, particularly when the race reached Mottet's Alpine backyard. 'Bernard knew the Grand Tours well,' he confirms. But while the partnership might have looked mutually attractive, not everyone believed in Mottet's promise. 'We already sensed he was not a three-weeks guy,' says the journalist François Thomazeau, at the time covering the Tour for the Reuters news agency. Whether Mottet could cope with the expectation of being a team leader was moot. He seemed to have doubts himself. 'I was leading a new team, so I was under pressure to perform for my new sponsors.' (France's other great white hope – Toshiba's Jean-François Bernard – was absent in 1989, at home recovering from a knee operation.)

Mottet had taken the world number one ranking from Sean Kelly, a position the Irishman had held for five years straight. A glance at Kelly's racing successes, his palmàres, leaves no one in any doubt as to why the man from Carrick-on-Suir enjoyed a half-decade of uncontested dominance. By the time he rolled his bike into the start house at the Prologue in Luxembourg in 1989, Kelly had amassed an astonishing 151 career victories since turning professional 12 years earlier. (The story of how he turned pro is a peach. He was driving a tractor along a rural lane in County Waterford in bleak midwinter, pulling a muck-spreading tank, when a taxi blocked the road. Out stepped legendary team boss Jean de Gribaldy, dapper in a pinstriped suit and Brylcreemed hair, and carrying a contract to sign for his Flandria outfit. 'Are you Sean Kelly...?')

Kelly's victories as a professional weren't small fry. Among them were 16 stage wins at the Vuelta a España (he also took the overall title in 1988) and seven back-to-back titles at Paris-Nice. That was just the stage races. He was also no slouch when it came to the one-day classics, with two victories apiece in Liège-Bastogne-Liège, Milan-San Remo and Paris-Roubaix. Then there were the five stage wins in the Tour, along with being crowned the green jersey points winner three times over.

In short, Kelly was a winner. But the *maillot jaune* had always eluded him, save for one day in 1983 when an overall lead of just a single second allowed him to don yellow for the one and only time. In 1989, at the age of 33, he was still upbeat as he headed into the late afternoon of a formidable career. He seemed to be enjoying himself more than before in the dimming of the day, a smile now regularly playing on his lips during interviews. Freshly signed to the well-financed Dutch team PDM after several years with the Spanish KAS squad, Kelly's eye was firmly focused on winning the green jersey for a record-breaking fourth time.

The PDM team had other contenders for high placings in the general classification. They were especially blessed in the climbing department, where two Dutchmen, often inseparable on the road, came as a pair. Steven Rooks had won the polka-dot King of the Mountains jersey the previous July, when his assault on Alpe d'Huez had helped deliver him to second place overall. But it was difficult to read too much into the early months of his 1989 season. PDM had steered clear of both the Giro and the Vuelta, its Grand Tour preparation exclusively reserved for those three weeks in France. Rooks' performances in the Spring Classics were solid if unspectacular, ranging from 2nd in La Flèche Wallonne to 14th at Milan-San Remo.

In the only pre-Tour stage race in which Rooks' climbing form could be gauged, he finished an underwhelming 20th in the Tour of Switzerland. With the likes of Delgado, Roche and Fignon all already having a Grand Tour under their belts by the time they congregated in Luxembourg, the hope for PDM was that both Rooks and his compatriot Gert-Jan Theunisse would be fresher and less fatigued once the race reached the Pyrenees and the Alps.

If Rooks' form in the Spring Classics was moderate, his team-mate and compatriot Gert-Jan Theunisse's was even more anonymous. His best performances were an 11th in Milan-San Remo and 15th in Liège-Bastogne-Liège. He was coming into the Tour with broken ribs, too, a souvenir brought home from the Tour of Switzerland. And, like Delgado, a fog of suspicion followed the enigmatic, long-haired Dutchman around ahead of the Tour's departure. In 1988, while in fourth place, he had tested positive for testosterone. The punishment at the time wasn't immediate disqualification. Instead, Theunisse received a ten-minute time penalty, which took him out of the top ten overall, although he still did make it a Dutch 1-2 in the King of the Mountains competition behind his pal Rooks.

Although the bookmakers placed him at 20-1 to win the yellow jersey in 1989, Erik Breukink was another Dutchman very much worth keeping an eye on. He possessed all the qualities required for overall victory. A great time trialist who could also keep up in the mountains, he also had the support of one of the strongest teams, the fiercely competitive Panasonic. The squad were under the tutelage of the brilliant strategist Peter Post, one of the most successful *directeur sportifs* of the period. His management style delivered results but was unyielding. His former charge Robert Millar once moaned that 'Post ran the team like an army'.

Post's methods clearly suited Breukink, though. Although 1989 would only be his third Tour de France, he had already shown a fine pedigree when it came to stage races. On his first Tour two years earlier, he outfoxed his rivals in a four-man break (which included Jean-François Bernard and the Colombian Luis Herrera) by sprinting for the line a kilometre from home and gliding to victory in the market square in Pau. The following year, Breukink took second place overall in the Giro, the highlight of which was his win on the famously snow-driven stage that traversed the Passo di Gavia. And his form thus far in 1989 was strong, having placed fourth at the Giro, a performance that included seven top-ten stage finishes. For his consistency over different terrain and formats, the blond-haired Breukink could prove to be something of a dark horse.

An entire continent was waiting for the man who beat Breukink to the *maglia rosa* in the '88 Giro to stamp his authority on the Tour. With LeMond deemed a curiosity, Andy Hampsten was expected to step up to fill the void. North America thought it was about time. Hampsten's best showing had been the quiet fourth place he took in his debut Tour in 1986, when his two La Vie Claire team-mates – LeMond and Bernard Hinault – were very loudly and very bitterly slugging it out for the overall victory.

The following year, Hampsten was ensconced as the leader of the American 7-Eleven team, but the squad's relative inexperience couldn't place him any higher than 16th in the general classification. While 1988 saw him blooming with that Giro triumph, he couldn't replicate it in France, finishing down in 15th and only making the top ten on one single stage. Doubts were still audible about his credentials for an overall Tour victory. Living in Colorado, the mountains were his natural habitat. Time trials on the flat – in which all those harbouring ambitions to be in yellow come Paris needed to show prowess – were Hampsten's Achilles heel.

The Canadian Steve Bauer was another La Vie Claire alumnus, but one who knew, unlike Hampsten, what it was like to have the *maillot jaune* on his back. In 1988, riding for the unfancied Weinmann-La Suisse team, he won the opening stage on a day that showcased his astute cycling brain. With a team time trial that afternoon, Bauer understood the reluctance of riders to do any chasing in the morning. He, though, was anything but reluctant. 'From the gun, I made sure to cover everyone.' His reward was the stage win and a total of five days in yellow.

While his overall placing of fourth place might have been slightly amplified by Roche's absence and Theunisse's time penalty, Bauer was nonetheless a combative rider more than capable of sneaking onto the podium come Paris. A third place in April's Amstel Gold Race, allied to fourth overall at the Tour of Switzerland, also suggested a man with form in his legs.

The rider who deprived Bauer of a podium place at the Tour in 1988, Colombia's Fabio Parra, was widely tipped to repeat the feat 12 months later, especially as the 1989 course included an increased number of mountain stages. Parra's solo win at Morzine was the defining moment of that third place, although he could have finished higher in the general classification had just one of his attacks on Alpe d'Huez not been frustrated by camera-bikes causing congestion on the narrow road up the mountain. With seven stages to look forward to in 1989 – two in the Pyrenees and five in the Alps – perhaps Parra could even deliver Colombia's second Grand Tour triumph, following Luis Herrera's capture of the Vuelta two years previously. He was certainly close to it in Spain in '89, his defeat to Delgado in the Vuelta being by the narrow margin of 33 seconds after three weeks of racing.

Herrera's form was notable too. The month before the Tour, the petit Colombian reached a landmark that would become his legacy in retirement. By winning the *maglia verde* at the Giro, he became only the second rider in history to win the mountains category at all three Grand Tours, after his wins at the Tour in '85 and '87, and at the Vuelta, also in '87. Only the legendary Spanish climber Federico Bahamontes in the late 1950s had previously managed the feat. With his principal ambition for this season achieved, the modest Herrera now had the freedom to stir things up in the mountains on the Tour, on what would hopefully be a seven-day feast of climbing excellence. The shackles were off.

Scotland's Robert Millar was another mountain man feeling the chimes of freedom flashing. Having been forced, by Stephen Roche's injury problems, to lead the dysfunctional Fagor team in the '88 Tour, the Glaswegian had jumped ship at the end of the season and retraced his steps. He was back in the fold at his first continental team, Peugeot, now co-sponsored by the French clothing company Z. Not only had he been relieved of the pressures of team leadership (Z's captain at the Tour would be the French rider Éric Boyer who had finished fifth the previous year), but Millar's preparation in '89 was much more to his liking. A procession of *directeurs sportif* had always insisted he ride either the Vuelta or the Giro before heading to France. This year, though, that duty had been lifted. Every inch, every ounce, of Millar's season could be focused on those seven mountain stages, the ultimate prize being a second polka-dot jersey after his King of the Mountains crown in 1984.

As he rolled his bike up to the start in Luxembourg, Millar would begin the Tour without fatigue already in his legs. 'Despite the signs,' he explained to the writer William Fotheringham, 'the managers I worked with didn't seem to understand that I was capable of doing one [Grand] Tour well each year. Maybe it was due to the fact that budgets got bigger every year, and they expected more and more. That was what it felt like. I tried to hide and take it easy in the Vuelta or Giro, but it's in my nature to compete when I can, so I'd find myself racing.' 1989 – albeit for one year only – would find Millar in the shape he wanted to be in come the Tour. And a second place in the week-long Dauphiné Libéré the previous month, where he came home behind Charly Mottet by just 18 seconds, sent a warning shot across the bows of his polka-dot rivals.

While there were contenders aplenty going into July, there were very few certainties. The neutrals were looking forward to three weeks of shocks and surprises, controversy and despair, triumph and failure. They weren't to be disappointed. It would be quite some month.

***

There was one man in particular whose actions helped to ensure that the '89 Tour was a humdinger, and yet who wasn't present when the race convened in Luxembourg. Jean-François Naquet-Radiguet had been dismissed from his job as Tour director more than a year previously, having only served 12 months in the role. But it was one particularly bright idea of his that ensured the '89 Tour went down not just to the wire, but down to the thinnest wire imaginable.

Naquet-Radiguet was by no means – and by his own admission – a man of cycling. What he was, though, was a salesman. Not a used car fast talker or an insurance policy hustler, but a man whose trade was concepts. He thought big. With an MBA from Harvard tucked under his arm, plus experience on the top floor of various food corporations (most notably cognac producers Martell), Naquet-Radiguet was something of a surprise choice for the role when his appointment was announced in May 1987. 'No one wanted to direct the Tour,' he later told the journalist Daniel Friebe. 'It took a poor idiot like me to say yes.'

He had big boots to fill and a tough double act to follow. Jacques Goddet, the founder of the French sports newspaper *L'Equipe*, had been at the helm of the Tour since 1936. In 1965, Goddet began sharing power with the journalist Félix Lévitan. They made a formidable pairing, their work largely divided up between business (the province of Lévitan) and sporting affairs

(Goddet's domain). In 1987, Lévitan left the Tour under his own personal black cloud following allegations of creative accounting. Goddet retired at the same time, although he was awarded the ill-defined role of race-director-at-large. The main benefit of this assignment appeared to be the freedom to criticise the methods of whomever his successor was.

In his mid-40s, Naquet-Radiguet was practically half the age of the octogenarian Goddet, but didn't baulk at revolutionising the structure underpinning the Tour. 'I came into a completely archaic world,' he told Friebe, 'a completely dictatorial world.' His first experience of the Tour at close quarters – the 1987 edition won by Stephen Roche – was supposed to be purely observational, a crash course in soaking up the culture of the race he knew so little about. But his grand plans were already taking shape in his head.

Like a stuck-in-the-mud, on-the-eve-of-retirement editor unwilling to relinquish his publication to a thrusting young buck with ideas, Goddet was protective of his legacy and regularly sniped about the new man's lack of cycling credentials. Naquet-Radiguet adroitly countered by appointing the recently retired Bernard Hinault as his cycling adviser. Who better to learn from – and who better to provide credibility by association – than the five-time Tour winner?

While his programme of reform dealt with obvious, long-overdue changes close to home (for instance, upgrading the decidedly parochial-looking finish-line banner and winners' podium), Naquet-Radiguet was mainly driven by a desire to globalise the Tour, to maximising its worldwide audience. This would be not only on TV but also in the flesh. Indeed, Grands Départs as far afield as Tokyo and Québec were mooted, plans that even the more liberal elements in cycling might have regarded a step too far.

The pace of intended reform was speedy. Goddet and Lévitan had a combined 73 years at the helm, during which time the race's progress and development was nowhere near as swift as it was in other sports. Perhaps Naquet-Radiguet's dreams were too big and came too soon for the traditionalist quarters. Certainly they weren't ready for a Tour director conducting interviews in English. Unheard of. Sacrilegious. As Daniel Friebe observes, his 'laconic self-assessment is that he merely "went into a stuffy environment and opened the windows and doors". More impartial judges maintain that he dragged the Tour kicking and screaming towards the 21st century.'

Naquet-Radiguet had long gone by the time the 1989 Tour de France course was unveiled in the October of 1988. Those two additional mountain stages reduced the overall distance to be covered over the three weeks; at 3,285 kilometres long, it was the shortest Tour for more than 80 years. The design generally met with riders' approval. 'It was a good, all-round, competitive course,' remembers Andy Hampsten, nearly 30 years on. 'When I won at Alpe d'Huez in 1992, it was one of only three mountain stages. During the Miguel Induráin years, there were what I thought to be a lot of dud, flat stages – not many mountains and long, too long, time trials. There were some uncreative courses in the 1990s, but 1989 was fantastic. And a mountain time trial was a gift to me that I had to make the most of.'

While Hampsten had earmarked that particular Alpine stage in the race's last week, it was a different time trial that was grabbing imaginations and scorn in equal measure. During his 12-month tenure, Naquet-Radiguet had privately declared that the final stage, that supposedly blue riband mass parade up and down the Champs-Élysées, would now take the form of an individual time trial every year. It wasn't possible in 1988, but the idea was made flesh for the following summer, despite its author's departure long before then. Rather remarkably, his final-day plan remained intact in his absence. It became his legacy, albeit one in place for just a single year and albeit thanks to the closeness of the general classification. It was helped by circumstances beyond his control.

The concept of a final-day time trial had been taken up before. In the 1968 Tour, the Dutch rider Jan Janssen overhauled a 16-second deficit to beat Belgian Herman Van Springel to take the yellow jersey and the overall title. The time difference – 38 seconds – was the shortest in Tour history. Yet, despite the cliffhanging conclusion, the format was never adopted again for the last stage of a race. Not until 1989, that is.

In a sense, Naquet-Radiguet's idea was simply the next evolutionary step for the race's final day. In 1975, Lévitan had been equally radical, bringing the Parisian finish into the city centre by relocating it from the Vélodrome de Vincennes, out beyond the Périphérique ring road, to the undeniably more photogenic Champs-Élysées.

It was something of a gamble, one that raised plenty of eyebrows and a few hackles. This was a race that didn't discard tradition lightly, after all. The race always signed off with a semi-competitive parade into the French capital, one that, in not affecting the general classification, offered the sprinters a moment in the Parisian sun. There was also the danger that – with every chance of the overall winner having already been decided before the final day – this new time trial format could become an even less consequential parade. One without, even, the excitement of a mass sprint finish. The dampest of damp squibs, the deadest of dead rubbers.

For every excited time trialist in 1989, there was a non-plussed sprinter. Other mildly dissenting voices could be heard too. Graham Watson was on his third of what would be 30 Tours as one of the photographers gamely balancing himself and his camera on the back of a speeding, weaving motorbike. For him, and his art, the notion of a final-day time trial wasn't a cause for celebration. 'The thought of a last-stage time trial filled me with dread. It took away the fun and colour of a peloton racing up and down the Champs-Élysées – the most important images for a seasoned Tour photographer. It was almost certainly going to be a bore, a simple coronation parade for the overall winner. At least, that's what I and most people thought. Indeed, many journalists would go on to bypass the Paris finish and get home a day early in the belief that the race was over.'

Praise be it was anything but.

TWO

LAZARUS RISING

'There was a ten-second pause as we reflected on the American's chances. The whole table erupted with laughter' – Paul Kimmage

GREG AND KATHY LeMond live in Tennessee these days. For 30 years, they endured Minnesota's bone-shaking winters, those months when the landscape slides into a deep, deep hibernation. It's a time when there's little to do other than strap on a pair of cross-country skis and head out onto frozen Lake Minnetonka, just across the street from the LeMonds' home in the Minneapolis suburb of Wayzata. It can be bleak round those parts. Indeed, the film-making siblings Joel and Ethan Coen, who grew up in the neighbouring suburb of St Louis Park, once referred to midwinter Minnesota as 'resembling Siberia, except for its Ford dealerships and Hardee's restaurants'.

The LeMonds will freeze no more; the first tenet of that legendary Southern hospitality is its clement weather. Today is the opening day of March and while Minnesota's temperatures remain below zero, the mercury in mid-morning Knoxville has already reached a very agreeable 26° Celsius. The couple recently moved south to be closer to the base of their carbon fibre company, LeMond Composites.

In short, life is good for the LeMonds. Such buoyancy is in deep contrast to the state of affairs the couple found themselves in the spring of 1987. Yes, the arrival of baby Scott undoubtedly brought joy, but father Greg, post-accident, faced a difficult and uncertain future, a journey that would be undertaken while his physical and psychological scars slowly healed. 'We were so lucky,' Kathy says of the helicopter rescue, three decades later. 'That was the silver lining of Sacramento being the murder capital. Those ER docs had a lot of experience with shootings. And they had an amazing female trauma surgeon. She saved him. She was extraordinary.'

Not that there wasn't more distress on the immediate horizon. Toshiba, the team with whom LeMond had won the Tour de France with the previous summer when they were known as La Vie Claire, had shown themselves to be both impatient and callous. With their flamboyant owner Bernard Tapie now having eyes for the young French rider Jean-François Bernard, LeMond was deemed surplus to requirements. Barely a month after the shooting accident, he received a letter giving him his marching orders.

'Oh yeah, we got that right away,' confirms Kathy. 'We were really pissed off. Greg had just won the Tour for them. But, honestly, we always felt that we were just grateful that he was alive, so we didn't dwell on it that much. Compared to not being alive, it really wasn't that big a deal.'

Tapie and Toshiba had obviously thought that the severity of the accident meant LeMond would never again be the rider he had been before the events of Easter Monday, 1987. But, due to his extraordinary physiology, and his resolve, his recovery was the speediest it could have been. 'That's because he's Greg,' says Kathy. 'If he were a normal person, it would have been months and months. He was better on his bike than he was walking. The bike was a good support. But he was skin and bones. Absolute skin and bones. He was 120 pounds. When he won the Tour in 1986, he was 145 or something. But he was back on the bike.'

As well as building those muscles back up, LeMond needed to restore his levels of blood. He hadn't been given any transfusions out of his doctors' fear that donated blood might be contaminated with the AIDS virus, and it took a full two months for his levels to be back to normal. But then, three months after the shooting, LeMond had to undergo an emergency appendectomy, one made difficult because of the scar from his shooting operation. 'It was a picnic in comparison to the accident...'

Not only did LeMond appear to be physiologically different from other riders, his outlook on life was decidedly more relaxed than that of more intense types in the professional ranks. This often brought criticism from conservative quarters within the sport; the writer Edward Pickering neatly compared LeMond to the outsider chess player Bobby Fischer, 'coming in from America to beat the established countries at their own game'. Simply substitute Russian grandmasters with the cycling traditionalists of northern Europe.

LeMond's motivation and commitment seemed to come under constant scrutiny, as he later told *Procycling* magazine. 'I'll never forget reading a Belgian newspaper story that said I got what I'd deserved in '87, because I was eating ice cream and hunting when I ought to have been racing and training. And yet they knew that I was back in the States because I'd fallen in Tirreno-Adriatico and wouldn't be able to race for six months. After the accident, there were some mean-ass letters and negative articles. Even today, you still hear the myth that I didn't train properly and that I was only interested in the Tour. The reality was that, physically, I wasn't the same after the accident. Before that, I raced balls-to-walls from February to September.'

Hope – elation, probably – came in the shape of PDM, the Dutch team who were arguably the strongest outfit in world cycling. They signed LeMond for the 1988 season, although the contract stipulated that he had to appear in PDM colours during 1987, presumably to measure the progress of his recovery. That September, five months after all that emergency surgery, he entered a criterium race in Belgium, just to honour this legal requirement. 'One lap, and I pretended to have a flat tyre.'

While his injuries denied him the chance of wearing the prestigious number 1 on his back at the '87 Tour as defending champion, LeMond didn't make the start the following year, either. A crash in a minor springtime race in Belgium prompted an enforced lay-off, the premature return from which brought about a case of tendinitis in his shin. 'Because I started riding on it too soon,' he later explained to the American writer Samuel Abt, 'it got irritated and then inflamed … After two weeks off my bike, I was really ambitious and did four races in the first week. I didn't finish any of them.' While the Tour was well under way, across the Atlantic, LeMond was under the surgeon's knife in his new home state of Minnesota. Another frustrating summer. The title he'd been so desperate to reclaim was instead pocketed by the first-time-winning Spaniard, Pedro Delgado.

One incident during that Tour, though, angered LeMond from afar: the positive drugs test of his PDM team-mate Gert-Jan Theunisse. 'My reaction was to tell the management that whoever had given him the drugs should be fired,' he told Daniel Friebe, 'and the same applied to Theunisse. I liked Gert, but I didn't want to be associated with any kind of doping. Of course, this was never made public, which gave them the licence to start rumours about me bad-mouthing the other riders and asking for a pay raise. They were all saying "How dare he ask for a pay raise when he's had no results and he never trains?".'

The relationship had soured and both parties welcomed his departure. 'They had lost total confidence in me,' he said at the time. 'They were trying to claim that maybe my liver was bad, my lung was shot up, maybe I had lead poisoning. They said, "Maybe you're not going to ever come back".'

'We felt that his training was not concentrated,' offered Harrie Jansen, the PDM team manager. 'His whole career, he has eaten hamburgers, not worrying about what he drank or how he rested. He has so much talent that he can live like ordinary people. He was too fat, and he was still eating his hamburgers, his pizzas, his beers, his everything.'

The Bobby Fischer figure certainly wrote his own rules, and much was often made of his less-than-saintly refuelling. *L'Equipe* was particularly dismissive of his diet. 'He could unearth a Mexican restaurant in the depths of the Auvergne,' the paper grumbled. Andy Hampsten, his team-mate during the La Vie Claire years, admires his compatriot's rebellious streak. 'He really loved to go to Italy and fret about his weight over two or three big plates of pasta,' he laughs, 'as we all would.' Another American rider, Joe Parkin, once noted how this kind of preparation didn't really affect LeMond's performances. 'He could climb off the couch and win races. He could come back from the off-season soft and doughy, and within a week he'd be ripped.'

With an exit from PDM looking imminent, LeMond put the feelers out for an alternative team for the 1989 season. He tested for the Fagor squad, before putting in a call to Johan Lammerts, a former team-mate at Toshiba. Lammerts, a Dutch rider with whom LeMond had struck up a firm friendship, was now riding for the small Belgian ADR team. The American had been offered a slot on their roster the previous year before he hooked up with PDM; at the time he had been dismissive of them, denouncing them as 'one of the weakest teams around' who could never help deliver a Grand Tour victory.

But now, having fallen from number two in the world rankings right down to number 345 in the space of two years, this beggar couldn't be a chooser. ADR owner François Lambert and *directeur sportif* José De Cauwer were enthusiastic about a former Tour winner joining their roster, and a salary, significantly lower than that which LeMond was on at PDM, was agreed. It was based on a comparatively meagre basic pay, with a $500,000 bonus should he confound the critics and win the Tour in ADR colours. The deal went down to the wire, with LeMond's father Bob finalising it a couple of hours short of midnight on New Year's Eve. Had the contract remained unsigned as the clock struck 12, another season at PDM awaited – and one on a much-reduced wage, to boot.

'ADR was a really crummy team,' Kathy LeMond remembers. 'They weren't paying him that much – and in the end they didn't pay at all. Going into the Tour, we hadn't been paid yet. But he had some freedom there. You really don't have to listen to the team owner if he's seven months late paying you.' ADR – the vehicle-hire firm All Drive Renting – had a Flemish nickname. It was suggested that its initials stood for Al De Restjes, or the Good-For-Nothings.

In order to cover LeMond's salary, ADR had entered into an agreement with the American Coors Light team, whereby he would race for them at events in the US. The arrangement gave Coors team boss Len Pettyjohn front-row insight into how the unscrupulous François Lambert operated. 'Very quickly, Lambert was running into money problems,' he explains. 'He wasn't paying the riders. He wasn't following through on his contract obligations. He had a huge fight with Greg, because Greg's contract required that he got a Mercedes as a personal car. He ended up getting some piece-of-shit Fiat or something like that. A Punto, or whatever. Greg was just furious and Bob LeMond was out-of-control mad about it.'

As Kathy LeMond clarifies, the couple didn't even get some piece-of-shit Fiat. 'We never got anything! He made us go up to Antwerp where we picked out a nice Mercedes and he took us to dinner. He kept saying "Yeah, yeah. Your car will be in next week, next week". He was a total, total conman.' LeMond even had to sign up, through a criterium organiser, a new co-sponsor, the lubrication gel manufacturer Agrigel. In return for cash to cover administrative fees, Agrigel received advertising space on the team jerseys. 'ADR didn't even have the $50,000 to enter the Tour de France. We came up with the money from Agrigel. And we didn't have the money either. We hadn't been paid.'

Having encountered salary issues while his son was with La Vie Claire, Bob LeMond had negotiated a front-loaded contract, whereby the first chunk of the annual wage would be paid on 1 January 1989, the day after the contract was signed, sealed, delivered. It never came. Not in January. Not in February. Not in March, April, May…

In fact, not a cent had been paid by the time LeMond lined up for the start of the '89 Tour. 'François was significantly in arrears,' explains Len Pettyjohn, 'so we sent a letter to him saying that he was in breach of the contract. The UCI had looked at the contract and the payments, and said Greg was free to leave the team. That was a shock to François. He thought he had it nailed down.'

Pettyjohn has the utmost sympathy for José De Cauwer. 'I felt sorry for him that he was tied to Lambert. He was the direct link to the riders. "OK, you're not getting your salary. You're not getting the things that have been promised to you." As a team director, that's a horrible thing to happen to you. I'd be sitting in his office and I thought there were times when he was just going to throw his phone through the wall. François was a crazy man. He had this ego that thought, just by his presence, he could will things to happen. And he was constantly lying to people. He didn't have any money. He was playing a shell game – always trying to shift the sponsorship around so he could pay for next week.'

Nothing ever seemed to be easy for LeMond. Not only was the team teetering on the shakiest of financial foundations, but the quality within its ranks wasn't the greatest, certainly not for a Grand Tour. For starters, there was only one ADR rider who could remotely be thought of as a climber. LeMond soon realised that he'd be getting minimal assistance when the race hit the mountains. 'We weren't a team that was aimed at the Tour de France,' says Johan Lammerts, by this time LeMond's room-mate. 'It was mainly for the Classics races at the start of the season. That changed when Greg joined. He was a little more progressive than others in the team. Belgians are sometimes very conservative and we had conservative riders in our team. But everybody had respect for Greg. He was a Tour de France winner.

'There were expectations, but not necessarily high expectations. Everybody was curious to see if he had recovered well and could perform at the highest level again. The hunting accident wasn't just a little thing; he still had pellets in his body. But he was still an incredible, super-good rider.'

Certainly LeMond's form in the early months of 1989 was lacking. Lacking to the point of provoking an existential crisis. Riding in the colours of co-sponsor Coors Light at the Tour de Trump – the inaugural stage race bankrolled by Atlantic City huckster/future US president Donald Trump – it wasn't a happy homecoming. Struggling on the climbs, LeMond trailed in 27th overall. 'He realised that he was attracting little attention as reporters flocked to interview the riders with impressive results,' reported the *New York Times* correspondent Samuel Abt. 'The message was unmistakable: he was yesterday's story.' Getting dropped at the Tour de Trump was, says Andy Hampsten, 'an absolutely unique experience for LeMond.'

It was an experience that would be repeated, back on European soil and back in ADR colours, at the Giro d'Italia little more than a week later. On the second day, on a moderate climb up the slopes of Mount Etna in Sicily, LeMond trailed the winner by eight minutes. Three weeks later, going into the final day time trial, he was in 47th place, nearly an hour behind the about-to-be-crowned champion Laurent Fignon.

'I remember talking to Greg and feeling sorry for him at the Giro,' says Hampsten. 'He was genuinely humbled about how terrible he was and was writing off his chances. He was an unknown quantity after his accident, but I wouldn't write him off. It was Greg LeMond, after all.' Kathy saw from the closest of quarters how the accident had changed him. 'He never really had bad days before, but after he got shot, he had a lot of bad days. He was a completely different rider.'

His team boss, José De Cauwer, was careful not to exert pressure on those vulnerable shoulders, though. 'We weren't expecting miracles,' he later explained to *Cycling Weekly*. 'The only question was, "Can we bring him back?". The Giro was bad. There were a couple of days when he was behind and the race radio would announce Groupe LeMond, six minutes down, seven, eight... I remember he had an insurance policy he could have cashed in if he'd stopped. Collect the money, retire, go do something else. I know he considered it.'

The low point of his Giro experience was in the wake of Stage 13, where he lost 17 minutes. He put a tearful call in to Kathy who, because of a health scare, had yet to fly to Europe for the racing season and was still in Minnesota. He was on the verge of not just quitting the race, but turning his back on the sport. 'I just asked him if he thought he'd given it everything. If he'd given it everything and he was really, really done, then OK. But if he hadn't *really* given it everything, then it was a momentary depression.'

A number of factors were coalescing. It wasn't simply his form on the bike. There was the lack of wages going into the bank account, and there was Kathy's health scare, which involved the couple's yet-to-be-born third child. 'It was a really down period,' she recalls. 'We had had a scare with the next pregnancy, my cousin had died in a helicopter crash that week, and Greg wasn't riding well. He was half a world away. He was depressed. But he was still a person.

'Fans forget that these are still just young men who have marriages and families. When you're a cyclist, it's not like being a baseball player or a basketball player. They live in really rough and lonely conditions. A trainer once told me that it takes almost all their human energy just to do their sport. They don't have a whole lot of extra room for stress. So if you've got pressures or your parents are ill, there's just not a lot of extra room. And your cycling will suffer. You can't do it all. And they're humans.'

Help was soon at hand, though, as dispensed by LeMond's long-time *soigneur*, a gentle giant from Mexico by the name of Otto Jacome. He spotted one of the causes of LeMond's woes; his grey skin suggested an iron deficiency. 'I told him he needed an iron injection,' Jacome explained to the author Guy Andrews, 'but he got mad with me because he never used injections and he was upset because I was suggesting it. The following day, a doctor from the Giro came over to see him and they told him the same thing, that he needed iron. He got a jab – iron with vitamins – and the next day he says "Hey, Otto. I feel so much better now".'

A corner had been turned, as Kathy notes. 'I flew over the night of the iron injection. The kids and I were there, the baby was OK. Everything got better that day. We hit a good patch.'

The final week of the Giro saw an improvement in LeMond's riding, culminating in an extremely promising result in the final-day time trial. José De Cauwer had formulated a plan for that particular stage. 'That day we put the heart rate monitor away and I said, "Give it everything. Let's see when the engine cuts out." After six kilometres, he caught one rider. Then another. He ended up taking seven riders that day.'

LeMond's second place on the stage naturally delighted him. 'I'd pretended that I was in contention for the Giro,' he told Daniel Friebe, 'just to see where I was compared to everyone else. I'd got myself psyched up and ended up ahead of Fignon. That result blew me away.'

Most saw that performance as an anomaly, a one-off, a result from which little significance could be extracted. Fignon was one, even if his analysis was at odds with that of his team boss Cyrille Guimard. 'On the evening after I had won the race in Florence,' his autobiography reveals, 'Guimard came to have a word with me. He looked even more worried than usual. He wanted to talk one-to-one and it was important, even though all I was thinking about was celebrating my triumph. He was already concerned about July and looked me straight in the eyes. "LeMond will be up there at the Tour." I didn't hide my amazement.'

Others would have been amazed had they been privy to Guimard's assessment. A rider damaged by a life-threatening trauma, and riding for a wildcard team, did not a Tour de France favourite make, no matter what his past achievements. That was certainly the opinion of British rider Sean Yates, by then enjoying his first season with the American 7-Eleven team. 'It wasn't the last-chance saloon at that point for him, but ADR certainly weren't a major team with a major contract. You're only as good as your last race and his last two years had not been great. In the Tour de Trump, he was just going nowhere, but he did show a little bit at the end of the Giro. After that, I rode a kermesse and he didn't look great in that, although he might have been building it back up after the Giro and taking it steady. He certainly wasn't considered a contender for the Tour.'

Yates's former team-mate, the Irish rider Paul Kimmage, recalled how, on the first morning of the Tour, the Fagor team organised a sweepstake at the breakfast table of their hotel. The object was to predict the winner of the Tour three weeks hence. All the obvious names were mentioned – Delgado,

Fignon, Mottet, Breukink, their own leader Stephen Roche. Then the team masseur, a Spaniard called Txomin Erdoiza, was asked his opinion and he plumped for LeMond. 'There was a ten-second pause as we reflected on the American's chances. The whole table erupted with laughter.'

The rider-turned-TV-commentator Paul Sherwen admits he shared the majority verdict on LeMond's chances on the Tour. 'I rode my last professional races in '87 and remember seeing Greg at the Nissan Tour of Ireland. His back was pockmarked. It looked like he had measles. Unless you saw Greg's back at that time, you can't imagine how bad it was. There was a pockmark every inch of his back. He was like a dartboard. It was pretty scary to look at. Other guys will have seen that. "This guy's been shot in the back. He ain't going to win the Tour de France any more."'

As François Thomazeau confirms, the press pack was also giving LeMond's chances short shrift. 'Nobody fancied LeMond at all. For all of us, he was finished and it was a miracle he managed to make it back on a bike. His team was simply dreadful. We were just glad to see him back and felt more pity than anything else at the start.'

There were a few dissenting voices, though. LeMond's room-mate Lammerts notes that, following the Giro, the ADR team took part in a small stage race in Spain, in which LeMond rode well. 'He could follow the best Spanish riders and that gave him a lot of confidence.'

And that confidence had also been spotted by the photographer Graham Watson. 'I knew that LeMond knew this Tour was a do-or-die race for him and that he had every intention of re-finding his winning ways. Only a photographer would have spotted it, but LeMond had a certain glint in his eyes, a sparkle we'd not seen since 1986 – this too went unnoticed by most observers. The French media in particular ignored LeMond because of Fignon's superior form, a small oversight that would come back to bite them. But, importantly, it let LeMond come into the Tour as an underdog and race more or less unnoticed for a few days.'

LeMond had never been such an underdog in the Tour before. And, drawing from his wide smile and twinkling eyes, it was fair to say he appeared to be relishing his new-found position.

It was time to let the games begin.

THREE

A MATTER OF TIMING

*'Only when the official pushed my saddle
did I realise I was late' – Pedro Delgado*

1 July
Prologue time trial, Luxembourg, 4.8 miles

AS HE GLIDES his Land Rover around the quiet, mid-morning streets of residential north Madrid, Pedro Delgado is laughing, his eyes dancing. Laughter shouldn't really be called for, though. After all, he's recalling one of the most damaging days of his career as a professional cyclist. And certainly the most embarrassing.

But time is a great healer. The passing of the decades means that the nerves are no longer raw, that the pain subsided many moons ago. But, nonetheless, the best part of 30 years on, almost all mention of the 1989 Tour's Prologue focuses on the mistakes of the Spaniard.

Delgado, wearing the yellow jersey as last year's champion, had the privilege of being the final rider to charge down the ramp of the Prologue's start house. And confidence was high following his recent triumph at the Vuelta. 'I thought I was going to win again,' he confirms. 'I was very, very confident about that. I knew I would have to keep an eye on Fignon in the first few days, but once we got to the mountains, there wouldn't be a problem. My weakest part of the race was always the time trial, sure, but I was very keen to improve at the Prologue. But it was a disaster.'

At 5.16pm, Sean Kelly – the Prologue's penultimate rider to set off – headed out along L'Avenue de la Liberté, a blur in his white and black PDM kit as he sped past the thoroughfare's elegant townhouses and rows of equally elegant trees. Just one rider left to go. The champion. The favourite. The man in yellow.

As Kelly disappeared into the distance, the eyes of the crowd and the lenses of the press pack returned their collective gaze to the start house. Everyone expected Delgado and his bike to be right there, a tight figure of concentration and intensity preparing the defence of his title. But he wasn't. The seconds ticked. The seconds dissolved. At 5.17pm came the pips that announced what should have been his departure time. Still no sign. The clock started its count. Seconds became a minute and not a yard had been pedalled. Time was waiting for no man, not even the reigning champion of the Tour de France.

The growing media throng that was gathering around the back of the start house awaited a glimpse of yellow to appear on the horizon. A besuited official, stopwatch in his left hand, paced up and down inside, all confused hand gestures and shoulder shrugs. The Prologue is supposed to be an incident-free ride that merely warms up the legs for the titanic struggle yet to come. For some, it offers up the chance of wearing the yellow jersey for a day or two, an opportunity they might not otherwise get in this race – in their career, even.

In short, the Prologue doesn't usually make headline news. On this day, though, Pedro Delgado ensured it did.

The start house used for a Prologue or individual time trial in the Tour at this time was little more than the shell of a small beige and cream caravan, albeit one with large picture windows and a seperate entrance and exit. But this tiny structure became the crucible for an incident that would shape the next three weeks – or the next three weeks of one man, at least. But at this point, the rider known as Perico was oblivious to what was occurring. And the clock ticked on, the time accumulating. 'Deux minutes! Deux minutes!' went the shout from the officials. Delgado, though, wherever he was, was clearly out of earshot.

Being a few hundred yards away does tend to put you out of earshot; Delgado had ventured beyond the closed streets reserved for rider warm-ups. 'A lot of people were crossing those streets,' he explains. 'People wanted autographs and photographs, so I felt it wasn't a very good place to warm up. I was there to win the race, to win the Tour again. So I went farther out from this area. And that's when the nightmare began.

'I bumped into Thierry Marie, the French time trial specialist, who had already finished. He's a very nice guy. "Hey Thierry! How are you? Tell me about the course." He explained that it was varied – up and down, left turns and right turns. "It will suit you well. Good luck!" We were talking a lot and I needed to get to the start line. I was very calm, but when I arrived there, everybody said: "Hey Pedro! Where have you been? You need to start the race!"'

There was a flurry of cameramen and a cacophony of gendarmes' whistles as the yellow jersey cut through the tightly packed crowd. Delgado charged up the five metal steps leading into the start house and, thanks to the hand of one of the huffing officials, was sent flying down the ramp. He had arrived two minutes and forty seconds late, although he was actually still oblivious to the extent of his mistake. The absence of race radios – that essential line of communication between rider and team management in years to come – compounded the problem. No one could get word to Delgado in his splendid isolation beyond the warm-up area.

'My team director, José Miguel Echavarri, said "Go! Go! Go!" I thought I was on time. Very close, but on time. I saw the clock said '40, 41, 42…' and expected to start once it came back to 60 at the top. Only when the official pushed my saddle did I realise I was late. I thought maybe it was only 40 seconds or maybe it was two minutes 40 or maybe it was five minutes 40. I had no idea.'

Kelly was unaware of the commotion that had erupted back down the road. 'When you're preparing for a Prologue in the Tour,' he explains, 'you're just focused. There are riders around you and you're not aware if something's happening. Even if a guy going off two places ahead of you misses his start time by 30 seconds or a minute, you don't really notice. You're in a tunnel beforehand. You don't notice anything. You're so focused doing your final warm-up, getting on the ramp and just going as fast as possible from A to B.

'It was big news, of course. When you heard about it later, you thought "How did he make that mistake?" It's something that riders do. They just get totally into that zone and they don't pay attention and forget a little bit about time.'

Stephen Roche was also a little incredulous as the gravity of Delgado's error began to sink in. 'I was sitting in the back of the station wagon, in the boot of the car. We were listening to it and it was very encouraging news. Delgado, one of the main rivals, was already minutes down before the start. It was great. That is the first thing you think about. The Tour is never won on any one day. Every day is another day. But you can lose it all on one day by having a really bad day.

'No one could believe it. But then no one would have thought that I would make the same mistake in 1991.' That year, Roche was eliminated from the Tour for missing the cut-off time at the team time trial. Then riding for the Belgian Tonton Tapis team, he and the squad had been told an incorrect start time. When the mistake was spotted, the riders were then all informed that they'd actually be leaving ten minutes earlier than stated – all but Roche, that is. He was still out on the warm-up circuit and remained out of the loop. Oblivious and forgotten. The team left without him, leaving the former champion to fend for himself and to ride alone once the error had been revealed to him.

What was a simple case of miscommunication then turned into a game of Chinese whispers. At one point on the warm-up circuit, Roche had stopped for a wee in a temporary toilet. The story mutated into one where he had suffered a case of chronic diarrhoea and had got locked in the toilet, unable to escape. But whatever the circumstances, the outcome was the same: Roche was out of the race and, within days, had left the team.

In 1989, though, he welcomed Delgado's inaccurate timekeeping with a degree of glee. This didn't mean that a major rival had been *eliminated* from the competition, but the whole episode had severely weakened Delgado's campaign to become champion for the second successive year. The Spaniard was, after all, a tough nut to crack. He had been leading the '87 Tour into its closing days, until Roche took yellow on the penultimate stage and overall victory the following afternoon. Charly Mottet, the newly anointed world number one eager to prove himself in a Grand Tour, agrees with

Roche about how Delgado's rivals would have viewed his misfortune in Luxembourg. 'It certainly helped,' he smiles. 'It didn't do me any harm.'

Even though Delgado hoped he was only 40 seconds late in leaving, worries began to infiltrate his brain, internal whispers suggesting that the deficit could actually be so much more. He had to put maximum effort into this, his weakest discipline. Failure to do so might have seen his rivals out of sight by the end of the Prologue. A title defence surrendered after just five miles.

Once riding and into his groove, Delgado looked good, glued to the road's centre white lines on the straights and neatly taking the racing line on the bends. Judging him on speed and riding style alone, no one would have thought that there was a problem. But the gap between Kelly shooting past the local Luxembourgers gathered out on the course and Delgado's eventual arrival hinted that something very wrong had occurred. That and the abnormally large flotilla of cars and bikes trailing in his wake. Hungry for the story, eager for blood.

The photographer Graham Watson was, for once, not perched on the back of a motorbike. 'I was about halfway round along the course. I'd chosen my spot somewhere on the big bridge that straddles the valley and separates old Luxembourg from new Luxembourg. Each of the 198 starters came by in one-minute intervals, but Delgado never came by, and being on foot for this stage, I had no radio to tell me what was going on. It took ages before a yellow-jerseyed dot came into view, followed by this enormous motor cavalcade of TV, photographers, officials and radio teams. I was pleased to see Delgado had actually started his title defence, but confused as to what had held him back. It seemed later as if his defence had ended there and then.'

Delgado himself takes up the story again. 'I did the time trial at the maximum I could and when I passed the finish line, a lot of people were waiting there. I was in fear. I didn't want to stop. I went straight to the hotel to find out what really happened.' He just kept riding. This was a man too confused – and possibly too embarrassed – to embark on a very public post-mortem in the full glare of the world's sports media. He would learn of his error in the privacy of his team's set-up.

But there was further embarrassment to suffer privately.

Despite Delgado's success at the Vuelta, chief sponsor Reynolds, the aluminium manufacturers, couldn't afford to completely fund the team.

The team management was forced to find another benefactor who would part with cash in return for their logo being added to the riders' jerseys. That benefactor was Banesto, the Madrid-based bank. 'All the top personnel at the bank were flown to Luxembourg,' recalls Delgado, with a visible shudder. 'They said "We are happy to be here to see Pedro Delgado win the Tour de France again". It was a disaster. They didn't understand what had happened at the Prologue. We have an expression in Spain about when you start the day with bad luck. 'Con el pie izquierdo' – you start the day on your left leg. That's what happened.' (In the end, Banesto couldn't have been too offended. They took over as the team's principal sponsor a few months later, an arrangement they kept for many years.)

There was no escape from the incredulous press corps for Delgado, either. If they weren't preparing scathing headlines for tomorrow's papers, they were entertaining themselves at the rider's expense. 'A close friend of mine is a Spanish journalist with *El Pais*, and he usually didn't follow the whole race – he thought the first week was boring with sprints and team time trials. He usually joined the race in the Pyrenees because it was close to his home. But he came to the Prologue that year because the newspaper wanted him to. "What can I write about the first day of the Tour de France? There's nothing. There's no news." Afterwards he came up to me. "So, Pedro. Did you do that for me…?"'

Bemusement was the overwhelming emotion on the press benches. As the man from ABC Television called it, 'in that handsome Spanish head are stories yet to be told'.

And there was always a story around Delgado. The events of Luxembourg represented the latest entry in a catalogue of misfortune and/or controversy for him at the Tour – aside, that is, from the probenecid affair the previous summer. In his debut Tour in 1983, he sat in second position behind fellow rookie Laurent Fignon but, after the Alpe d'Huez stage, consumed a milkshake that caused him stomach problems and saw him lose 25 minutes the next day. The following year he crashed when on a breakneck descent of the Col de Joux Plane in the Alps, suffering a broken collarbone. Then, in 1986, he again retired on an Alpine stage after he was informed of the death of his beloved mother. And then came 1989.

Even though the time Delgado had lost while he made his way to the start house was only a third of his winning margin the previous July, when he finished more than seven minutes up on second-place Steven Rooks, some of his fellow riders thought the writing was already on the wall for Delgado in '89. Paul Kimmage's contribution to the pages of the *Sunday Tribune* noted that the Spaniard had 'presented the other race favourites with a gift voucher towards victory in the Tour de France worth two minutes and 40 seconds'. He was not alone. Admittedly writing several years after his retirement, Fignon mused on the effect of the incident on Delgado on the night of the Prologue, noting that 'victory in the Tour was already a distant memory for him'. While possibly an assessment made through the prism of hindsight, it was almost certainly his take on things that very evening, so supremely confident/arrogant (delete as appropriate) he was.

If, as Delgado's *El Pais* pal suggested, the first week of a Tour is underwhelming when it comes to blood-and-thunder action, human error made sure that the first day of the 1989 race stood out from the pack. It may have even set the tenor of the three weeks to come.

'Nowadays, it's probably better for the teams and the riders to have radios,' says Perico, 'but for the spectator it's a pity. Now there are no mistakes. It's all controlled, blocked off. It's another race altogether.' A grin and another Delgado chuckle. 'Mistakes are good for the race.'

***

Before Delgado's debacle, the other 197 riders had stretched their legs over the Prologue course, the first time the cobbles and tarmac of Luxembourg had been under the Tour's wheels for 42 years. Five miles was way too short a distance on which to judge a rider's condition and form, but psychological markers could be put down, a chance for the more demonstrative members of the peloton to carve out an edge over the more mentally fragile.

Andy Hampsten, the gaze of North America focused on him, was a mixture of bullishness and caution beforehand. 'We're here to win the race but we know enough about racing to make too many plans. Right now, there's nothing holding us back. It'll be a real competitive race, which is good for us.' As a man for whom the early days of the Tour – when the roads were flat, the racing fast – were an exercise in staying within an arm's length of his main rivals for the overall general classification, Hampsten's time of

10:12.01 fitted the bill. He was far from being cut adrift – and, crucially, had come through unscathed.

LeMond, the man about whom attention had waned, was more wistful. 'What I'd like to do is start the Tour de France with hope and finish it strong,' he had told one of the few television crews giving him attention in the days before the race. 'If I can place in the top ten, I'll be very satisfied this year.' Anyone within earshot might have raised an eyebrow. Some might have raised both.

But, as he waited in the start house in the last seconds before his departure, LeMond looked the part of the serious contender. In his wind-slicing teardrop helmet and trademark Oakley shades, he didn't look down the avenue at what was before him – both in the next ten minutes and over the next three weeks. He tightened the fixings on his shoes and then backpedalled to get into the optimum position from which to push hard down, to catapult himself down the start ramp and into the race. As the countdown climaxed, the former champion stared intently at his handlebars and front wheel. One pedal stroke at a time. Play it by ear. Test whether that great final day in the Giro was indicative of anything.

As a man who, with three Tours under his belt, had yet to finish outside the podium places, he was riding into the unknown. What was the final destination? Glory? Mediocrity? The abyss? LeMond wasn't concerned with legacy, with keeping that phenomenal record intact. If that's what he was after, he could have just never bothered returning to the Tour, quietly seeing out his days in Minnesota in all that snow and ice. That wasn't Greg LeMond, though. This was a man living in the now, a man using the first week of the Tour as a measure of recovery.

As he had declared, LeMond did indeed start the race with hope. His riding style on the Prologue was smooth and direct, his body generating plenty of power. Indeed, his speed suggested a man who had never been away. And so did the time he recorded over the bends and climbs of Luxembourg (a country helpfully put into context by ABC's fabulously named anchorman Al Trautwig, who described it as 'smaller than the state of Rhode Island'). LeMond was just nine-tenths of a second beyond the ten-minute mark, putting him in second place behind the standard set by Erik Breukink. LeMond had cut the Dutchman's lead down to six seconds.

In being the only rider that afternoon to dip under ten minutes, Breukink – unlike LeMond and Laurent Fignon – had decided to ride without his aero helmet, relying on his close-cropped hair to provide the streamlining. That seemed to suit him, as did the Prologue course, all five miles of it. It was a close fit with the Panasonic rider's strengths. While he showed his out-and-out prowess on the flat section, when the road headed upwards for a 900-metre climb that sharply coiled around the Cote de Pabeiebierg hill (one that the man from the *Guardian* scathingly described as 'a mere pimple compared to what awaits them in the Pyrenees and Alps'), Breukink was flying. His performance sent a message to all of those around him, those riders more fancied to take overall victory, those who'd forgotten about him wearing the leader's jersey for five days at the recent Giro. Ignore me at your peril.

Breukink wasn't the only rider replicating his form from Italy. Fignon's ten minutes on the serpentine streets of Luxembourg showed all the smoothness and form that had delivered him to glory 20 days earlier. He didn't assume quite such a tucked position as LeMond, preferring a more upright profile, seemingly keen to scrutinise the approaching tarmac through those distinctive oval spectacles. But it worked, with the Frenchman knocking LeMond back to third, albeit by just four-tenths of a second. The pair's proximity to each other on the Prologue seemed to set the tone for the race's remaining 2,036 miles.

Sean Kelly was also applying the squeeze. While the green jersey was the longer term goal, he also recognised how the first few days could reunite him with the overall race lead after his fleeting acquaintance with it back in 1983. 'As a sprinter,' he recalls, 'if I'd done a really good Prologue, I could pick up some time bonuses on the early stages and maybe get the yellow jersey for a period in the early part of the race.'

And a really good Prologue is exactly what he did. While he couldn't dislodge Breukink from his perch, Kelly did split Fignon and LeMond to take third. All three had finished within half a second of each other. As *Cycling Weekly* correspondent Keith Bingham noted in a delightfully era-specific observation, the trio recorded 'a series of times only a good electronic watch could separate'.

Not all Irish eyes were smiling, though. Stephen Roche, arguably the most consistent time trialist in the whole peloton, found himself 24 seconds down on Breukink, a significant loss over such a short distance. This was his first appearance in the Tour since standing atop the podium in Paris nearly 24 months previously and perhaps suggested that he needed to recalibrate his chances of a successful race. LeMond's post-stage interviews suggested he was recalibrating his own expectations, although in the opposite direction to those of his old adversary Roche. 'I said to myself if I could finish in the top five in the Prologue, I could finish in the top five overall,' he beamed. After the dark, soul-searching days of the Giro, optimism was flowing fast through LeMond's blood.

And Delgado? He came in 2:54 down on Breukink, to whom he surrendered that yellow jersey. Most significantly, he found himself in the humiliating position of propping up the peloton. 198th of 198 riders – and a minute and a half adrift from the next man, Greg LeMond's team-mate Philip Van Vooren. Had he left the start house when he was scheduled to, his time would have put him into 16th place. But, of course, without the mental strain coursing through his head, that Prologue position would likely to have been even better.

The degree to which the day's events not only defined his race but also his career is revealed in one particularly acute Delgado anecdote taken from 2002, the next time the Tour rolled up in Luxembourg. He had just landed from Madrid, ready to take up a three-week tenure in the commentary box for Spanish TV. 'When I arrived, there were three television crews – Belgian, Dutch and French – in the airport.

'Oh, who was on my plane? Maybe a famous person is here.'

'Hey Pedro! Come over here and tell us about that start of yours all those years ago…'

General classification
1. Erik Breukink (Panasonic/Netherlands) 9'54"
2. Laurent Fignon (Super U/France) +6"
3. Sean Kelly (PDM/Ireland) +6"
4. Greg LeMond (ADR/USA) +6"
5. Steve Bauer (Helvetia-La Suisse/Canada) +8"

FOUR

DOUBLE TROUBLE

'It was like trying to ride behind a rocket' – Bjarne Riis

2 July (morning)
Stage 1, Luxembourg – Luxembourg, 84 miles

'HEY PERICO! YOU still in the race? If I were you, I'd be at home, not here.'

'Oh, thank you, Laurent. Thank you!'

After the debacle in the Prologue, the first full day of the Tour brought further humiliation Pedro Delgado's way, this time from within the peloton, from among his own kind.

Three decades on, it clearly still smarts as he recounts how a gloating Laurent Fignon, wearing the points competition green jersey bequeathed to him by Erik Breukink who was busy wearing the more prestigious yellow, dropped back through the peloton to take a toilet break. There he spied the Spaniard who'd opted for the anonymity of the peloton for the first stage proper. Fignon couldn't resist having a pop. 'I liked him as a rider,' Delgado says, 'but he was disagreeable as a man. He did this not just once, but on two or three stages.'

Whether intended as fraternal teasing or, as seems more likely, a heartless attempt to further weaken the Spaniard's mental stability, Fignon's words achieved the latter. 'I was very, very down,' Delgado admits. 'I was in last place. My morale was…' He pauses, then shakes his head. 'I had no morale. Below zero!'

Delgado could have studied the time deficit with a rational, scientific brain. For a rider with such phenomenal climbing abilities as he, not to mention the prospect of those seven mountain stages stretching out ahead of him, retrieving the three minutes he trailed by was eminently possible. Indeed, that morning he appeared to have made peace with his predicament, at least for the cameras. 'It was only the Prologue,' he insisted to the media tracking his every pre-stage move. 'The whole Tour de France lies ahead and I'm fine. It was just a setback for me but not my hopes for this first day. I think the rest of this Tour will be very much better.'

But privately Delgado couldn't see the woods for the trees. His brain had refused to do the maths; it wouldn't tell him that there were still three weeks to go.

There was a reason why his brain couldn't rationalise it. 'I was hating myself after the Prologue,' he now admits. '"It's my fault, it's my fault. Why did I do that?" And my mistake was not taking a sleeping tablet. I normally sleep very well and don't need anything. I had only taken a sleeping tablet once before – when my mother died in 1986. But that night, all night long, I turned left in my bed and I turned right. Maybe I got one hour's sleep.'

And one hour's sleep proved to be anything but ideal preparation for a day's racing, particularly when that day contained two separate stages – an 84-mile anticlockwise circuit of Luxembourg's south-eastern quarters, followed by a post-lunch, high-velocity 28-mile team time trial.

Not only did Delgado opt for the anonymity of the peloton for the majority of this first stage, but back at the start line – on L'Avenue de la Liberté, scene of his blunder the previous day – he had even chosen to roll out from right at the back of the bunch in an attempt to avoid the stares and finger-pointing of both media and fans. Perhaps it was also to punish himself a little.

The morning was one for the chancers, for those seeking to capture a moment of glory while the big names all conserved their energy for the team time trial a few hours later. Søren Lilholt, a 23-year-old Danish rider on the French Histor team, clearly fancied his chances. After just eight miles, he made his move at the first catch sprint, an interim sprint offering those time bonuses Sean Kelly fancied bagging. Lilholt was gunning along. As a previous winner of the Tour of Luxembourg, these were roads he knew well.

The response from the peloton to Lilholt's attack was muted to the point of being non-existent. Erik Breukink's Panasonic team fanned themselves out across the road to control the tempo of the pack, protecting their man in yellow from any other acts of insurgency from more serious contenders for the general classification. If the Dutch team thought Lilholt didn't have the stamina to stay out front on his own, they might have underestimated his breakaway pedigree. The Dane had made a solo tilt at a stage win in the '88 Paris-Nice race, holding off the peloton for 100 miles. This stage only covered 84. Well within his capabilities.

Or perhaps the Panasonic team, wanting to conserve energy for the team time trial later, weren't too concerned about losing yellow – at least, losing yellow to someone who wouldn't be a contender in Paris. Had the break come from one of the main favourites for the overall title, their response would have been somewhat more energetic. Keep your enemies closest and all that.

Lilholt built up an advantage of nine minutes over the lethargic peloton, making him the virtual *maillot jaune* on the road. But if the star-laden bigger teams didn't want to know, a couple of other riders sprang out from the pack to hunt him down: Portugal's Acácio da Silva, riding for the Carrera team, and the Frenchman Roland Leclerc from the Paternina squad, the newly renamed team led by the vastly experienced Spanish climber Marino Lejarreta.

As the race traced the vineyard-heavy left bank of the Moselle River northwards, with West Germany a couple of hundred yards away on the opposite bank, da Silva and Leclerc caught their prey. But Lilholt didn't slide back, instead clinging on to the latter's wheel. The chance of the young Dane taking the stage win, and with it the yellow jersey, had been significantly slashed; da Silva would be the favourite if it came to a three-way blast for the line. But this would be offset by the cooperation of the trio to stay out in front, away from the hungry reach of the peloton, into whose anonymous depths each man would doubtless have otherwise faded.

And evade the pack they did. With around 30 miles to go, the breakaway still held an 11-minute lead. They were going to survive. It was now simply a case of which rider most fancied trying on the yellow jersey for size. The effort required to bridge the earlier gap to Lilholt was a debt that Leclerc was now forced to repay and he slipped back when da Silva made a bolt for it on the same climb that had ended the previous day's Prologue. It would take the Portuguese rider a second attack to also slip free of Lilholt's clutches, before he took an ecstatic victory in the city where he spent many of his formative years. Having lived in the grand duchy for 14 years from the age of seven, this was nothing short of a triumphant homecoming for da Silva and was ecstatically received by his former neighbours.

Not that it was a one-off stage victory on a Grand Tour for him. No stranger to wins in the Giro, da Silva was also actually recording his third Tour triumph in as many years. In 1987, during the race's detour into West Germany, he held off the Swiss rider Erich Maechler to take the third stage in Stuttgart, while the following year he confirmed his appetite for first-week stage victories by taking the fourth stage into the Normandy town of Évreux, where he outrode the world's top sprinters in a mass finish. More recently, he'd also won the second stage of the '89 Giro, up the slopes of Mount Etna, just five weeks before.

Those first two Tour victories were achieved while he was with the Spanish KAS team, where he was a team-mate of Sean Kelly. 'Acácio showed unbelievable talent in the early part of his career,' Kelly remembers. 'He was an all-rounder. He was pretty good in the sprints, he was able to climb and he was able to put in a good time trial performance. He looked like a rider who could win a big Tour. He had the quality to do that, but he never achieved it. He was a rider who just enjoyed cycling and who was maybe a bit too relaxed at times. The performances that he should have achieved are greater than he has on his palmàres.'

The Mexican rider Raúl Alcalá lived near to da Silva in Switzerland and the pair would go on regular training rides. 'He was a tough rider and a good sprinter,' Alcalá recalls, 'but more suited to shorter races like the Dauphiné. To ride the Tour de France to win is difficult. Not so many guys have the capability of being in the top ten all the time. He was a rider for six or seven days.' Alcalá's assessment is completely consistent with da Silva's three first-week Tour stage victories. In each year, he rendered himself invisible come the second half of each race.

That third victory – in the colours of Carrera after KAS's dissolution at the end of the 1988 season – was different from the first two. There was that additional prize. Coming home nearly five minutes ahead of the peloton, da Silva also inherited Breukink's yellow jersey. 'If you're a rider who can keep within 15 or 20 seconds on the Prologue, you never know what can happen,' says Kelly. 'If you can get into a breakaway in the next day or so, then you can take the yellow jersey. That's how it worked out for da Silva.'

As da Silva was being mobbed by the media at the finish line, the peloton's frontrunners were still jockeying for position on that final climb. The most notable protagonist was the *lanterne rouge*, the last man in the race – Pedro Delgado. Trying to use the sharp gradient to scrape a few seconds back overall, he found his attacks suppressed. They represented a pointless waste of energy when really he should have sat tight and been patient. Other stages, other opportunities.

'I tried to break away towards the end,' he acknowledges, the memory of the stage remaining crystal clear. 'But it wasn't normal for a rider like me to try that in that kind of stage. All you end up doing is losing your strength.' Delgado's sleep-deprived brain was making bad decisions. And a loss of strength is far from the ideal preparation for a team time trial just a couple of hours later.

Stage 1
1. Acácio da Silva (Carrera/Portugal) 3:21:36
2. Søren Lilholt (Histor/Denmark) +8"
3. Roland Leclerc (Paternina/France) +1'41"
4. Etienne De Wilde (Histor/Belgium) +4'40"
5. Sean Kelly (PDM/Ireland) +4'40"

General classification
1. Acácio da Silva (Carrera/Portugal) 3:31:44
2. Søren Lilholt (Histor/Denmark) +13"
3. Roland Leclerc (Paternina/France) +1'54"
4. Erik Breukink (Panasonic/Netherlands) +4'26"
5. Laurent Fignon (Super U/France) +4'32"

***

2 July (afternoon)
Stage 2, team time trial, Luxembourg – Luxembourg (29 miles)

'It's the cruellest, most nerve-wracking thing you can do.'

Sitting at home in Colorado, the bright sunshine reflecting off the snow outside and filling his house with light, Andy Hampsten is recalling one particular horror from his riding days: having a team time trial on the same day as another stage.

'You're trying to conserve energy in the morning and stay out of trouble, but then people attack. You can't over-estimate how extraordinarily difficult and chaotic those team time trials were.' Not that, as Hampsten observes, they needed to be held on a double-stage day to qualify as a horrific experience.

'I love the event, but more as a spectator than a rider. Professionals, in my opinion, are terrible at team time trials. They're all so nervous and there's probably some new bike or new wheels or new aerodynamic thing to try out. A nine-person time trial is so much different from the four-man ones we were used to as amateurs back in the day. The speed is so incredibly high. If you're doing well, you have ten or 15 seconds to sprint at the front of the group and then sit up to get out of the way because your team-mates are all over the road, especially on the tiny roads the Tour likes to put us on. Then you have to sprint again to get on the back.'

This was the theory, at least. No one told Pedro Delgado ahead of the afternoon's team time trial. Just as Søren Lilholt took things easy on the back of the Histor bunch after his exertions that morning, Reynolds' leader was also shying away from taking his rightful turn at the front of his team. But, aside from that attempt to slip away from the peloton in the final uphill mile or two of the earlier stage, Delgado couldn't blame it on the effects of a Herculean effort a couple of hours earlier. Not helped by the lack of sleep the night before, his problems were psychological. And he was inadvertently putting an even larger dent in the defence of his title.

Those problems manifested themselves very publicly. Around the halfway point of the stage – so only 14 or so miles in – Delgado began to slide off the back of his team. He was mightily fortunate that, in those radio-free times, one of his faithful domestiques, the Basque rider Julián Gorospe, had spotted the demise of his great leader. Gorospe, with all the instinct of the selfless servant, instantly dropped back, cajoling Delgado and offering him a drafting opportunity to bring him back into the bunch. This he managed. Job done.

Or so Gorospe thought. Delgado remained at the back of the Reynolds pack but, as his team-mates fluidly negotiated a right-hand bend, he again dropped off. And this time there was a significant margin between him and his eight team-mates. The instinct of Gorospe, or any of the other domestiques, was much slower to kick in. When they finally realised Delgado had jettisoned himself, the scene was comedic. The team was in disarray – freewheeling, spread out all over the road, waiting for their man.

The Reynolds team never recovered that afternoon. Having been treated to the indignity of being overtaken by Z-Peugeot, who had started out three minutes after them, they limped home in the slowest time of all 22 teams. Again, as he crossed the line, Delgado was the bait in a feeding frenzy. The Tour's photographers, microphone men and notebook-clasping reporters still had an appetite for the Spaniard's destruction.

At the day's end, he had only avoided still being in 198th position because two riders had been eliminated from the race for finishing beyond the time barrier. He was merely 196th out of 196 now. When they consider the champion's demise in '89, many observers simply believe Delgado lost the Tour on the Prologue. He didn't. He lost the Tour on the team time trial. Stage 2 and he was already almost ten minutes down on the yellow jersey.

Delgado admits it himself. 'The real problem was the team time trial. I became very, very weak. I hit the wall. The team were saying "Oh Pedro, come on!", but I lost another five minutes. I was still in last position. Everybody – Spanish journalists, people on the team – were saying "What do you want to do? Do you want to retire from the race?" But I thought that if I did that and went home, I'd feel even worse than if I stayed in the race. I understood I'd made big mistakes, but I needed to recover mentally. And it was better to do that in the race than at home. It was 100% mental.'

It would have been the easiest thing to slip away quietly from the race, citing some phantom physical complaint that explained everything away.

But Delgado – perhaps unwilling to play into the hands of those doubting his win the previous year – stayed in the race to save both face and reputation.

His commitment impressed Paul Sherwen, the seven-time Tour rider who was by then co-commentating alongside Phil Liggett for Channel 4. 'Psychologically, he'd lost it. He was gone,' he remembers. 'The whole thing was totally destroyed. He couldn't stay with the guys, with the boys he was thrashing all year in road races. They had to drag him and nurse him along to try to keep him in contact with the race.

'You're last overall. What do you do? What can you do? Anybody would say "OK, let's go home. Done. Finished." But Perico never complained and he climbed up the general classification every day after then.'

There was also some sympathy among the peloton. Sean Yates, the time trial specialist who'd recently jumped ship from Fagor to 7-Eleven, and who had powered the American team towards sixth place that afternoon, attempts to dissect the Reynolds team's tactics to restore Delgado's confidence and get him moving up the general classification.

'These were the days before proper planning of a team time trial. Nowadays, you'd be thinking, "OK, we need to do it like this. Pedro's not feeling great. He needs to sit on and we mustn't drop him at any cost. We need to protect him blah blah blah." But they must have gone out hell for leather with three or four guys in the red, and everything just went tits up. That just wouldn't happen these days. Control the controllables. Think about what could go wrong and plan for it. In those days, it was a case of going out there and smashing it. There was no Plan B. If it went tits up, it was "OK, bad luck" – even though a team time trial could make the difference between winning and losing.'

Some were reminded of that on that particular afternoon, Stephen Roche especially. Possibly because Sean Yates's power and metronomic pacing hadn't been satisfactorily replaced over the winter, Fagor only finished 15th, dropping Roche down to 95th position. At the end of the second day, he was already raising the white flag on his GC aspirations. 'I'm not going to win this Tour,' he freely admitted at the finish line. 'I've got lots of doubts. I've not recovered from the Giro.'

Steve Bauer's slide down the general classification – aka the GC – was, on paper at least, quite dramatic, dropping from eighth to 56th. RMO's

Charly Mottet also departed the top ten for now, finding himself down in the anonymity of 35th place.

While Sean Kelly also temporarily vacated the top ten, his PDM team would have been satisfied with fourth place, especially as their strengths would be truly revealed when the race reached the mountains. But the surprise performance of the day probably went to LeMond's ADR squad who, sneered at for their weaker riders, came fifth. It was a performance that may have quietened a few doubters, although several pointed out how it wasn't that surprising, bearing in mind the flat racing pedigree of the team's six Belgian riders. The mountains remained LeMond's true test, especially as he had only that single specialist climber in the ADR ranks to help him.

The likes of Kelly, Mottet and LeMond may have dropped down the general classification, but most would find themselves rising back up in the coming days. Their respective demises were – as is usually the case after a team time trial, certainly after one won so comprehensively – a temporary statistical blip. The winning team finds all its riders accelerating into the upper echelons of the overall standings, an artificial amplification of their individual abilities and of where they should actually be in the rankings. Equilibrium would be restored in a few days' time.

Hence, at the end of this double-stage day, Laurent Fignon's Super U team celebrated having five riders in the top eight places of the GC after their victory. The last team to set off, they flew along the course like an absolute juggernaut, their leader – as all leaders should – setting the mood and ambition of his team. And, as he keenly explained himself, setting the pace too.

'Apart from a few fleeting moments,' Fignon would later write, 'on the final part of the loop no one was able to share the pace-making with me. I could feel the power inside me, the power that was there on my best days.' Super U swooped back into Luxembourg City the most unified, purposeful and, most importantly, fastest of all 22 teams. The performance wasn't so much a warning shot across enemy bows as a big, booming explosion of intent.

If he wasn't already aware, Bjarne Riis, Fignon's recently recruited right-hand man, received confirmation that afternoon that he had joined a team that was both seriously talented and seriously ambitious. This was a team with the primary goal of winning the Tour by smashing the opposition. 'With Gérard Rué, Thierry Marie and Fignon at the head of affairs,' he recalled, 'we hammered away from the start. We rode fast. Really fast. I was flying and was giving it absolutely everything every time I took my turn at the front of the line. Fignon and Marie were among the world's best time trialists and could ride fast for long turns at a time. Every time they took over at the front, it was like trying to ride behind a rocket.'

Riis had won a stage on his very first full day on the Tour. 'That was fantastic,' he remembers now. 'These guys were phenomenal. Fignon was strong but Thierry Marie was – ahhh – exceptionally strong on this stage. It gave us a great boost and an advantage over the rest.'

As the best-placed Super U rider, Fignon moved into third overall behind da Silva and Lilholt. And his advantage over his GC contenders was also a psychological one. With the likes of Delgado, Roche and LeMond all, in different ways, on the comeback trail, each was wrestling with a set of variables, whether mental (Delgado), political (Roche) or physical (LeMond). They had distractions. They had concerns. They couldn't just simply get out there and ride.

Fignon on the other hand – despite being on the comeback trail himself after five years of stuttering Tour appearances – had cured himself of his ills and injuries. He had neutralised his own variables. In fact, on the evidence of the team time trial, he had blasted right through them.

It had taken him a long time to recover the form and condition of his early years in the professional ranks. In 1981, Fignon had entered the Tour of Corsica as an amateur and was delighted to find he could keep up with two-time Tour winner Bernard Hinault on one particular stage on the mountainous Mediterranean island. Hinault's team boss Cyrille Guimard spotted the potential in Fignon's 20-year-old legs and swiftly offered him a professional contract for the following season, one that would place him alongside Hinault and LeMond on the Renault team. (Fignon later referred to Renault at this time as 'the Oxbridge of cycling'.)

Having briefly led the Giro in his debut pro season, Fignon's first Tour was the '83 edition which, remarkably, he won, albeit in Hinault's absence. There was, admittedly, a degree of good fortune about the victory. Long-term leader Pascal Simon broke his shoulder blade on the tenth stage and, after battling on with it for a few days, eventually abandoned and handed Fignon the yellow jersey. With the 1980 champion Joop Zoetemelk having tested positive, the 22-year-old Frenchman enjoyed a comfortable, pressure-free ride into Paris.

Fignon's 1984 win was much more of a test, and therefore offered much more glory. Going head-to-head against his former team-mate Hinault (now leader of Bernard Tapie's La Vie Claire team), Fignon saw off the older man, his winning margin of more than ten minutes secured thanks to five stage wins.

He was a rider at the very top of his game – and with another ten years or so of potential glory stretching out before him. 'In 1984,' he later told *Cycle Sport's* Edward Pickering, 'I wasn't far from perfection … Sometimes I spoke with my team-mates, who told me their legs hurt all the time. During races, during training. I didn't understand it – they had never gone a day when their legs did not hurt. I can say that, during the 1984 Tour de France, my legs pretty much did not hurt the whole way round.

'In fact, at the start of 1985, I was much stronger than the year before. If I hadn't had the injury which stopped me then, I can promise you that my career would have been a different story. I was incredibly strong, and it was easy. Then it stopped, just like that.'

That injury – an Achilles problem that required major surgery – then introduced Fignon to more barren times in the Tour, a period when he would finish the race only once in four years. Having missed the '85 race, the following year he retired in Pau after the team doctor's thermometer recorded Fignon's temperature being 39 degrees. A seventh place in 1987 suggested a return to the days of glory could be imminent, but these hopes were dashed 12 months later when he again abandoned; this time he was suffering from the after-effects of a tapeworm.

His anxiousness to record a third Tour victory were exacerbated by the fact that not only was Fignon Super U's leader, he was also the team co-owner. In 1985, Renault had pulled out of all their commitments to sports sponsorship. But the response of Fignon and Guimard wasn't to sail off into the sunset in search of contracts with other teams. Instead, they turned the traditional formula of cycling team ownership on its head. Rather than the usual arrangement whereby a sponsor owns the team, the pair set up their own marketing company that would own the team; the sponsors subsequently signed up would simply be buying advertising space on the team's jerseys.

This meant that they could operate without other personnel offering their opinions and advice on the way the team was being run. They weren't employees subject to the whims of their paymasters. They were the owners who could choose their own path for the team.

As long as the pair agreed with each other, of course. The Reuters journalist François Thomazeau explains that 'there really was a father and son relationship between them. They were very close, much closer than Guimard ever was with Hinault. Both were headstrong and they made decisions together, but my feeling was that Guimard was really the mastermind. He was the first modern manager in many ways – very keen on scientific and technical improvements. He really knew what he was doing. But he wasn't very diplomatic and his sponsors were getting tired of him. Super U left at the end of the 1989 season.'

Fignon's own lack of diplomacy was the stuff of legend, with him often portrayed as a fiery ball of impatience and volatility. 'He was not very popular,' says Thomazeau. 'I saw him refuse to sign autographs to young kids in the rudest manner. I don't think he was really a bad guy. He was a bit shy and I don't think he liked the media attention that much.' Thomazeau points out that Hinault too, despite five Tour wins, didn't exactly unite the country behind him either. Instead, France retained a fondness for those who never won the Tour, riders like Jean-François Bernard and Ronan Pensec. 'We were still partial to losers at the time...'

Not that the lack of public or media support would have bothered Fignon. He simply wanted it from within the team ranks, that unflinching respect and commitment from his Super U riders. 'Fignon would give instructions in a neutral and friendly tone,' Bjarne Riis later wrote. 'There was no shouting or swearing. He was always calm and a complete gentleman.

'If he'd been an idiot, I doubt I would have been willing to sacrifice myself for him the way I did. You need to be as willing to fight for your team leader as you are to fight for yourself. And victory for your leader is good for your bank account, too. For every decent result Fignon attained, it meant a share of the prize money for me.'

After five years of turbulence and misfortune, Fignon was the GC
contender in the best position after two days of the '89 Tour. He was strong
and his team equally so. A deep, easy sleep would have come quickly that
night, the Super U team dreaming of future glory – and quite possibly of
prize money too.

It was surely a different matter over at the Reynolds team hotel.
Having had very little rest the night before, Pedro Delgado must have
considered taking a sleeping pill after the further indignity of that
afternoon's team time trial. He would definitely have taken one had he
known the newspaper headlines being printed at the very moment that
he was turning in for the night.

Stage 2
1. Super U 53'48"
2. Panasonic +32"
3. Superconfex +49"
4. PDM +50"
5. ADR +51"

General classification
1. Acácio da Silva (Carrera/Portugal) 4:27:27
2. Søren Lilholt (Histor/Denmark) +26"
3. Laurent Fignon (Super U/France) +2'37"
4. Thierry Marie (Super U/France) +2'41"
5. Pascal Simon (Super U/France) +2'48"

FIVE

THE MAN FROM MONTERREY

'I attacked hard and they let me go. I went full gas' – Raúl Alcalá

3 July
Stage 3, Luxembourg – Spa-Francorchamps, 150 miles

THE MORNING NEWSPAPERS were brutal, spelling out the depth of despair that Pedro Delgado had brought on himself in Luxembourg. 'FIGNON EXECUTE DELGADO' shouted the headline in *L'Equipe*, stressing that Super U's efforts the previous afternoon had effectively killed off any suggestion of the Spaniard arriving in Paris in yellow. The Spanish *AS* paper was a little less dramatic in its tone, but the message was unequivocal nonetheless: 'PERICO, ADIOS'.

The previous day's tumult had recalibrated expectations over the identity of the future champion, forcing the continent's bookmakers into action that Monday morning as soon as they unlocked their doors for business. Blackboard rubbers were reached for, and clouds of chalk dust created, as a new favourite was feverishly installed for the overall title. The name now scribbled in chalk at the top of their list was, of course, that of Laurent Fignon.

The team time trial had dictated this rewrite. Not only had Delgado's worries and woes cast doubt on his ability to even finish the Tour, but the

Super U squad were displaying attributes in polar opposition to those shown by the faltering Reynolds leader. The power and resoluteness of Super U's performance the previous afternoon was hard to bet against; it had worn an air of inevitability from the first time-check onwards. Accordingly, Fignon's odds had dropped to 9-4, while Delgado found himself slipping to an undeniably realistic (in fact, possibly optimistic) 4-1.

The third stage was a chance for the main GC riders to conserve energy and keep their powder dry for the long individual time trial later in the week. Accordingly, this lengthy stage into Belgium – one that would finish at the Formula 1 racing circuit at Spa-Francorchamps, having travelled through the undulating forests of the Ardennes – offered the chance for others to shine.

There was one rider who took that chance with open arms and a big smile. His name was Raúl Alcalá.

Alongside Sean Kelly, the Mexican was one of PDM's new signings for the '89 season. Until then, he had been one of the leading lights of the 7-Eleven team. At the '87 Tour, he won the white jersey awarded to the best young rider, as well as placing third in the King of the Mountains. He was both a very useful and popular member of Jim Ochowicz's set-up.

'I liked having Alcalá on the team,' says Andy Hampsten. 'It was nice having more than one leader. The idea was to try to win the Tour de France and it was better to do so having two climbers, not just one. We certainly understood that he couldn't say no to going to a big team like PDM and getting a big salary. I missed having him around.'

Sitting on his sofa at his home in Monterrey, with his partner Mercedes alongside him offering reminders of certain moments in his career, Alcalá remembers how 7-Eleven had been the perfect breeding ground during his formative professional years. 'That was my first team and I tried to stay with them as long as possible. Those guys there – Jim Ochowicz, Mike Neel – gave me good protection.

'As a small team, we didn't have any big responsibilities. There was less pressure. When you grow up in a small team, it's nice to develop slowly – to take time to gain experience and to not have the same pressure that was on the big guys like Hinault and LeMond. In my third year there, though, I had more and more responsibilities. They gave me a schedule for the year. "Which one do you want to win?" I always preferred to win the Tour de France, but that was a difficult one for a young rider. But I always tried to win it.'

As well as PDM offering a stronger foundation for a tilt at the Tour's GC, the difference in conditions turned Alcalá's head. 'They had everything,' he laughs. 'When I was at 7-Eleven, I was always looking up at them. They had big trucks and a big bus. "Wow! I want to be on that team one year…"'

It was small wonder Alcalá wanted to switch. He holds up his phone screen to show off a picture. It's a shot of several professional cyclists bedding down in a school gymnasium when the Tour reached the Pyrenean ski resort of Superbagnères. But this isn't a scene from the austere 1940s or '50s. The presence of Pedro Delgado on a fold-up bed in the foreground of the picture confirms it actually to be of 1986 vintage. Other riders from Reynolds are identifiable, as are the teams of Hitachi and 7-Eleven. That these were the conditions that the world's greatest cyclists were expected to endure as recently as the mid-1980s is a little shocking. And 'enduring' is exactly the right word. 'Everybody's snoring and coughing,' laughs Alcalá. 'Oh man! Cold water all the time. I couldn't take a shower like that. Impossible. It was terrible.

'With 7-Eleven, you would travel around in a small car all the time and you'd have to change your clothes in it after a race. We even did our own laundry. At PDM, we had our laundry collected and we had showers on the bus. That was a big difference.'

Alcalá would have made a strong addition to any team at that time. He was a compact, deceptively strong rider who showed immense talent as both climber and time trialist. Beneath that easy smile lurked steely ambition, suggesting someone capable, with a year or two's more experience, of a podium place in Paris. Indeed, several teams were making a play for him. But there was only really one destination. 'I talked a lot with [PDM's managers] Jan Gisbers and Manfred Krikke. Every day they'd talk to me like I was their son. They charmed me and that's why I went there.' Plus, the economics couldn't be ignored. 'I was on a bigger contract,' he confirms. 'I was earning four times more than at 7-Eleven. It was a lot at that time. It was one of the best contracts in cycling. It was close to a million dollars. Very close.'

7-Eleven understood it was an offer Alcalá couldn't refuse. 'Jim Ochowicz and Mike Neel were very open about it. "Raúl, if you'd prefer to ride for them, that's up to you. Go ahead. Whatever you want. You're free to leave." Things were always clear with those guys. It was always straight on, very honest. Nothing behind your back.'

If 7-Eleven had been conspicuously laid-back, Alcalá's PDM contract came loaded with expectation and pressure ('they expected a lot of things, including winning the Tour de France one of the years'). And on Stage 3 of the '89 Tour, a long stage somewhat surreally ending on a motor racing circuit, the young Mexican gave his new team reason to believe his signing had been extremely judicious. The race was barely 48 hours old.

Despite the distance, the early parts of the stage were dominated by some notably aggressive riding, as Alcalá recalls. 'The attacks started right from the gun, for 30 or 40 kilometres. It didn't stop. It was just attack, attack, attack.' These weren't conditions that necessarily suited Alcalá's team-mate Sean Kelly, who had been expected to challenge for the intermediate sprints in order to earn a few seconds here and there that would chip away at Acácio da Silva's overall lead. Instead, as the race finally left Luxembourg and moved into Belgium, the Panasonic rider John Talen bagged the maximum time bonuses on offer at the first three sprints. Perhaps the Irishman had an ulterior motive. The sharp, uphill finish at the racing circuit certainly suited the power of a Kelly sprint.

As the stage unfolded, though, it was the other new boy who represented PDM's best hope for the stage win. Alcalá had been involved in one of those early attacks and went with the flow. 'I was there at the front and I saw that nobody had come to close it down. That was a big break, with 15 guys or so.'

As the break eventually got within a few miles of the Spa-Francorchamps circuit, it had slimmed down to a nine-strong group. And they were being allowed to get on with it. Back at the head of the peloton, both the PDM and TVM teams had spread themselves across the road and slowed the pace right down, giving their men in the break the strongest chance of both surviving and taking the stage win.

By the time those first riders reached the tarmac of the circuit, they numbered only four. PDM weren't the sole Dutch squad represented; TVM had the Danish rider Jesper Skibby, while Patrick Tolhoek wore the colours of Superconfex. The other rider was Super U's Thierry Marie, later joined by his compatriot, Toshiba's Marc Madiot, to make a five-strong group gunning for victory. What was most surprising was that there wasn't a single Belgian among them, no one ready to take the win in the only stage this year on home soil.

As Formula 1 circuits go, Spa-Francorchamps very much has its own identity – a combination of long, wooded sections and some serious gradients. The following month, defending Formula 1 world champion Ayrton Senna would tame the circuit in wildly wet and windy conditions; the day before the Tour arrived, Eddie Lawson had won the 500cc race at the Belgian Motorcycle Grand Prix. The Tour, however, unlike the two motorised races, chose to tackle the circuit in an anticlockwise direction.

Alcalá had watched the motorbike race the previous day and, on television, the hills didn't look so fierce. The effortless ease with which man and machine powered up the inclines seemed to smooth them out. Sean Kelly, resigned to sitting in the peloton on account of his team-mate's presence in the front five, notes that he found anything but a mildly undulating circuit. 'It was very, very difficult. When you see Formula 1 cars going round it at x miles an hour, you don't realise how steep the bloody hill is. But when you go round it on a bike, that's when you get a real feel for the circuit. When we came down the hill and into the finish area, even on the bike it was amazingly fast.'

The stage finished with two laps of the 4.5-mile circuit and, as they approached the bell, the breakaway group got its first sense of how quick the descent 500 yards before the uphill finish really was. Alcalá – the main instigator of the break and the man who still looked the freshest – drove them through the bell and into the last few miles.

The Mexican had two objectives for the last lap: to win the stage, of course, but also to take as much time out of the peloton in order to catapult himself up the GC. That's why he was driving the group along and not simply hanging on the wheels of others, ready to dart out when the final sprint went into motion. A stage win was welcome, of course, but the longer game was also being played.

As the group's best-placed rider, Thierry Marie wouldn't have complained about the pace and propulsion. It gave him the best chance of being in yellow that evening and was infinitely preferable to being part of a group that reduced its speed as riders played games with each other. As it was, though, the group's lead was insufficient for Marie to take the *maillot jaune* from Acácio da Silva. The peloton was now charging around the circuit, a mass murmuration of riders swarming one way and then the other, collectively trying to find the kind of racing line that the likes of Senna, Alain Prost and Nigel Mansell had done many times over on this circuit.

While Alcalá and Marie were considering the bigger picture, for the other three riders – Skibby, Tolhoek and Madiot – it was all about the day, all about the stage win. As the mile count decreased, the kidology increased. Skibby invited Tolhoek to take a stint on the front of the group, to which the Dutchman blew out his cheeks and declined the kind offer, trying to suggest that the unexpected sharpness of the hills had emptied his energy reserves. Perhaps.

As they began the long drag up the big hill, the group started to slow and to spill across the road. This was partially to do with geography, but mainly psychology. Glances were exchanged, minds were read, cards were kept close to chests. Who was going to show their hand first? Alcalá, still looking the freshest of the bunch, didn't need a second invitation. As the road bore left, he nipped away on the inside – a perfectly timed attack, on which he was hotly pursued by the motorbike cameraman. The other four riders reacted, but didn't sustain their effort, their response falling apart as they came off the pedals and pleaded for each other to maintain the chase. Their indecision and petty squabbling played into Alcalá's hands who belted off down the long Kemmel Straight, his legs eating up the yards.

Once under the Stella Artois-branded banner denoting one kilometre to go, the first Tour de France victory by a Mexican rider was all but assured. Alcalá hurtled down the final descent, careful not to touch the red and white striped kerbstones on the inside of the bend, and back up the other side to take the win. The belated response from the rest of the group had brought the gap down to five seconds, but the games they'd played earlier had deprived them of the stage win that their efforts on this long stage might have earned. Skibby took second, pipping the actually-not-so-tired-after-all Tolhoek.

You get the sense that Alcalá has replayed that last lap of Spa-Francorchamps many, many times in his mind over the decades since, revelling in the beauty of his neat escape. 'I was in the moment and in the right position,' he recalls. 'I attacked hard and they let me go. I went full gas, otherwise those guys would have beaten me. Jesper Skibby was faster than me in the sprint. I had two options: go alone, or wait until the uphill sprint. So I went on a longer attack and that was the right moment to do it.'

When the peloton powered home less than a minute after Alcalá, the massed spectators really got a sense of the sharpness of that final descent. Like the cars of a rollercoaster, the pack flew down the downslope of the parabola, touching speeds of around 50mph, before being fired up the slope on the other side towards the line. 'Even on a bike, it was amazingly fast,' says Sean Kelly.

Kelly had put his ambitions – whether for a stage win or for an improvement on his position in the GC – on hold for the day. So had the other main contenders, who broadly kept their overall positions, aside from having to now accommodate Alcalá, who moved up from 26th to sixth. Fignon was on the move too, albeit dropping out of the top three. His replacement? His team-mate Thierry Marie, who now led his leader by 40 seconds.

Stage 3
1. Raúl Alcalá (PDM/Mexico) 6:34:17
2. Jesper Skibby (TVM/Denmark) +5"
3. Patrick Tolhoek (Superconfex/Netherlands) same time
4. Thierry Marie (Super U/France) +6"
5. Marc Madiot (Toshiba/France) same time

General classification
1. Acácio da Silva (Carrera/Portugal) 11:02.34
2. Søren Lilholt (Histor/Denmark) +24"
3. Thierry Marie (Super U/France) +1'57"
4. Laurent Fignon (Super U/France) +2'37"
5. Pascal Simon (Super U/France) +2'48"

***

4 July
Stage 4, Liège – Wasquehal, 158 miles

On the fourth day of January 1989, Bjarne Riis was contemplating life, the universe and everything. The Dane's problems couldn't quite be defined as an existential crisis, but he was certainly analysing his future as a professional cyclist, having spent the previous season as an anonymous – and little-used – domestique with the Toshiba squad. 'A disaster' is his assessment of his time with the French team. 'Nothing went well.'

During the winter months, he was forced to take an office job in his temporary home of Luxembourg in order to pay the bills. No team had expressed a desire to hire his services. The sport appeared to have given him up. The feeling was mutual. Returning to Denmark and putting his bike into storage was high on his agenda.

And then his phone rang.

Six months to the day later, Riis found himself part of a three-man breakaway in the fourth stage of his first-ever Tour de France. That he was wearing the white, yellow and red of Laurent Fignon's Super U team gave a clue as to who made his phone ring that January day.

The previous September, Riis had been riding in the Tour de la Communauté Européene, the French stage race more often called the Tour de l'Avenir. It was his only ride for Toshiba since the Giro d'Italia that May. Fignon, still on the mend after the debilitating effects of that tapeworm, approached Riis and a couple of other riders as, according to the Dane, he 'needed some help on one or two days. We gave him a hand – we had to earn some money! He seemed pretty impressed and I suppose he spoke to Cyrille Guimard about having me on the team.

'I didn't hear from him but then, suddenly, on the 4th of January, they called me. You should normally be sorted with a team for the new season by then. "We have a spot. Come on our training camp."' Accepting the offer of a monthly wage of 12,000 Danish kroner (around £1,000), Riis passed the audition and was selected by Fignon to be his faithful lieutenant, his bodyguard, his protector.

'Guimard had originally picked out a different rider to be Fignon's right-hand man,' Riis once wrote, 'but he had been forced to change his mind when Fignon himself told him that he wanted it to be me. Him choosing me meant that Guimard quickly gave me even more attention, keen to help me be as good a bike rider as I could be. And he didn't hold back on telling me what I needed to do.' Riis was a clear beneficiary of Fignon's dual roles, those of team leader and co-owner.

The partnership bore fruit very quickly. And rich fruit at that. 'We won the Giro,' he says, with some pride. 'I was very strong and helped Fignon a lot. I was the guy sitting in front of him every day, guiding him through the peloton. Somehow I was good at that. I thought "That's the job for me". He was safe when he was on my wheel. Always in a good spot, always in the right position. That was my job.'

And the faithful lieutenant even got his own moment in the sun when he took victory on the Giro's ninth stage into the Umbrian town of Gubbio. 'I'll remember that day forever. I'd been sitting in front of Fignon for eight days, just riding and riding. That stage was long and tough, and at the end there was a long, long, long false flat. Everyone was attacking and I was looking around. Fignon suddenly came up to me and said, "Bjarne, go for it. Just go." He didn't need to say that twice. I ended up sitting there with Dimitri Konyshev and I beat him in the sprint.'

The confidence that the Gubbio stage win gave Riis was now showing in the fourth stage of the Tour, where – in the company of his former Toshiba team-mate Martial Gayant and Federico Echavé of the Spanish BH team – he was powering along the narrow lanes of rural Belgium. While this might have been surprising terrain for Echavé, the winner of the Alpe d'Huez stage in 1987, the stage suited the more powerfully built Riis. Having ridden the Classics that spring in the service of Fignon, the stage from Liège into northern France returned the Dane to familiar ground, including nine sections of cobbles as the riders approached the Belgian border, nine opportunities to sample 'the hell of the north'.

The race most famous for these cobbles – Paris-Roubaix – offers a particular challenge when it's held every April, its competitors often emerging soggy and mud-caked thanks to the dampness of early spring in northern France. The cobbles represent something different in the dry warmth of early July.

Plus, the gladiators of Paris-Roubaix are all out for victory. It's a one-day-only blast for individual glory. What it isn't is a stage race, with one eye on tomorrow and the next day and the next…

This partly explains why the cobbles on this particular stage didn't offer up as much drama as the organisers might have been hoping. Aside from Riis's breakaway group, whose attack was launched with around 30 miles left, the majority of the peloton was largely still together as it roared over the pavé. 'The conditions were dry on the cobbles,' remembers Sean Kelly, 'so not an awful lot of surprises. It didn't really break the race apart. We were still quite a big group. Wet conditions would have suited better a rider like me who was a Classics man, but then again it's so dangerous when it's wet. You can get taken out in crashes.' Certainly, each and every *directeur sportif*, when they assessed the weather forecast that morning, would have been secretly pleased about what looked like being an anticlimactic day. Many of the peloton weren't Classics riders, so survival for them was everything. There had to be a tomorrow.

Not that the cobbled sections were without incident. Sean Yates might have been a contender for the stage win, especially as he knew the streets into the finish at Wasquehal very intimately, having won the individual time trial into the town the previous year, when he set a new record average speed for a Tour stage. However, hopes of a second Wasquehal win evaporated when he caused a heavy crash with about 20 miles left to race. Sporting a new haircut that day courtesy of a razor blade wielded by team-mate Jeff Pierce ('I had a bit of a mohican going on. Marginal gains!'), Yates brought down himself and a couple of other riders, including Thierry Marie, while on domestique duties.

'It was my job to look after Andy Hampsten as he wasn't very adept at riding the cobbles,' he explains. 'I was probably the best for that job – I was big and strong and could keep him out of trouble. This was doubly important as the next stage was the long time trial which, if you're going for GC, is absolutely crucial.

'I'm sure he would admit this, but Andy wasn't the greatest at staying in the right place at the right time. You'd bring him up to the front, he'd stay there for five minutes and you'd look round and he'd be gone. So you had to go back and get him. That was quite frustrating. I distinctly remember being on the cobbles and I kept looking round – "Where's Andy? Where's Andy?" By the time I looked round, I touched the wheel in front of me, which belonged to Thierry Marie. I came down and cut myself big time, which wasn't ideal. It made me curse Andy, but ultimately it was my fault.'

Hampsten is certainly quick to concede his limits on this particular terrain. 'Yates was super. He was so good. On that cobbled stage, I had armchair service. I felt terrible because he crashed thanks to me being so timid. With all the argy-bargy going on, I wouldn't shout when I was on his wheel or off his wheel. In looking over his shoulder for me, he crossed wheels and fell. But to keep me out of trouble on the cobbles or in the cross-winds of the last few kilometres of a stage, he was a dream team-mate to have. He was funny, too. His family showed up and there were all these little girls, his sisters, hanging on him. We thought he was some ferocious, man-eating beast, but he's just a big teddy bear.'

The ferocious, man-eating beast had been tamed – admittedly, by his own mistake – but at the front the Riis group was still firing along. The Tour organisers might have expected a degree of caution and a slower day, with energy conserved for the individual time trial to come, but the race was half an hour ahead of schedule. Locals wanting to catch a glimpse as the peloton bolted and jolted past their farmhouses may well have missed the spectacle. The pace was relentless, the riders dropping into the shade of numerous copses and back out again in an instant. And these twisting lanes left barely room for two-abreast riding, with the very real prospect of a spill into the ditches running on either side. Helicopters distractedly added to the intensity, buzzing low over the flat, open fields, like giant, attention-seeking mosquitoes.

Riis, Echavé and Gayant were still out in front, with an advantage of 35 seconds, as the race crossed the border and headed towards Roubaix. But then the Frenchman – a former national cyclo-cross champion who would have made this stage, with its uneven surfaces, his principal target for a victory in the entire three weeks – made his move. He shot away from the other two as they approached a railway bridge on the outskirts of the town, the bridge's design offering the perfect chicane on which to attack.

Echavé couldn't respond but Riis, eager to hold onto any chance of a second individual Grand Tour stage win in the space of a couple of months, gave it a dig for a few hundred yards before being swallowed up by the rapidly advancing peloton. Gayant had around four more miles to survive. He was still in front as he took a six-second bonus in the catch sprint outside the factory of La Redoute, the sponsors of Stephen Roche's team when he came third in the Tour in 1985.

Then Søren Lilholt, second place in the GC since the first stage, bridged the gap to Gayant. This was a smart move, one not anticipated by Acácio da Silva's Carrera team. By forming a Danish-French alliance, Lilholt could possibly stay clear of the peloton to the tune of 25 seconds or more. If he did so, he would be in yellow. And not just in yellow, but in the privileged position of being last man to go in the next stage, the individual time trial.

However brave, the pact lasted little more than half a mile before the peloton absorbed them. But that wasn't that. An even braver attack was then launched by the Dutchman Jelle Nijdam, the Superconfex rider who had struck out in similar solo fashion the previous year to win the seventh stage into another north-eastern France town, Liévin. Now, thanks to a dummy attack from his team-mate Gert Jakobs, Nijdam countered with his own on the other side of the road. It looked an impossible task, though. The run-in to the finish in Wasquehal, the neighbouring town to Roubaix, was along a wide, arrow-straight boulevard, and Nijdam would be a sitting target for the peloton to fix in their sights.

But the snapping jaws of the pack didn't capture their prey. Nijdam held on to win by three seconds, leaving the race's speedsters gnashing their teeth, again denied a mass sprint thanks to individual endeavour. Jesper Skibby was second man home for the second day running, while the yellow jersey remained on da Silva's back – for one more stage, at least. 'I was afraid of this stage,' he admitted afterwards. 'It was very important for me to keep the yellow jersey. That will allow me to ride the time trial in yellow and also be the last man off. It's a real honour.' Da Silva sounded like a man who knew the game was almost up, who understood he had just one stage left in the *maillot jaune*. A realist.

And while the sprinters were harrumphing about being unable to joust each other for the stage win, the GC contenders were expelling a long, collective sigh of relief. The cobbles were now in the rear-view mirror. Ahead of them, after a rest day during which they would transfer to Brittany, was the game-changing individual time trial. For them, the race would only then truly begin.

Stage 4

1. Jelle Nijdam (Superconfex/Netherlands) 6:13:58
2. Jesper Skibby (TVM/Denmark) +3"
3. Johan Museeuw (ADR/Belgium) same time
4. Jérôme Simon (Z-Peugeot/France) same time
5. Søren Lilholt (Histor/Denmark) same time

General classification

1. Acácio da Silva (Carrera/Portugal) 17:16:37
2. Søren Lilholt (Histor/Denmark) +14"
3. Thierry Marie (Super U/France) +1'57"
4. Laurent Fignon (Super U/France) +2'37"
5. Pascal Simon (Super U/France) +2'48"

SIX

THE AMERICAN EXPRESS

'When you see a rider do a time trial like that over 73 kilometres, you know they are in good form. Everyone noticed' – Sean Kelly

6 July
Stage 5, individual time trial, Dinard – Rennes, 45 miles

AMONG THE MANY thousands of fabulous photographs of the Tour in the archives of *L'Equipe*, there is one from the fifth stage of the 1989 race that's particularly fascinating. Despite it capturing the long individual time trial, when its competitors hit the road at regular intervals, three riders are in the frame, all shot from behind.

As the road curves to the left, in the distance is the blurred outline of an unidentified Panasonic rider. To the right of the carriageway is the Super U rider Christophe Lavainne. It's unclear whether he's out of the saddle because he's powering towards the Panasonic man or because he's struggling and has just been overtaken. Judging by his position on the road, it's the latter; Lavainne is far from taking the racing line through the bend. In fact, it appears he's heeded the line markings in the middle of the road, specifically the white arrow that normally compels motorists to keep to the right-hand side.

Lavainne has moved across for a reason. For commanding the road – and commanding the centre of the photograph – is a juggernaut, an American express. This express wears the number 141. The number of Greg LeMond. His pace and momentum is palpable, even in a photograph shot from behind. Unlike the struggling Lavainne, LeMond is glued to his saddle, a fixed, unmoving position. He's not looking across at the Frenchman, a former team-mate during their Renault days. The Super U rider is just another target that the charging LeMond has gobbled up on this time trial through Brittany. The Panasonic man 50 yards ahead is his new prey.

Not only is the photograph a study in the respective form and fortunes of three riders, it's also a study in the concentration of the spectators lining each side of the road. Their initial pleasure at seeing compatriot Lavainne coming round the bend has been usurped by even greater pleasure at seeing LeMond in full cry. They know this is a special performance, a pivotal moment in the Tour. Cameras are raised, flashbulbs pop. Illumination on a grey day. One spectator, on the nearside grassy verge, seems particularly taken by the scene. In his late fifties/early sixties – white shorts, tanned legs, orange cagoule – he's perfectly aware that history is unfolding before his eyes. Slightly crouched and offering encouragement, he doesn't bother reaching for his camera. He wants to soak it all in with the naked eye. The moment Greg LeMond became a contender.

***

If heightened levels of relaxation are an indicator of the arrival of form for a cyclist, then Greg LeMond would have had a strong idea of what was coming next. After the finish in Wasquehal two days before, he took advantage of the rest day to follow by retracing his steps back into Belgium. Here he would spend the evening – and, of course, share a Mexican meal – with Kathy and the kids in Kortrijk, their hometown during the racing season, little more than 15 miles away across the border.

The rest day was set aside to transfer the entire race across to Brittany and not even lengthy delays caused by a transportation mix-up could affect a relaxed LeMond. The Tour administrators had chartered two planes to fly the riders from Lille to Dinard on the north Brittany coast, but one had developed a fault on its way to Lille from Paris. A little before midday, a Boeing 727 took off with eight teams aboard, leaving 14 squads to argue over who could take advantage of a nearby 48-seater Fokker. Super U, Panasonic, RMO and, to LeMond's satisfaction, ADR were the lucky ones. Although arriving several hours later than expected, the American did at least get to put in some practice on the following day's course – unlike the remaining teams stranded at Lille, who were forced to wait for the arrival of a third plane, which had to come all the way from Toulouse.

As they flew westwards, riders had the chance to plan for the following day's time trial, to contemplate the weather forecast and fashion a strategy accordingly. This would be a day for the likes of Stephen Roche or Erik Breukink to shine, to make more of an impression on the GC. Roche knew exactly what a strong ride against the clock could do. In 1987 he had won the long time trial into Futuroscope, a victory that set up his charge towards the yellow jersey and the title. The following year had seen another English-speaking rider win the long time trial. Not that this rider had his eye on the GC; individual glory on one particular day was his singular aim.

In a modest, mid-terrace home in a modest, mid-Sussex town, Sean Yates stands before a wall of cycling books and a growing tower of cycling magazines. Most of them are pristine, unread. For Yates, cycling is more about the doing than the analysis, the pontificating. Pride of place, though, goes to the framed yellow jersey on the wall, the ultimate souvenir of a 20-year relationship with the Tour de France as both rider and *directeur sportif*, the memento of the single day he led the race in 1994. One day in yellow, just like his more decorated namesake Sean Kelly.

The day that would rank second-best among his golden Tour memories would be that July afternoon in 1988 when he furiously rode his bike into the time trial finish in Wasquehal. Back then, he was part of the English-speaking brigade at Fagor, which also included Roche and Robert Millar. But his stage win was a rare happy moment while there. A diamond in the dirt. 'It was the super-team, but it all went pear-shaped right from the start.'

Yates's escape route from Fagor had already been planned before the Wasquehal time trial. Before the '88 Tour, in fact. 'Dag-Otto Lauritzen, who was a close friend since our Peugeot days, was in 7-Eleven and I got my dad to ring him up and ask if he could get me out of this team. Fagor found out and threatened not to pick me for the Tour. But I signed during the Tour anyway. 7-Eleven turned out to be my team. I found my position.'

After the raging civil war at Fagor, the American outfit was much more in keeping with the laconic Yates. 'At 7-Eleven, it was more of a fun thing. They weren't embedded in the European culture of cycling. When we'd do a training camp in Santa Barbara, we were given a certain amount of money to go out and eat, and we'd stuff ourselves with Mexican food and a few beers. It was much more relaxed. The sponsors didn't know too much about the sport, so we weren't under a huge amount of pressure to deliver big results. It was more like a fun adventure.'

That said, the team – under the guidance of *directeur sportif* Jim Ochowicz – had helped deliver Andy Hampsten to the *maglia rose* in the '88 Giro. Expectancy was growing and, with the arrival of the Tour into Dinard, Yates would be expected to push hard to repeat his time-trialling success of the previous year. 'The team was climbing up the ladder,' he admits. 'They'd climbed every rung before that. And we'd had a decent build-up. Dag-Otto had come third in the Tour of Flanders, I'd come second in Gent-Wevelgem and we won the Tour de Trump with Dag-Otto. We were hoping that Andy would really perform and get us a decent result. He had high hopes.'

Although unbeknownst at the time, 7-Eleven's presence at that May's Tour de Trump would dramatically contribute to the result of the Tour de France two months later. Aside from the sizeable protests against the titular entrepreneur ('Die Yuppie $cum!', yelled the placards), the inaugural stage race, visiting five states on the Eastern Seaboard, was notable for one particular innovation being introduced to road-racing: aerobars.

Also known as tribars on account of their growing use in triathlon (where the legendary triathlete Dave Scott had pioneered their adoption), this elongated, U-shaped tube, complete with elbow rests, clipped to a road bike's existing handlebars. They allowed the rider to assume a comfortable, tucked position; the irresistible theory was that this lower profile met with less resistance from the wind and thus allowed greater speeds. The theory was both irresistible and pretty watertight. Windproof, too.

While he huffed and puffed to the not so dizzy heights of 27th place in the Tour de Trump, Greg LeMond saw these aerobars in action on the final-day time trial, clipped to the bikes of some of the 7-Eleven team, including the winner of the stage, the Coloradoan Ron Kiefel. LeMond liked what he saw. Their unveiling, and their use on a road bike, would be the only positive he took from the race.

Yates takes up the story. 'Somehow we got hold of these tribars of Dave Scott's. We figured out they were good, but Andy [Hampsten] did not want us to use them in the Tour de Trump, as the world would have seen them ahead of the Tour. But Dag-Otto was in a position to win the race in America for an American team. This wasn't an opportunity we were going to throw away. So he used them and won the overall. Also in the race was Greg LeMond, racing for Coors Light, and he spotted them. He was open to ideas. At that race, he was going like a bag of shit.'

'It was definitely a debate,' confirms Hampsten. '"Should we keep these hidden for the Tour de France?" That wouldn't have been too clever in hindsight as it would have meant I wouldn't have been training with them. But we definitely wanted to use them on the Tour de Trump for Dag-Otto to protect his lead in the ghost town of Atlantic City. If we hadn't been looking to win that race in that last time trial, we might have kept them secret.

'I then had the opportunity of using them at the Giro when there was a flat time trial at the end but, probably foolishly, decided not to as I hadn't been training with them because I'd been racing. I could have used them to try to move up from third place, but I didn't – which was too bad.'

Len Pettyjohn, for whom LeMond was riding in the colours of Coors Light at the Tour de Trump, insists that that wasn't the first time LeMond had seen these acrobars. He had already been approached by their inventor, a guy called Boone Lennon who had been the USA national ski coach during the mid-80s. Lennon's invention simply drew from his experiences on the slopes, where the more tucked position a downhill skier adopted, the quicker he or she would go. 'We look at this now and go, "How could we not have known this?",' sighs Pettyjohn. 'Everyone who's ever ridden a bike, who gets down in a tuck, goes past people. I'm sitting here thinking "Why didn't I think of that?". It's so simple…'

As simple as the idea was, there were doubters, whether it was those who believed the gains it offered to be practically non-existent or those who argued that the bars contravened the Tour's rules and regulations. Although back in '89 he saved his dissent over the technology for the final-day time trial, Fignon remained indignant about others' use of the bars when he wrote his autobiography 20 years later. He believed that the bars used had four contact points, rather than the permissible three. 'For reasons that still elude me, [Cyrille] Guimard and I didn't make a formal complaint,' he moaned. 'The idle commissaires shut their eyes. The rules were being bent and the consequences would be way beyond anything I could have imagined.'

Fignon was actually wrong in suggesting the Tour authorities closed their eyes on the issue. The two teams to use the aerobars in the Rennes time trial – ADR and 7-Eleven – made separate visits to the authorities to secure official clearance. The day before, José De Cauwer had spoken with the head of the race jury, to whom he'd presented LeMond's aerobars. 'I went early,' he told *Cycling Weekly*, 'so no one from any other team would see we were intending to use them. I said, "LeMond wants to use these bars." The chief judge said, "OK, you can use them. No problem." I carried on. "He has a problem with his back. This is more comfortable for him." The judge replied: "I said it's OK. He can use them."

'Then I got out of there.'

7-Eleven also sought official clearance. Jim Ochowicz and his team made their case to the commissaires, taking with them arguably the greatest Tour rider ever. 'Having Eddy Merckx supplying your bikes has its advantages,' laughs Hampsten. 'We were not obscure people approaching the jury.'

The fact that those seeking to use the aerobars were representing either an American rider or an American team is not coincidental. 'Boone Lennon had offered them to PDM and Panasonic,' wrote the *New York Times*' Samuel Abt, 'and had urged riders on both teams to try them. He had no takers among the Europeans.'

Len Pettyjohn offers his thoughts on why that might be. 'Most Americans were not bound by tradition. They were more willing to see something new and different, and try it. Try to put those bars on a European bike at that time? Wouldn't even hear of it. But Greg was open to that. Whatever he could do to go faster.' The new order was butting up against old Europe. 'The language of cycling was French. "We're not going to change. We're not going to broadcast anything in English. It's French. If you don't know French, fine." I was told multiple times that France was the centre of the universe of cycling and that we were just interlopers.'

'The Anglo-Saxon people do love to try and to taste new things,' observes Delgado. 'In old Europe, we like to be more conservative. "I know this new technology is good for me, but maybe later, maybe tomorrow. Not now." It's a typical personality across France, Italy, Spain… We don't like quick change. We like to get there step by step.'

Sean Yates, one of the four enlightened 7-Eleven men to clip on aerobars for the Rennes time trial, had seen the resistance to new innovations when he and other British riders, alongside those from the US, Ireland, Australia and Canada, went abroad to race on the continent in the early 1980s. 'We used to turn up to breakfast with our cereal and the French would be like "What's that bloody horse feed?". When I turned pro, everyone had steak for breakfast. Steak and rice. Eating steak at 4am can't be good for you. Twenty years later, though, they were all eating cereal…

'There would have been a point where they said "These bloody English-speaking people are a pain in the arse". Then there would have been a period of acceptance. It was a gradual acceptance over the years until now when the English-speaking people are winning left, right and centre.'

If José De Cauwer was keeping the matter of aerobars close to his chest, so too was his main rider on the day of the time trial. LeMond was out warming up around the streets of Dinard, hiding – whether consciously or not – those aerobars away from the scrutiny of questioning eyes. He was all smiles as usual, making him as difficult to read as the most sombre, poker-faced competitor.

Hampsten also elected to ride with aerobars attached. Hiding his eyes behind a very large pair of royal blue-lensed wraparound shades, he still appeared nervous as he glided around the warm-up area in small, tense circles, biting his bottom lip. He was worried about not allowing the other GC contenders, those with stronger time-trialling pedigrees, to put too much daylight between themselves and him at this early stage, to be disappearing into the distance ahead of his more natural habitat of the mountains.

Fignon, fourth overall and thus the highest-placed main contender, looked relaxed and at ease in the Brittany sunshine. If he was concerned about both Americans' adoption of aerobars, there was no trace of it on his face.

That morning, Delgado had enjoyed the benefit of a silver lining. Still down in 134th place, he rose early, ready to depart among the domestiques in the depths of the GC. He would be gliding down the start house ramp – the one that had defined his Tour thus far – a good three hours before the other big guns. But, nearly ten minutes down on the yellow jersey, there was an advantage to this. The weather, warm and dry as he departed, was due to get much worse that afternoon, pretty much at the time when the main players would be setting out.

And he made hay while the sun shone. As he set out from Dinard, Delgado had a breeze at his back, those light winds blowing in off the English Channel. By the time he reached Dinan and its impossibly quaint quayside, he was already more than three minutes faster than any of the 60-odd riders who'd already passed that point. The gulf in class was unavoidable as Delgado hurtled down the town's narrow streets and over its hump-backed bridges.

The rest day had clearly agreed with him; a time to reflect, to reboot his brain, to restore his confidence – and to leave the horrors of the previous week out of sight beyond France's eastern borders. The immediate past was a foreign country.

The arrival of a headwind during the second half of Delgado's ride meant the split time registered at Dinan hadn't grown correspondingly by the finish line in Rennes. Still, arriving with a lead of more than four minutes over everyone else was an impressive performance from the new, demon-vanquishing Delgado. And, with the Brittany weather very much on the turn, his was a time that would be decidedly tricky to overhaul.

Roche the all-rounder was having a go at doing just that. At the 13-mile mark, he had shaded Delgado's interim split by a single second. But then that headwind found accompaniment in the form of hard and heavy rain. Accordingly, the second half of his ride was less fruitful, losing three minutes to the Spaniard. As Roche rode into Rennes, there was a marked difference in the pair's respective body languages. Where Delgado had charged to the line to gain as many seconds as possible, Roche timidly came round the final left-hander on Rennes' now-greasy streets, as if riding on thin ice.

The aerobars didn't do a great deal for Andy Hampsten. Encountering the worst of the weather, he was three minutes down on Delgado at the Dinan time split. This rose to in excess of four minutes by the time he took the line in gloomy Rennes, the headlights of his support car shining golden on the glassy, wet tarmac. Bad conditions or not, he looked like he was riding well within himself. If Hampsten was at all a gambler, he was a patient, conservative one. A cool head, deploying reason over rashness. Any gambit was usually modest, certainly on these early flat stages. Higher stakes would surely be placed on better-suited days.

Yates, injured from that crash two days previously when he was searching for Hampsten over the cobbles, failed to repeat the exceptional performance of that '88 time trial. The aerobars may well have helped though. Despite his injury – the wounds on his leg remained bright scarlet – Yates was into second place. No new record, no champagne. But a job well done nonetheless.

Neither Hampsten nor Yates plumped for aero helmets, but possibly wished they had when the wind changed direction. Using the holy trinity of aerodynamic aids – teardrop helmet, rear disc wheel and those controversial aerobars – LeMond punched through the headwind as if it were nothing more than a light breeze. Although in touch with Delgado's impressive time throughout, it was during the stage's last quarter that he reeled in the Spaniard, screaming through the gloom to register a time 24 seconds quicker.

The TV cameramen, who thought they had recorded the story of the day several hours earlier when Delgado finished, leapt up to pursue the American as he poured over the line, a forest of microphones engulfing him when he came to an enforced standstill. Whistles, jostling and more flashbulbs. Helmet off and forehead plastered with wet hair, he looked uncharacteristically non-plussed by the media scrum. More truthfully, it was that he was dazed from exertion, from a titanic effort in worsening weather. And, quite possibly, from the realisation that he could be in yellow by the day's end.

Delgado was sanguine at the state of affairs, at what *Cycling Weekly* correspondent Keith Bingham described as 'fate switching horses at the last moment'. Perico was at ease with his belated return to form. 'I finished in first position and needed to wait at the finish line for, maybe, two hours,' he remembers. 'Spanish television wanted me to be with them towards the end of the stage. "Pedro, you will win the stage because it has started to rain. You had the advantage of the good weather." I said, "Maybe not. In the last part of my time trial, the wind was in front. I hope I'll win, but it's not easy to know if I'll win or not." I only lost by a few seconds.' (The gap was a little more substantial than Delgado remembers. But when you've started the day the best part of ten minutes adrift, 24 seconds probably feels like 'a few seconds'.)

'For me, the Tour de France started again in this long time trial. My morale was very low, but that day I found I was physically very, very good. At that moment, I started to think: "Maybe I can do something in this race…".'

Fignon, ever the practitioner of kidology, was quick to dismiss Delgado's intentions, despite the fact that, now standing 28th overall, he'd gained 170 places in the GC over the last few days. 'It's impossible for him to make up seven minutes and win,' he sniffed. 'Even two minutes will be hard. Delgado is in an impossible situation. If he goes all out and attacks one day and gains five minutes, he'll be committing suicide because he'll have to collapse. And if he goes around trying to snatch 30 seconds here, 30 seconds there, he won't be able to get enough of them.' Fignon seemed to suggest Delgado needn't bother trying. Fortunately for the neutral spectator, the Reynolds man instead dug his heels in and offered a masterclass in resilience and resistance over the following two weeks.

Sean Yates was another man buoyed by a strong ride. Fifth place on the stage translated into fifth place in the GC too, a position to please both sponsor and team management. There were other benefits as well, to be enjoyed on the following day. 'From the point of view of your car's position, it's nice to be up there as it means your car is very near the front of the convoy in case of emergencies. If you're 20th, it's impossible for your car to get to you and service you if you have an accident.'

And 20th place happened to be the position that another Sean – Kelly – slipped to after a disappointing time trial. 'I really weakened in the final 20 kilometres,' he recalls. 'I started to suffer majorly. I don't know if it was dehydration or hunger, but I did fall to pieces in the final 15, 20 kilometres. I lost a lot of time.' He wasn't the only PDM rider to under-perform. The two Dutchmen, Steven Rooks and Gert-Jan Theunisse, both slipped down the GC to 36th and 39th respectively. Both had elected not to fly to Brittany the previous day; instead, they travelled in a team car before riding the last 90 or so miles to Dinard.

Fignon fared better. Ten places and 51 seconds ahead of LeMond at the start of the day, he took third with an impressively strong ride, even if he did ship the best part of a minute to LeMond. Acácio da Silva soon followed Fignon home, but the Portuguese, despite overtaking second-placed Søren Lilholt, was forced to relinquish the yellow jersey that had been in his possession for nearly a week. But the recipient wasn't Fignon. Remarkably, amazingly, and by a margin of just five seconds, Greg LeMond was the new leader of the race.

'It was like winning the world championship,' LeMond gushed afterwards to Samuel Abt. 'It was my best moment in many years. I'm happier than when I won the Tour in 1986. This is the most wonderful day of my life. It's almost a miracle.' He set out his ambitions to ABC Television. 'I was going to be happy to be in the top 20. Now I'm shooting for the top five and, who knows, maybe even better.' The smile was the broadest it had been for at least two years and those cobalt eyes hadn't sparkled so much for that long too. 'I can't refuse a victory and I can't refuse the yellow jersey.'

Cutting a windproof figure through the poor conditions, the aerobars had definitely helped. 'I didn't even know if they would make a difference or not,' LeMond later told the writer Daniel Friebe. 'The first time I saw them was when [7-Eleven rider] Davis Phinney rode past me at the Tour de Trump that year. I thought "Hmmm, he looks more aerodynamic than me". So I used them in that first time trial in Rennes and won.'

Whether assisted artificially by technology or not, LeMond had returned to cycling's top table. 'You'd be an idiot if you didn't think he was back,' says Hampsten. 'I'm sure he was playing it down, but he was really honest and frank with his friends on 7-Eleven. He'd say, "I didn't really expect to win, but I haven't felt like that for two years or more. That felt really good. I'm psyched. I'm back in the hunt." We knew he was back.' Sean Kelly was also an astute judge. 'That wasn't a one-off,' he later said. 'When you see a rider do a time trial like that over 73 kilometres, you know they are in good form. Everyone noticed.'

Channel 4 co-commentator Paul Sherwen was a little more circumspect. 'LeMond indicated that he was in good form, but there had been no serious difficulties in the Tour up to that point. "Good job. Well done. But what's going to happen next?".' Kathy LeMond shared that caution. 'The one thing he kept saying was, "I haven't climbed anything. I have no idea if I can climb."' Another person close to him – his room-mate Johan Lammerts – agrees. 'Winning the time trial was great for him, but now he had to wait and see how it would be in the first stages of the Pyrenees. Greg still had some doubts that he might not be able to follow the best climbers.'

That night, the LeMonds were twin balls of excitement. 'We didn't know this was going to come back into our lives,' explains Kathy. 'We could hardly sleep. We were so happy. We could not believe it.'

At the same moment that the happy couple were struggling to sleep, *L'Equipe*'s printing presses were lurching into action. The next morning's front page was one very few thought imaginable. Not only was LeMond pictured in the yellow jersey for the first time in three years, but the headline confirmed what had seemed impossible just a week previous: 'LEMOND : LA RESURRECTION'.

Stage 5
1. Greg LeMond (ADR/USA) 1:38:12
2. Pedro Delgado (Reynolds/Spain) +24"
3. Laurent Fignon (Super U/France) +56"
4. Thierry Marie (Super U/France) +1'51"
5. Sean Yates (7-Eleven/GB) +2'16"

General classification
1. Greg LeMond (ADR/USA) 18:58:17
2. Laurent Fignon (Super U/France) +5"
3. Thierry Marie (Super U/France) +20"
4. Erik Breukink (Panasonic/Netherlands) +1'51"
5. Sean Yates (7-Eleven/GB) +2'18"

SEVEN

THE GREAT ESCAPE

'There were 180km left. On your own, that's suicidal' – Joël Pelier

7 July
Stage 6, Rennes – Futuroscope, 161 miles

THE WAITING STAFF at the hotel hadn't seen anything like it before. With several hundred anonymous breakfast shifts under their belts, serving coffee and croissants to the holidaymakers of Brittany, this was one they wouldn't forget in a hurry. The reason? The legions of television crews that had invaded the dining room, making service a little more challenging that morning.

The focus of the cameras' attention, the target of their lenses, was the skinny young man in the baggy Coors Light T-shirt. With a freshly poured black coffee and a small pile of yogurt pots in front of him, he was self-consciously trying to ignore their presence, concentrating on carefully chopping a kiwi fruit. The man with the knife was the new leader of the Tour de France.

Greg LeMond was calm and considered that morning. Not allowing himself to get over-excited, his words were tempered. Whilst naturally thrilled to be in yellow, he was unsure just how long his tenure as the leader of the pack would last. A five-second lead is just a five-second lead, after all.

The jersey might only be on his back for a matter of hours. The first time he had got to wear it in the last three years might also be the last time he ever did.

'The mountains' – this mythical barrier, this test of both body and mind – was a motif that peppered his conversation that first week. Although hopeful that his form thus far would travel with him at altitude, LeMond was acutely conscious of the embarrassment that a very public capitulation would bring, especially if his climbing form continued in the vein of those underwhelming performances he'd put in on the high roads of Italy during the Giro. LeMond simply didn't know how strong he was. While the Pyrenean and Alpine mountain passes selected for the Tour would be familiar territory to him, he'd nonetheless be riding into the unknown.

This uncertainty painted those sky-blue eyes a little darker that morning. After breakfast, an interview with ABC outside the hotel showed a man whose customary effervescence was on hold, whose mouth wasn't readily forming the smile it usually did at the end of each sentence. Some gentle joshing with the 7-Eleven boys at the riders' sign-in, plus even a handshake from Laurent Fignon, couldn't distract him. Until this point, LeMond's days that week had all represented something of an experiment, a test to gauge recovery and strength. No pressure, no expectation. But he was no longer the rider with nothing to lose. Even if – as expected – the GC contenders would be taking things easy following the time trial and with the prospect of the Pyrenees looming in a couple of days' time, LeMond and his team had to go into defensive mode. They had to keep their wits about them.

And the first day of that defence of the yellow jersey coincided with the longest stage of the entire three weeks, as the race took a windy, southerly route from Rennes to Futuroscope, a slightly bizarre, apparently futuristic theme park near Poitiers. This one had potential. There was a full 161 miles of tarmac between on which a stage-winning break could be launched. The one that was indeed launched became something of a classic breakaway.

It was fair to say that, prior to 1989, Joël Pelier's Tour de France career wasn't exactly drowning in glory. Indeed, the Frenchman was probably best known for collapsing on the Col du Granon at the end of one of the 1986 Tour's Alpine stages and being airlifted off the mountain, having slipped into a coma that would last seven hours. After a subsequent ill-fitting season with Cyrille Guimard at Système U in 1987, the following year Pelier joined the Basque-based BH team who, among all their bantamweight climbers, needed a sturdier rider to put some serious legwork in on flat stages in the Grand Tours, specifically the Tour de France.

On the first stage of the '89 Tour, his second in BH colours, Pelier fancied abandoning his domestique duties and putting in a surprise attack. His team boss, Javier Mínguez, overruled him, reminding him of his job description. But it was a different scenario less than a week later as the peloton huddled together in the wind and rain en route to Futuroscope. Mínguez performed a U-turn.

'I don't know why,' Pelier later explained to the author Richard Moore, 'but he gave me carte blanche. During the stage, I went back to the car to get a rain jacket and bidons [water bottles]. There were about 180km left and he asked me why I didn't attack. It was like he was challenging me. He told me he didn't think I had the balls to attack because there were too many kilometres left. He was laughing, but it was like a bet or a challenge.'

Pelier took the bait. With rain jacket and bidons safely delivered to his team-mates, he made his way to the front of the peloton and simply kept riding. The break for glory wasn't exactly dramatic. It was almost apologetic in the manner he slipped away. Unobtrusive, inconspicuous. It was far from an eyeballs-out, stand-on-the-pedals attack. Pelier just rode calmly away, backside still in the saddle. The peloton seemed fine about it. Compliant, even.

Pelier wasn't just making a point to Mínguez; he was also doing the same to Cyrille Guimard, taking the chance to show the Super U boss what he no longer had control over, after releasing him at the end of the '87 season. And Pelier rapidly created a substantial lead over the peloton, the pack seemingly content to keep the pace pedestrian on a grey day when the sunflowers in the adjacent fields bowed their heads with no sunshine to reach up to.

The peloton's compliance was actually blurring into complacency. As Pelier crossed the Loire, the race commissaire's red Fiat pulled alongside him. In the back seat, an elbow hanging out of the open window, was Bernard Hinault, now gainfully employed, of course, as a race official. Hinault informed Pelier what the time gap was. Seventeen minutes. It may or may not have come as a surprise, but the information would certainly have inspired and emboldened a rider who started the day nearly ten minutes down on LeMond. As things currently stood, and with the pack remaining ambivalent and non-committal a few miles back down the road, Pelier was the virtual yellow jersey on the road.

If his riding style looked solid, internally he was somewhat less secure. 'Your mood is changing all the time,' he told Richard Moore. 'You believe, you don't believe, you believe, you don't believe.' Faced with such a tantalising scenario, Pelier's brain was playing tricks. 'I tell myself that I'm going to win, then I hear the gap is falling quickly and I think "I'm fucked. I'm going to be caught."'

But the gap wasn't falling all that quickly. A crash on the wet roads had brought a new degree of caution to the field; the ferocity of the team cars' windscreen wipers was an indication of how unwelcome the conditions were. But ADR, aiming to avoid surrendering the yellow jersey after just one day – and to a mere domestique at that – made sure that Pelier's lead was cut to within an acceptable boundary, one that wouldn't remove LeMond from the top of the GC. Panasonic also assisted in forcing the pace, eager to preserve Erik Breukink's fourth place. Although the gap shrank considerably in the final few miles, Pelier held on to finish more than a minute and a half ahead of the pack. Having been out on his own for in excess of four hours and 110 miles, he had recorded the second-longest solo break in Tour de France history.

But the story didn't end there. Unbeknownst to Pelier until he crossed the line, his parents had travelled across from eastern France to watch him race. His mother was the dedicated carer of Pelier's disabled brother, who was on a holiday break at a specialist medical centre. This allowed her a few days' grace to watch her other son in action for the first time in six years. It appeared to be a happy coincidence that it was on the day that he delivered one of the race's all-time great individual performances. Or had, thought the odd suspicious mind, Mínguez, the Pelier-baiting BH team boss, known all along?

Either way, the outpouring of emotion from the Pelier family was irresistible. His father hung over the railings of the grandstand, nearly doubled up as he embraced his son, while Pelier's mother tenderly cradled her offspring's flushed face. Up on the podium, the victorious rider made a futile attempt at strangling his tears. It was the only thing he'd failed at all day.

Stage 6

1. Joël Pelier (BH/France) 6:57:45
2. Eddy Schurer (TVM/Netherlands) +1'34"
3. Eric Vanderaerden (Panasonic/Belgium) +1'36"
4. Adrie van der Poel (Domex/Netherlands) same time
5. Rudy Dhaenens (PDM/Belgium) same time

General classification

1. Greg LeMond (ADR/USA) 25:57:38
2. Laurent Fignon (Super U/France) +5"
3. Thierry Marie (Super U/France) +20"
4. Eric Breukink (Panasonic/Netherlands) +1'51"
5. Sean Yates (7-Eleven/UK) +2'18"

***

8 July
Stage 7, Poitiers – Bordeaux, 161 miles

Another surge southwards. Another marathon stage. Another day dictated by the weather.

The seventh stage was only half a kilometre shorter than the previous day's monster journey into Futuroscope but, thanks to the continuing wet and blustery conditions, it would mean around 25 minutes longer in the saddle. Transparent waterproof capes were the order of the day and those riders who chose not to wear them suffered the consequences. Greg LeMond was one; he had to ask for special dispensation to swap his sodden yellow jersey for a regular ADR top.

Unlike the day before, this wasn't a stage for individual heroics. Setting off from Poitiers ('where Joan of Arc first started getting into trouble,' as the man from ABC helpfully informed his viewers), the destination was Bordeaux, scene of more than 70 stage finishes in the Tour's history. Across those years, Bordeaux had become synonymous with mass sprint finishes. In '89, the race's 71st visit to the city, the inability of any of the attempted breakaways to sustain themselves in the grey gloom ultimately ensured it would be another day for the sprinters, a rare chance in this Tour to go into battle against each other.

At journey's end, four riders were very slightly clear of the peloton – Histor's Etienne De Wilde, Helvetia-La Suisse leader Steve Bauer, Jean-Claude Colotti from RMO, and Superconfex's Patrick Tolhoek, last seen in a meaningful capacity coming third at the Spa-Francorchamps racing circuit. In Bordeaux, it was De Wilde who took the line from Colotti, in the process registering Belgium's first stage victory of the race.

The blanket finish ensured that there was no movement in the upper echelons of the GC, but the presentation ceremony did reveal one significant development: Sean Kelly, winner of the points competition in 1982, 1983 and 1985, had been reunited with the green jersey. That he achieved this after getting involved in a nasty crash two-thirds into the stage, one that also injured his team-mate Raúl Alcalá, was a measure of the man's commitment and quality in his 11th Tour.

Joining PDM in the close season seemed to have done Kelly the world of good. At 33, he was the most senior rider on the team by a clear five years. Indeed, he also had a good few years on the race's big three – Delgado, Fignon and LeMond – all of whom were still in their twenties, having been born within 15 months of each other. Fignon, with that thinning hair and spectacles, might have looked like the elder statesman of the bunch, but was actually born in a later decade than Stephen Roche, the boyish-looking Irishman with those butter-wouldn't-melt brown eyes. This age gap made Kelly's evergreen form and consistency all the more impressive. By the time Delgado, Fignon and LeMond had each reached the age the man from Carrick-on-Suir was in 1989, each had already raced his last Tour de France.

Kelly's performances, though, represented anything but the elder statesman seeing out his career. 1989 was in danger of becoming his finest Tour ever. Five top-ten stage finishes in the first week had helped secure the green jersey, as had 11th place in Bordeaux. He was very much delivering on his PDM contract, one signed only after Greg LeMond's departure from the team. While they were a well-financed team, they couldn't afford both the American and the Irishman.

'I had a contract to continue with KAS,' he explains of his shift across to PDM at the end of 1988, 'but they stopped team sponsorship. Their boss

Louis Knorr, a big cycling fan, had died that year and they decided not to continue with the bike team. I had no choice.

'I'd done a few years with KAS. Being a Spanish team, it was always important that we raced the early-season races like the Tour of the Basque Country and the Tour of Catalonia. I had to ride them, and then the Vuelta a España at the end of April and early May. The programme I was doing at KAS was very busy because I wanted to do the Classics as well as the Vuelta and the Tour. It was so hectic with the team wanting to do all the Spanish races. PDM's programme was much lighter. When the Classics campaign finished, there would be a rest period.

'PDM were in contact with me pretty much immediately after KAS announced they were pulling out of sponsorship. They made me aware that signing me was about winning the Classics and the green jersey in the Tour de France. Those were the performances they were expecting from me. There was an understanding that to win the Tour or to get on the podium was going to be difficult because I had tried and failed so many times. Maybe I didn't say it out loud, but in the back of my mind I had that doubt too.'

PDM didn't enter Paris-Nice in '89, so Kelly's run of seven consecutive wins was brought to a – perhaps premature – end. But there was early success in the team's colours when he took his second victory at Liège-Bastogne-Liège, the one-dayer affectionately known as 'The Old Lady'. The race provided Kelly with the opportunity to assess the loyalty of his new team-mates. There was no clear hierarchy in the PDM ranks; he had to share leadership duties with fellow new boy Alcalá, Steven Rooks and Gert-Jan Theunisse. 'I'm sure you've heard the saying about too many chiefs and not enough Indians...

'Rooks and Theunisse were good guys,' he later wrote, 'but I knew I'd have to keep an eye on them because if I worked for them in one race, I couldn't be sure they'd return the favour. They couldn't help it. Dutch cyclists at that time loved a double-cross.

'I knew how political it was. I knew that whatever was agreed in the team meeting before a race was not necessarily binding. And I knew that sometime I'd have to stitch them up before they had a chance to do the same to me.'

And that was how Kelly scored his first victory in PDM colours. 'When I won Liège-Bastogne-Liège,' he recalls, 'I struck out early, maybe 30 kilometres from the finish. I had it in the back of my mind that if I waited and waited and left it down to the sprint, Rooks or Theunisse would go on the attack before then. It was a risky one. I didn't say it at the time but I did admit, a number of years later, that that was why I went in an earlier breakaway, which is something that as a sprinter I wouldn't have been doing.'

In order to secure that fourth Tour green jersey, Kelly would need to put in some good performances in the Pyrenees and/or the Alps. Just how this would play with his hard-climbing team-mates remained to be seen. Fascinated observers who had a taste for a little in-house fratricide were salivating at the prospect.

Stage 7
1. Etienne De Wilde (Histor/Belgium) 7:21:57
2. Jean-Claude Colotti (RMO/France) same time
3. Patrick Tolhoek (Superconfex/Netherlands) +2"
4. Steve Bauer (Helvetia-La Suisse/Canada) same time
5. Jean-Paul van Poppel (Panasonic/Netherlands) +4"

General classification
1. Greg LeMond (ADR/USA) 33:19:39
2. Laurent Fignon (Super U/France) +5"
3. Thierry Marie (Super U/France) +40"
4. Eric Breukink (Panasonic/Netherlands) +1'51"
5. Sean Yates (7-Eleven/UK) +2'18"

***

9 July
Stage 8, Labastide d'Armagnac – Pau, 98 miles

Father Joseph Massie was all smiles. It was a day he'd been waiting for for 30 years, 30 years of hopeless dreaming – and, presumably, rather a lot of praying. But, whether divine intervention or simply the work of the mortal race administrators, those prayers were being answered, those dreams were coming true. The latest stage of the Tour de France was departing from his village.

Massie was no ordinary priest. Massie was a fanatic – a fanatic about cycling. And this fanaticism took him to extraordinary lengths. In 1958, he repurposed the 12th-century chapel in the small fortified village of Labastide d'Armagnac, turning it into a shrine-cum-museum that celebrated life on two wheels. A year later, Pope John XXIII made it official; the chapel would henceforth be known as Notre Dame des Cyclistes, a 'national sanctuary of cycling and cyclists under the protection of the Virgin, Our Lady of cyclists'.

The chapel became an extraordinary place of pilgrimage for the cycling community, its interior walls adorned with hundreds of cycling jerseys, many of which were donated by the sport's biggest legends, among them Eddy Merckx, Jacques Anquetil, Luis Ocaña and Raymond Poulidor. The Tour had passed by the chapel five years previously en route to Pau, but 1989 was its crowning glory: to be the point of departure for the 188 riders still left in the race.

Eighty-five miles south of the previous day's finish in Bordeaux, the village was a hive of activity that morning. Brass bands played, drum majorettes marched. And, most importantly, Father Massie had an audience with some of his cycling heroes. Stephen Roche, Pedro Delgado, Luis Herrera and Greg LeMond were among those lining up to meet the bike-mad priest, with the American presenting him with a yellow jersey to add to the chapel's collection.

Not that everything went swimmingly that morning. Before the peloton departed, anti-nuclear protesters took advantage of the media circus that had descended on Labastide. They padlocked themselves together, forcing the riders to pick a single-file path through the protest to get to the start line, either pushing or carrying their bikes. From the back seat of the commissaire's car, Bernard Hinault cast a weary eye over proceedings. A fiery Breton not known for his sympathy for Tour-delaying public protest (on occasion, he got decidedly hands-on with protesters during his riding days), the clothes of officialdom meant he was now a man with responsibilities, a man trapped in his job. Hinault stayed put in his car. The race left the village 15 minutes behind schedule.

After the previous two marathon stages, the day's itinerary – a much shorter route that broadly traced a due-south path – was warmly welcomed by those requiring recovery and recuperation ahead of the Pyrenees stages.

While the GC contenders would still watch each other closely, moves by the race's main protagonists were unlikely. So an open invitation was issued to the race's lesser lights: this was a chance for someone who was likely to struggle at altitude in the coming days to etch their name into Tour history forever. Tomorrow would be a struggle, but today could be glory.

With 50 miles of the stage left, there was a strong possibility that that lesser light would be one of four men who had combined to create a significant break. They included the RMO rider Éric Caritoux, wearing the jersey of the French national champion; Michael Wilson, one of two Australians in the Tour; Z-Peugeot's Philippe Louviot; and the Irishman Martin Earley, another of PDM's close-season signings.

With the gap between the break and the peloton getting close to three minutes, ADR began to take action and stepped up the pursuit. Their nervousness was caused by the presence of Wilson in the lead group and they took action to reduce, or even extinguish, his position on the road. Of the four breakaway riders, he was the one closest to LeMond, starting the stage five minutes down on the yellow jersey. And he had pedigree that marked him out as a danger. He won the second stage in the 1982 Giro by outsprinting Fignon; he also took a stage in the Vuelta a year later.

Elsewhere, teams took care of their leaders. Delgado was particularly well-protected, cocooned within the protective seal of his domestiques. The objective was to deliver him safely into Pau before he would unleash himself in the mountains the following day. Fignon, though, was his usual self, a mixture of playful and dangerous. He surprisingly attacked the first of the four fourth-category climbs, presumably with the aim of snatching enough seconds back to allow him to arrive in the mountains in yellow.

Fignon's attack meant the pace of the chase was high and the front group's lead was reduced to just a minute with 12 miles left. Within three miles though, Louviot, riding his first Tour, made what looked like being the decisive break. Job done. But the other three, rather than surrendering to the approaching pack, instead pulled Louviot back in. As Caritoux slightly relaxed, presumably thinking that the four would slug it out in a sprint, Earley attacked with more than half a mile to go. As he arrived in the market square, the Dubliner glanced back a couple of times before raising both arms to take a famous victory. The smile admitted that this was his career highlight, the defining moment. Right here, right now.

'I knew I had to attack because I was strong,' the bespectacled Earley explained at the finish. 'If I'm ever riding for fourth place, I like to think I can get first just as well. And they weren't such great sprinters there, so my chances were as good as the rest.'

Earley was a popular winner. The perennial third man of Irish cycling behind those high-achievers Roche and Kelly, it wasn't his first taste of Grand Tour success, though. That came in the Giro in 1986 when, then riding for Fagor, he again showed his sharp tactical acumen, outfoxing LeMond and ultimate winner Roberto Visentini to take a stage victory in the mountains.

'Martin was always a great rider,' says Roche. 'A great team rider. He was ambitious, but he knew where his limits were. He recognised he wasn't going to win the Tour, but he knew that on his day he was capable of winning stages. But he wasn't going to win a stage without looking after his team-mates and his team leader first. He was a guy that a leader – whether in the Classics or the Tour – could count on. Everyone was delighted for Martin when he won that stage. It was compensation for all of the other work he'd put in.'

When he signed for PDM, Kelly had insisted, so strong a domestique was he, that Earley be brought across from KAS too. 'They had a lot of riders already signed, so it was very limited for places. Martin was the only one I managed to take with me. Everyone within PDM was so excited by Martin winning. He was a helper in the team a lot of the time, but there were occasions when he would be able to ride his own race, but that would be a minimal number of races throughout the year.'

That day's entry in the diary of the fourth Irish rider in that Tour, Paul Kimmage, also hinted at a sense of national pride at his compatriot's success. 'I knew he was going to win. I said it to Kelly about an hour from the finish. I just got this gut feeling he was going to do it. As we arrived in Pau, I strained my ears to the commentary of race speaker Daniel Mangeas. When I heard him shout M-A-R-T-I-N E-A-R-L-E-Y, I waved a triumphant fist in the air.'

With four compatriots in the Tour, cycling in Ireland was in extremely rude health. And there wasn't really a clear reason why it was so. As the author Ed Pickering has noted, 'Irish cycling's run of success in the 1980s was a statistical outlier. In Sean Kelly and Stephen Roche, Ireland had two of the best four or five cyclists in the world.'

Certainly, those two cyclists have never been able to explain why the riches were so great in that particular era. 'I don't know,' shrugs Roche, after being asked about it for the umpteenth time in his life. 'Maybe it was the genes or maybe it was what we ate – potatoes and cabbage! Whether it's in the water or it's in the air, there's definitely something in Ireland that breeds champions. We're a small nation and it's amazing that we do so well. It's something that's in the culture and the land and the mentality.'

Kelly draws upon Irish success in other sports at the time to attempt to make sense of it – the Irish national football team under Jack Charlton or the medals won by the country's distance runners, athletes like Eamonn Coghlan, Sonia O'Sullivan and John Treacy. 'It was amazing that we had so many riders at the top level. We all just seemed to come along at the same time – it's something that happens in sport. And when we finished up, there was nobody else there for quite some years. That's just the way it goes. We had a number of very talented riders at the same time. Of course, if they see another Irish guy who's doing well, it does motivate them a bit more.'

The degree to which Earley's victory in Pau was a result of success breeding success is moot. What it definitely represented was an acknowledgment that, within the domestique ranks, lived some riders of great guile and ability.

For the next day, however, the focus would shift back onto the big boys, the stars, the GC contenders. Arriving in Pau, the gateway of the Pyrenees, unscathed and unharmed, the combatants were ready. It was time for those mountain-top battles to commence.

Stage 8
1. Martin Earley (PDM/Ireland) 3:51:26
2. Éric Caritoux (RMO/France) +4"
3. Michael Wilson (Helvetia-La Suisse/Australia) same time
4. Philippe Louviot (Z-Peugeot/France) +6"
5. Laurent Bezault (Toshiba/France) +8"

General classification
1. Greg LeMond (ADR/USA) 37:11:25
2. Laurent Fignon (Super U/France) +5"
3. Thierry Marie (Super U/France) +40"
4. Erik Breukink (Panasonic/Netherlands) +1'51"
5. Sean Yates (7-Eleven/UK) +2'18"

ACT II
THE SECOND WEEK

EIGHT

MOUNTAIN MEN

'It's not for me to push. It's for Laurent' – Greg LeMond

10 July
Stage 9, Pau – Cauterets, 91 miles

FROM THE BOULEVARD des Pyrénées, in the hilltop city of Pau, look due south and the spiky, blue-grey silhouettes of the Pyrenees gaze back at you from the distance, gathering like sharp-toothed giants on the edge of the horizon, on the edge of oblivion.

They're a welcome, overdue sight for the slight, jinking mountain men of the Tour de France, those who had to suffer the wind and the rain and the miles of the last few stages as the race powered its way south. The only consolation was that those roads brought them to their preferred terrain. The foothills, the slopes, the summits.

For many others in the Tour – the sprinters and the time trialists – the presence of the Pyrenees is a cause for questioning their own sanity. Two days of torture and torment, of agony and anguish, before the roads flatten again and equilibrium is restored. That's if the torture and torment, the agony and anguish, isn't so bad that they've gone beyond the stage cut-off time and are out of the Tour, asked to leave, surplus to requirements.

Ever since the Prologue and the team time trial, and his decision to stay in the race where others might have gone to ground, Pedro Delgado had been wishing the days away to get to this point. And for a rider who was well known for going faster the harder the climb, the first day in the Pyrenees had served up a doozy. Two first-category climbs – the 1,035m Col de Marie Blanque and the 1,320m Le Cambasque – bookended the day's absolute monster: the Col d'Aubisque. The Aubisque had been designated an HC climb – *hors catégorie* or 'without category'. It was an ascent so severe that it was simply *beyond* categorisation, 12 miles (20km) of muscle-straining, lung-busting endurance. And all with the most spectacular, unprotected drops in the whole race just a matter of feet away.

The first rider to show his hand was the Fagor domestique Robert Forest, who led the race over the Marie Blanque, 25 seconds clear of the Dutchman Adrie van der Poel, who himself was 25 seconds clear of compatriot Gert-Jan Theunisse. Forest's undoubted career highlight to date was a stage win in the '87 Giro, but the Frenchman had only secured that solo victory in the final kilometre, meaning that it couldn't be viewed as a portent of what he might achieve over the rest of the day's climbs. More than likely, he was sent off to stretch, and prematurely tire, the rivals of his leader Stephen Roche, a tactic that his still-fresh team captain could take advantage of on the stage's later climbs. An elite group – featuring LeMond, Fignon, Delgado, Rooks and Kelly – were indeed keeping an eye on Forest (and on Theunisse), rolling over the Marie Blanque summit a minute and a half back. Markedly, though, the group didn't actually contain Roche.

Then the day's true star emerged. Miguel Induráin, a 24-year-old domestique earmarked to be a Grand Tour team leader of the future, attacked at the bottom of the Aubisque. No one could doubt his ambition, striking out for home this far out and with huge climbs to surmount on his own. His star was certainly in the ascendancy within the Reynolds team; he had won Paris-Nice earlier in the year, holding off Roche by 13 seconds, when he had shown an aptitude for climbing. Until then, his forte was believed to have been the time trial, a discipline suited to his comparatively chunky build. Induráin's physique certainly wasn't that of the gravity-defying climber dancing on his pedals.

Home for Induráin was a village on the outskirts of Pamplona, just 80 or so miles from the day's stage finish. 'This was his home territory,' noted the Spanish writer Javier García Sánchez of that day's Pyrenean stage. 'He knew the landmarks, he knew that his people were waiting in Cauterets. The beech groves spoke to him once more, and history, too.' Delgado had noticed Induráin was itchy that day, a restlessness to make an impression on the race. Perhaps, having followed his Paris-Nice win with a disappointing Vuelta, where he crashed on the 15th stage and broke his wrist, he had a point to prove.

So, with the insurance policy of domestiques Abelardo Rondón and William Palacio taking care of their leader, Delgado allowed Induráin to slip his moorings and strike out. 'This was his day,' wrote García Sánchez. 'That afternoon, he was really going to test his relaxed heart. He was relaxed himself, because he knew Pedro had Rondón and Palacio with him.'

If he were to take the stage win, it would undoubtedly be the greatest climbing performance of Induráin's career. And, heading up into the mists enshrouding the Aubisque's peak, his attack was strong. Over the top, and pushing newspaper up his jersey to counteract the chill of the descent, Induráin was two minutes and 19 seconds ahead of the next two on the road, Luis Herrera and Theunisse. That elite group were in attendance a further ten seconds down. Robert Millar, however, the man with two Pyrenean stage wins in his palmàres, had punctured on the Aubisque's slopes and faced a hefty challenge to bring himself back into contention.

Induráin's lead stretched as he put in a nerveless descent, before comfortably dealing with two lesser climbs. When he reached the valley town of Pierrefitte-Nestalas after 81 miles, a motorbike pulled alongside him, its passenger holding up a mini-blackboard onto which the latest times were scribbled in chalk. Induráin now had a six-minute hold on LeMond, Fignon and the rest. Another minute and a half, and the American's yellow jersey would be his.

Between Induráin and the elite group were two other Spanish riders, the BH team-mates Anselmo Fuerte and Javier Murguialday. While the pair looked strong and were confident of retrieving him, it was indicative that, such was Induráin's imperious performance, it would take two riders to make an impression on his lead.

But, content in his own company, Induráin kept pounding out that steady, metronomic cadence that would become familiar throughout the Tours of the early '90s. That same pain-free facial expression. Those nutcracker thighs. That backside glued to the saddle, irrespective of the gradient.

At the 10km banner, Induráin still looked strong. By the time Fuerte and Murguialday went under the same banner two and a half minutes later, it was down to a one-man pursuit. With his team-mate fading, Fuerte was handed sole responsibility to rein the Reynolds man back in.

On arrival in the centre of Cauterets, the freshness was still there in Induráin's legs. The only thing was that the stage wasn't ending just yet. The finish was a few more miles up the road at the ski station – 'up' being the important word. It would take conquering another first-category climb to take the victory.

But, with three miles left, Induráin was running out of juice. The climb was tightening – and so were his legs. Unusually, his mouth was open too, sucking up all the oxygen it could find. The grimace could be mistaken for a smile. But it wasn't time for smiling. Not yet, at least. And, in another departure, he occasionally rose out of the saddle, desperate to find some elusive rhythm. 'By that time,' García Sánchez wrote, 'Miguel could no longer see anything. All he wanted was to fly, even though he felt as if he were treading water.'

Back down the road, that group of elite riders was beginning to rupture. William Palacio put in an unlikely attack, trying to stretch the bunch, a manoeuvre from which his leader Delgado could profit. But everyone was wise to the plan. No one took the bait. Fignon and LeMond only had eyes for each other, although – sat on the Frenchman's wheel for most of the day – the American was out of Fignon's eyeline, much to the Super U man's aggravation. 'He sucked the wheels as best he could,' he later complained of LeMond, 'and made it obvious he was just going to be a spectator.' His team's attempts to test LeMond, including an impressive, hard-riding spell on the front of the bunch by Gérard Rué, couldn't dislodge him.

Once this group headed out of Cauterets and onto that last brutal climb, Charly Mottet flew off the front, the assassin in the mirror shades. It was as if he had been abiding by a speed limit when riding through the town centre and, once back on the open road, was permitted to floor it. His raw pace and distinctive out-of-the-saddle riding style, his hips shimmying like those of a ballroom dancer, saw him fly past Palacio at double the Spaniard's speed.

The lead of the rapidly tiring Induráin over the yellow jersey was down to four and a half minutes and dropping, thanks to the injection of pace from this elite group. Delgado hit the pedals to bridge to Mottet, shadowed by the vigilant Theunisse. Very shortly, though, just as the trio captured Murguialday, Delgado rode away from his companions. The other BH rider Fuerte was in his crosshairs.

By now, Induráin's legs were so tight and tired that the flag-wielding fans running alongside him barely had to break into a jog to keep up. In marked contrast, so sharp was Delgado's attack that his admirers had to sprint with all their might. Would the leader catch his team-mate? And, if so, what was the plan?

As the Cambasque's inclines began to reduce in their severity, Induráin found something of a second wind. Passing the 2km banner, there was enough left in his tank for one last out-of-the-saddle effort. The crowd, delighted by the gutsiness of the young prince, were nonetheless even more ecstatic when the incumbent king Delgado made an appearance a couple of minutes later. Cameras flashed and Basque flags waved even more fiercely at the reigning champion, despite Induráin's home turf being significantly closer than that of Delgado, the man from Segovia. The fact that the man splitting them, Fuerte, was also Spanish only increased the collective pleasure.

With the comparative plateau of the last few hundred metres easing the pain, Induráin summoned sufficient energy to lift one hand off the handlebars and acknowledge his first Tour stage victory with a partial salute. He was spent after an astonishing individual effort that no one thought was within him.

Paul Sherwen, from his vantage point in the Channel 4 commentary box, hadn't foreseen Induráin's potential. 'He just looked like a big, strong domestique,' he concedes. Andy Hampsten similarly didn't think back then that the Spaniard would turn out to be a serial Tour champion. 'I certainly hadn't caught on to that, no. I missed it.'

The journalist François Thomazeau, a man with the ear of Reynolds team boss José-Miguel Echavarri, had some inside information. 'Echavarri told me in March at the Critérium International [which Induráin won] that he was a rough diamond he had been polishing for years. He told me that he still wanted Miguel to learn a bit in the 1989 Tour, but that he believed he would win at least five Tours. And he did.'

Despite Induráin's endeavours, the roars that accompanied Delgado's last mile were even louder. It was as though he had won another precious Vuelta title. Instead, he had merely taken third place in the first mountain stage of a Tour de France in which he had started the day in 28th position and nearly seven minutes down on the yellow jersey. Not that you'd know the action was taking place on the French side of the Pyrenees. There wasn't a tricolour in sight. The red, green and white of the Basque flag dominated.

While there was obvious delight for Induráin's maiden victory, the resurrection of Delgado had given the crowd even more pleasure. The Spanish retention of the ultimate crown in cycling could still happen. The key, though, was the extent of his time gap over the other GC contenders. What damage had Delgado done? How much time had he recouped that he could take off that self-made debt?

The answer came precisely 27 seconds later. The group had rallied on the last climb and the green jersey of Kelly brought that group over, one that also contained Rooks, Theunisse, Fignon, Mottet and, most significantly, LeMond. The American, having fretted about the mountains all week, had passed his first test. He had matched Fignon pedal-for-pedal up and down a series of truly testing climbs and had found himself to be not wanting, even if the Frenchman was indignant about his refusal to respond to Induráin's initial attack. 'LeMond didn't blink,' he sniffed. 'I was the one who was forced to keep them within reach. All he did was sit tight and take advantage of the work I put in. To be honest, it was extremely frustrating.'

LeMond was resolute in defending his tactics, reminding reporters of the leaderboard. 'It wasn't for me to ride behind Induráin. He is more than seven minutes behind in the standings. It's not for me to push. It's for Laurent. I have to protect the lead I have on him.'

Nearly three decades later, the LeMonds are still responding to accusations that Greg didn't ride with style in the mountains in '89. 'It bugs me when people talk about the tactics,' says Kathy, 'when they say Greg didn't attack. Well, if you've got no team and you've not climbed a Tour mountain in two years and you don't really know your ability any more, you would be an idiot to ride in a show-off way. You're not going to win! He rode the way he rode because he had to. He rode really smart.'

As he answered questions at the finish on the Cambasque, LeMond was pleased about how his fitness had held up over four and a half hours in the saddle, much of which was spent going uphill. 'Today's stage shows that I am in better form than the Tour of Italy. I had a good day. That was reassuring for me. But that doesn't say that the next stage is going to go as well. Now it is a problem of recuperation, for me and the others, too.' The message? Ask me in the morning.

For now, he would wear the *maillot jaune* for another day, for another blue-chip mountain stage. Two days into his leadership, LeMond appeared at ease in yellow. On the podium, Miguel Induráin was a little less comfortable. He looked a little lost, a little shell-shocked. Yet to master the art of publicly putting on a jersey with the world's media watching him, he needed help getting the polka dot jersey of the King of the Mountains leader over his head. Then the presentation women had to give him his first lesson in how to hold a Coca-Cola-branded bouquet to get maximum exposure for the sponsor. But he would learn. The future Tour legend had plenty of opportunities over the years to come to get it right.

***

There was one notable absentee from the finish enclosure. More than five minutes after Sean Kelly had been presented with yet another green jersey, his compatriot Stephen Roche limped over the line, quarter of an hour after Induráin. As much as the stage truly announced the Spaniard's arrival in the Tour, an injury to the Irishman effectively drew the curtain on this Tour grandee's season.

On a cold, crisp January morning in Antibes on the French Riviera, Roche – the silver-topped, 57-year-old version, the one more than double the age he was when he won cycling's Triple Crown – has just returned home from a two-hour ride. He's in better shape than he was on that July afternoon in the Pyrenees twenty-seven and a half years earlier.

Having missed the '88 Tour with a debilitating knee injury, his race hit trouble. It was all down to his ascent of the Marie Blanque. While his Fagor team-mate Robert Forest was the first rider to reach the summit, Roche was suffering back down the mountain. 'I slipped a gear and hit my knee on the end of the handlebar. Boomf. It wasn't too bad going over the climb and down the far side. But at the bottom of the next hill, it was so, so, so painful.

'I got to the finish and the doctor looked at me. "Maybe tomorrow it will be OK." I never abandon a race. You might not start the next day, but you never abandon. Once you climb off, you're going to wonder what might have been. And I couldn't have a Did Not Finish on my CV. A DNF wasn't an option. I never wanted to cry off or pull out for a stupid reason. And you're taking the place of someone else when you're riding the Tour. As a mark of respect for these guys, you go to the limit. You push yourself over the barriers. You're lucky enough to have a place on this Tour and you cannot justify not going until the finish.

'And the next day could be better, you know?

'But the next morning, I walked down the steps to breakfast and it was so painful that there was no point even thinking about getting on a bike. It was just such a stupid thing. It was that same knee again. Had it been the other knee, you never know. But it was the bad one, which was still fairly fragile. There wasn't so much damage. But it was a bruise on an already damaged knee.'

Roche's team-mate and compatriot Paul Kimmage was riding alongside his leader at the time. 'It was giving him fierce pain,' he subsequently wrote in his book *Rough Ride,* 'and we called the race doctor. The spray can was produced but we all knew that the solution was not to be found in an aerosol. He was cooked, it was over. The *bête noire* had struck again.

'Stephen was in terrible pain and riding on one leg. We were quickly distanced by the leaders, but left a lot of struggling bodies behind us – men with two good knees. I stayed at his right shoulder, Eddy [Schepers] on his left. I never once put my bike in front of his, riding all of the time a half-length behind – I didn't want to insult his dignity any further. Photographers and television crews surrounded us, like vultures waiting to be called to dinner. They all wanted to capture the moment when the great champion puts his foot to the ground and abandons the race. But he wasn't going to give them that pleasure. Roche's golden rule was that he never abandoned. He was riding to Cauterets.'

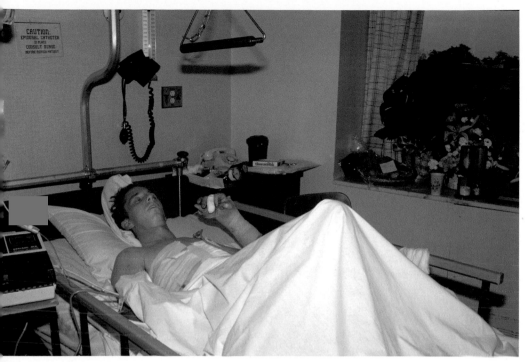

In April 1987, Greg LeMond lies in a Sacramento hospital bed following extensive surgery after being accidentally shot in a hunting accident by his brother-in-law. His wife Kathy describes his body, decimated by buckshot, as being 'like a colander'. *Offside/Presse Sports*

After arriving at the Prologue time trial in Luxembourg nearly three minutes late, defending champion Pedro Delgado finds a long, lonely road ahead of him if he is now to challenge for the yellow jersey. *Offside/Presse Sports*

The following morning, last-placed Delgado discusses his predicament with the new Tour director, Jean-Marie Leblanc. That afternoon, he would lose even more time after a disastrous team time trial. *Offside/Presse Sports*

Laurent Fignon (centre) is in jubilant mood after leading his Super U squad to an imposing win in the team time trial. Tour debutant and future champion Bjarne Riis (far left) has just won a stage on his first full day in the race. *Offside/Presse Sports*

Stage 5 finishes in Belgium, in the unlikely setting of the Spa-Francorchamps motor-racing circuit, home of the Belgian Grand Prix. 'When you see Formula 1 cars going round it at x miles an hour,' says Sean Kelly, 'you don't realise how steep the bloody hill is.' *Offside/Presse Sports*

Raúl Alcalá takes the applause following his victory at Spa-Francorchamps. Having recently moved from the American 7-Eleven team to the Dutch PDM squad, he becomes the first Mexican rider to win a stage of the Tour. *Offside/Presse Sports*

After an encouraging start to the race, Greg LeMond sits in quiet contemplation ahead of Stage 5, the time trial between Dinard and Rennes in Brittany. The American has earmarked the 45-mile stage to be a measure of his form and fitness. *Offside/Presse Sports*

On the road to Rennes, LeMond overtakes the Super U rider Christophe Lavainne, one of several riders he passes on the time trial. Not only does his phenomenal ride give him his first Tour stage win in three years, it also puts him in the yellow jersey. *Offside/Presse Sports*

Roared on by thousands of flag-waving Basques, Miguel Induráin launches a surprising solo attack on the first day in the Pyrenees. He manages to sustain his advantage until the finish in Cauterets – the first of only two non-time trial stages the Spaniard would win in a career that saw him take the overall Tour title five times. *Offside/Presse Sports*

Escorted by his Fagor team-mate and compatriot Paul Kimmage, Ireland's Stephen Roche limps towards the finish at Cauterets after banging an already injured knee on his handlebar. He withdrew the following morning, but had been determined to finish the stage. 'You might not start the next day, but you never abandon.' *Offside/Presse Sports*

Robert Millar nips past Pedro Delgado to take the stage win at the ski-station of Superbagnères. A classic mountain stage, it was also the Scotsman's third – and probably best – win in the Pyrenees. *Offside/Presse Sports*

On the scorching hot Bastille Day stage between Montpellier and Marseille, Frenchmen Charly Mottet and Laurent Fignon launch a joint attack, much to the surprise and consternation of their rivals near the top of the general classification. *Offside/Presse Sports*

Steven Rooks of the Netherlands wins the mountain time trial into Orcières Merlette, showing exactly why he finished runner-up to Pedro Delgado in the 1988 race. *Offside/Presse Sports*

Sean Kelly had a superb Tour, taking the green points jersey – for the most consistent finisher – for a fourth time. For a big man more familiar with duking it out in sprint finishes, he climbed the race's sky-high peaks brilliantly. *Offside/Presse Sports*

Wearing the polka-dot jersey of the King of the Mountains leader, Gert-Jan Theunisse scores a classic victory at Alpe d'Huez, the latest in a series of Dutch riders to win big on the totemic mountain. *Graham Watson*

Laurent Fignon leads the race's top five riders – (left to right) Greg LeMond, Gert-Jan Theunisse, Pedro Delgado and Marino Lejarreta – into Aix-les-Bains. The order in which they finished on the stage mirrored the order in which they finished overall in Paris. *Offside/Presse Sports*

Facing a 50-second deficit – but with the advantage of those controversial aerobars – Greg LeMond considers the task at hand as he leaves Versailles on the heart-stopping final-day time trial. *Offside/Presse Sports*

As the last man to go in the final time trial, Laurent Fignon knows how quickly LeMond is riding on the road ahead. Powering along the banks of the Seine, the Frenchman is nonetheless shedding significant time to the American. *Offside/Presse Sports*

Having safely negotiated the hairpin in front of the Arc de Triomphe, LeMond now rides flat out down the Champs-Élysées. Does he dare to believe that he's making the impossible possible? *Getty Images*

LeMond is flabbergasted at receiving confirmation that Fignon has fallen short by just eight seconds after three weeks of intense racing. It is one of the greatest sporting comebacks of all time. *Offside/Presse Sports*

Having collapsed at the finish line, Fignon is inconsolable at learning that his fastest-ever time trial was still not enough to prevent defeat. He describes himself as being 'like a boxer who's concussed'. *Graham Watson*

For just a few fleeting seconds on the podium, Fignon manages to share a smile with LeMond and Delgado. The pain, though, would remain with him for the rest of his life. *Graham Watson*

Ever the family man, LeMond poses for post-stage pictures back in his hotel room, alongside the ever-supportive Kathy and two-year-old Scott. *Getty Images*

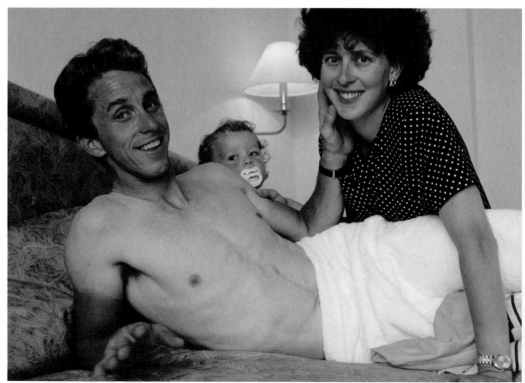

Fignon tries to exact revenge on LeMond at the world championships in Chambéry the following month, but the American outsprints everyone to take an incredible double. *Offside/Presse Sports*

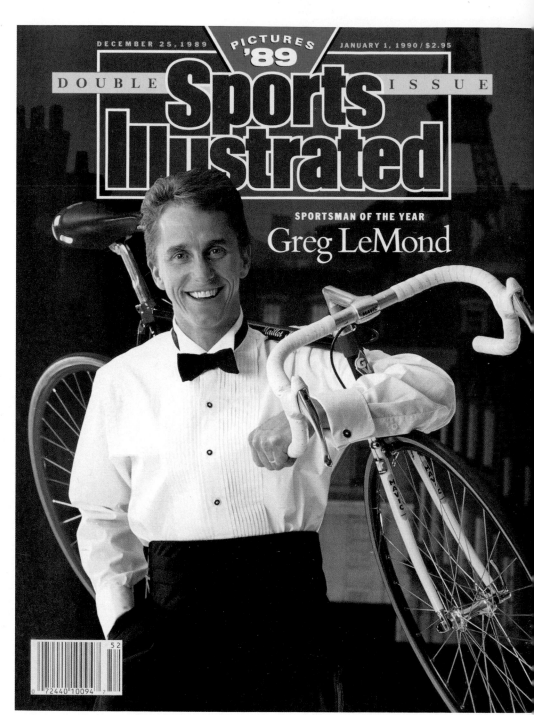

LeMond's extraordinary year is capped in December when *Sports Illustrated* name him their Sportsman of the Year, beating much more established names from American football, basketball and ice hockey. *Getty Images*

The pain was heightened by the fact that the Aubisque had previously been a happy hunting ground for Roche. In 1985, in one of the most defining performances of the ten Tours he rode over the years, the Dubliner scored a terrific win on the mountain, a courageous solo ride that took a minute and a half out of yellow jersey Bernard Hinault and all but secured Roche a place on the podium come Paris. Four years on, his wounded struggle up the Aubisque's slopes was a long way from that thrusting, almost cocky ride to victory.

Roche's problems ran deeper than a bang on the knee. After that Aubisque triumph in the colours of the La Redoute team, and the Triple Crown for Carrera in '87, his second year with Fagor wasn't panning out the way he'd hoped. After Roche's injury and poor form in '88, the squad had been severely weakened by a few departures, especially from the English-speaking quarter – the likes of Robert Millar, Sean Yates and the Sheffield sprinter, Malcolm Elliott. 'To get a podium finish [in '89], those are the riders I would have needed,' Roche explains. 'It wasn't that the team wasn't a good team, but if you're riding for a leader who's going to win a stage or the GC or a podium place that brings in a couple of extra dollars, you'll always dig that little deeper. You know something's going to be coming back from it.'

Because Roche's form wasn't good, his influence when it came to recruitment had been weakened. Signing the riders he wanted on the squad, or even recommending them, was difficult to the point of impossible. 'For '88, I was able to bring riders in because I was world champion. But when you're the wounded ex-world champion, you've no real power to impose someone you really want on the team. My power didn't go very far. I was in the passenger seat.

'You're basically told, "Well, get results and you can talk. For the moment, it's the way we want it. We know what we're doing." That's the way a lot of teams worked in those days. Generally, when all goes well, everything is great and you can ask for a lot. When things start going wrong, you have to roll in with everyone else.' The usurping of Roche ally Patrick Valcke as *directeur sportif* was a further measure of the team leader's declining influence.

'Equipment was also a big thing. When the management of a team goes to suppliers looking for equipment, if they know what they're talking about and are respected, they get a lot more. But the Fagor management weren't very highly respected and weren't getting good deals. They were going for equipment that wasn't the best. We had very heavy bikes. Nothing was going well for us.'

It was a scenario that Yates would recognise from his first year on the team. 'At Peugeot, there had always been a real sense of professionalism,' he later wrote of his first pro team. 'The mechanics at Fagor were gleefully free of that kind of responsibility.'

Chaos seemed to seep into the workings of the team, from the top brass downwards. 'The whole Fagor management had the potential to do a lot of good things,' reasons Roche, 'but everyone was fighting, looking for power. It was all about being seen, about putting the blazer on. They didn't realise there was more to it than putting the money in. The equipment, the psychology…'

The highest-profile exit thus far, Roche's departure from the race the morning after Cauterets was swiftly followed by his departure from the turmoil of Fagor. Some sweet release after two years of sanity-shredding decisions. Out of the madhouse. A free man.

That July morning, Roche's name was removed from the general classification. The leaderboard was getting rewritten in other ways. After days of stagnation, as expected the first Pyrenean day had reordered its upper echelons, with time trialists like Thierry Marie and Sean Yates now banished into the murky depths of the peloton. Erik Breukink surrendered his fourth place rather meekly, down 14 minutes after trailing home in 75th position. The Panasonic assistant boss Ferdi Van den Haute put the underwhelming performance down to Breukink being 'too nervous. This is his third Tour and each time he started with great hopes but his nerves let him down.'

As well as seriously stretching his green jersey lead over the increasingly distant Etienne De Wilde and Søren Lilholt, Kelly's fourth place on the stage also delivered him to fifth place overall, his highest position since finishing fourth in 1985. Could the Irishman dare to dream? Could he really make a credible challenge for that elusive yellow jersey?

For that matter, could Pedro Delgado? At the end of the stage, he probably harboured some disappointment that his attack hadn't yielded even 30 seconds on his main rivals. There was also the feeling that he'd not gone as full throttle as he might. 'I didn't know the Cauterets climb,' he now reveals. 'I thought it was going to be harder than we actually found it. It was easy. It wasn't steep enough for long enough for me to really break away, except towards the end. But Miguel won the stage, so we were very happy. Plus, my mind was always focused on the next day into Superbagnères...'

The first day in the mountains had offered intrigue and incident by the barrow-load. The second day would offer even more.

Stage 9
1. Miguel Induráin (Reynolds/Spain) 4:32:36
2. Anselmo Fuerte (BH/Spain) +27"
3. Pedro Delgado (Reynolds/Spain) +1'29"
4. Sean Kelly (PDM/Ireland) +1'56"
5. Steven Rooks (PDM/Ireland) same time

General classification
1. Greg LeMond (ADR/USA) 41:45:49
2. Laurent Fignon (Super U/France) +5"
3. Pascal Simon (Super U/France) +3'56"
4. Charly Mottet (RMO/France) +4'09"
5. Sean Kelly (PDM/Ireland) +4'52"

NINE

YELLOW PERIL

'Our hand-to-hand combat had begun' – Laurent Fignon

11 July
Stage 10, Cauterets – Superbagnères, 85 miles

THE MODEST SKI resort of Superbagnères continues to be held in untarnished reverence by certain quarters of the cycling cognoscenti. This is despite the Tour not having visited its heights in nearly three decades. Quite possibly, its cherished position may actually be *because* of its absence from the race's schedule. As a stage finish, the mountain is effectively trapped in amber, a relic of a golden era of adventurous, gung-ho individual riding before team-focused defensive tactics – those of control and containment – became the dominant *modus operandi* of the Tour peloton.

The race's abandoning of Superbagnères was a remarkable state of affairs considering the excellent racing and multiple levels of intrigue it offered up the last time riders pushed themselves up its slopes. That year was 1989.

Perhaps Superbagnères wasn't beautiful enough. As the writer Edward Pickering has described, the resort consists of 'a cluster of rickety-looking chalets, crêperies and shed-like hotels in a desultory semi-circle round a rocky, unpaved car park where puddles, once formed, last for weeks'. Or perhaps the geography of its ascent wasn't sufficiently spectacular. Where

Alpe d'Huez bewitches and beguiles its attendant masses with its 21 hairpin bends, the approach to the Superbagnères summit, certainly in its last couple of miles, is broadly a long, straight, unsheltered slog. But in 1989, it was the crucible of not one but two battles royal, providing one of the best days of the Tour de France in the entire decade.

Not that the stages the resort previously hosted were remotely anonymous. First selected as a Tour finish in 1961, the following year Britain's Tom Simpson wore the yellow jersey in a time trial up the mountain. It was the only day Simpson would hold the race lead in his entire career; he lost more than six minutes that day to stage-winner Federico Bahamontes and dropped out of the top five in the GC. Other Tour legends have climbed its slopes in the *maillot jaune*, among them Jacques Anquetil, Eddy Merckx and Bernard Hinault. Hinault was in yellow on the Tour's penultimate visit in 1986, a day of attacks and counterattacks that climaxed with Greg LeMond taking his first-ever stage victory in the Tour's mountains. It brought him within 40 seconds of his team-mate Hinault, providing the springboard for the American's overall victory, in the infamous race where his biggest rival had been his allegedly double-crossing team-mate.

Robert Millar was second to LeMond that day in 1986 and fancied his chances of going one better on his return visit three years later. His two Tour stage wins to date had both been in the Pyrenees. In 1983, he pipped Pedro Delgado at the finish in Luchon, just down the mountain from Superbagnères, while in 1984 his solo attack outfoxed and outpowered everyone on the climb up to the Guzet-Neige ski station.

A hat-trick of Pyrenean wins was what Millar had in mind in 1988 when the race returned to Guzet-Neige – and it looked likely to happen before he and Philippe Bouvatier took a wrong turn 300 metres from the finish. Bouvatier had misinterpreted the signals of a gendarme who was actually directing the team cars, not the riders. Millar followed the Frenchman into a side turn, allowing third-placed Massimo Ghirotto to coast to victory. In 1989, Millar needed to erase the embarrassment of the previous summer, to correct an injustice. The previous day's puncture – when he had had to wait on the roadside for assistance for quite some time – had denied him a tilt at a stage victory. So, in his happy hunting ground of the Pyrenees, this second and final day would need to be the one.

The route from Cauterets to Superbagnères took in some totem climbs: the Col du Tourmalet, the Col d'Aspin and the Col de Peyresourde. Millar was champing at the bit and, together with Charly Mottet, launched an early attack as they approached the Tourmalet. The pair worked together well, similar builds but different styles. The ponytailed Millar was largely hunched over his bike letting his legs do the work, while the faster that Mottet pedalled, the more his body bobbed up and down. The Scotsman led the Frenchman over the summit, gratefully accepting a spectator's offer of a copy of that day's *L'Equipe* to put up his jersey to keep out the cold wind on the descent.

As Millar and Mottet gained some respite on the Tourmalet's down-slopes, something was afoot on the other side of the summit. In a group containing most of the main GC contenders, Laurent Fignon, so imperious thus far in the race, was struggling on the first stiff climb of the day. For all his bluff and bravado, he couldn't disguise his weakness – even if he thought he had.

'I felt as if I was having a massive off-day,' Fignon later wrote, 'particularly on the Tourmalet where the attacking was brutal and I had no answer. I was going nowhere. But as I put on a bit of a show as I went along and didn't give any sign that I was in trouble, my rivals didn't notice my real state.'

Fignon was wrong. His rivals had noticed he was in trouble, the first of just a handful of public displays of weakness from the Parisian throughout the entire three weeks of the race. It was crystallised by one particular incident on that first climb, an episode noticed by both LeMond and Andy Hampsten. It involved one of the motos, the motorcycles on which cameramen and photographers ride pillion.

'Theunisse and Rooks were doing a super-hard tempo on the Tourmalet,' Hampsten remembers, 'and a photographer on a motorbike, Graham Watson, was just trying to get by. There were eight of us taking up the road. The race director's car, with the head commissaire in it, was the first car behind us. It couldn't be more front-seat, all-eyes-open. Fignon was hurting. I was watching him, LeMond was watching him. "This is great. He's having a really bad day." But Fignon then put his hand on Graham Watson's forearm. LeMond and I exchanged looks. "Are you seeing what I'm seeing?"

'It wasn't for just a second. It was 20 seconds, half a minute. It was a long, really helpful pause. Yes, it wasn't that Fignon then attacked and won the stage, but it was more important than that to him. He was getting dropped and hung on to not get dropped. LeMond and I both looked back at the race director's car, four metres behind us. They must have seen it. We both thought that we didn't need to attack because he'd be thrown out of the race. It was so obvious, so blatant. But nothing happened. Nothing. Maybe Greg could have held on and not got thrown out. But I don't think so. It was a very telling moment in a French sporting event.'

'If Andy says he saw it,' says Graham Watson from his home in the northern reaches of New Zealand's South Island, 'then for sure he saw it. But I don't recall this incident at all. Riders grabbing hold of motos back then was commonplace. But it rarely happened when the going got tough and officials could see more clearly what was going on. When it did happen, and when I was aware of it, I tended to look away from the cyclist, as if by doing so I was pretending to be unaware of the illegal tow. It would have been hard to penalise the driver – and certainly not the innocent passenger! – as he was hardly offering his moto as a catapult for Fignon. But back then, the Tour would have looked the other way if its French race leader had taken a tow. That's how it was.'

You didn't need to be a soothsayer to know Pedro Delgado's intentions that day. Everyone knew he would make his move at some point, buoyed by the phenomenal levels of Spanish support on the roadside and vexed by the fact that his efforts at Cauterets had gained him fewer than 30 seconds, a small reduction in that sizeable time deficit. He couldn't delay his move until the Alps in a good few days; the second and final Pyrenean stage had to be the time and place for a performance that he hoped would make a serious dent in the GC.

Aided by his faithful domestique Julián Gorospe – the bodyguard who had brought his leader back into the fold at that fateful team time trial – Delgado bridged the gap to Millar and Mottet on the descent of the Tourmalet. With nothing more than a nod and a glance, an alliance was formed, an unspoken acknowledgement that, at least until the final climb up to Superbagnères, all three riders would work together and not attack each other.

With Mottet and Delgado's shared objective being to recover as much time as possible on LeMond and Fignon in order to catapult themselves up the GC, Millar led the trio over each of the day's summits, unheeded and unchallenged in his collection of the maximum King of the Mountains points. Things were working out very nicely for all three of them. As the gap back to LeMond, Fignon *et al* rose and rose, Mottet – four minutes and nine seconds off the yellow jersey at the start of the stage – now found himself the new race leader on the road.

'I'd had an idea that I might have been *maillot jaune virtuel*,' he explains, 'but there were no radios and, anyway, these were the first mountain stages of the Tour. We still had many kilometres to go. I wasn't particular interested in making the *maillot jaune* anyway. I was among the favourites but I wasn't the favourite and this gave me more freedom to go on the attack. Fignon and LeMond were marking each other. It was their responsibility to control the race, so I and others could take advantage of that situation.'

For a man in such mental turmoil just a week before, Pedro Delgado looked every part the keen-eyed optimist in control of his own destiny. He was at absolute ease with the situation, even dropping back for a toilet break at one point before calmly coming back into the fold. No panic. And no one taking advantage. The mutuality was clear; at one stage, Delgado offered a thirsty Millar his water bottle.

And, were anyone in any doubt about the stage's proximity to the Spanish border, Delgado was being roared on by a partisan crowd. The names painted on the narrow roads further confirmed the main nationality in attendance. 'Pedro', 'Miguel', 'Pablo', 'Marino'…

And then the end game. On the final climb up to Superbagnères, the exuberant, vociferous support began to overwhelm and annoy Delgado. There was a constant stream of fans who felt the need to run alongside him at extremely close quarters, crowding in and invading his space, their faces inches from his. On a stage where his temper had been even, he cracked. Reaching down to pull his water bottle from the down tube of his bike, he hurled it at a pair of runners keeping pace on his right-hand side. Despite the bottle reaching its target, they continued their pursuit – until, that was, the less athletic one stumbled to the ground, his legs unable to cope with the steep gradient. The commissaire's car just avoided making contact with his head.

In anger, Delgado pushed hard on the pedals and took off around a steep left-hand bend. Maybe, just maybe, the whole incident was an elaborate conceit – throwing a bottle to distract Mottet and Millar, before flying off towards possible glory. Whatever the motivation, the move finally did for Mottet, the man who, in the early stages of the break, had asked Millar just why he was riding so fast. He had finally run out of gas.

Desperate to avoid a runners-up spot in successive years, the Scotsman managed to reel Delgado back in. The higher the pair climbed, the more they gasped for air, and the more the neighbouring peaks were smudged by clouds of mist. At the kite banner signalling the last kilometre, they caught the first glimpse of the Grand Hotel beyond the throng of spectators, a vast L-shaped affair that seemed to cling to the very side of the mountain. Its out-of-season eeriness was immediately reminiscent of the Overlook, the hotel whose underpopulated corridors were prowled by a psychotic Jack Nicholson in *The Shining*.

With the finish line just in front of the hotel, Delgado knew what was left to do. He started to pull away from Millar again, not with any sudden injection of pace but with purpose nonetheless. The stage win looked on. But the crowd again seemed to distract the Spaniard, the sporadically placed gendarmes unable to cope with a tag-team of young men eager to demonstrate their athletic prowess by charging up the mountain on foot. When he should have been rocketing to the finish line, Delgado's mind seemed to get diverted from the task at hand, unaware that Millar had ghosted up behind him. The two riders came together again with 800 metres to go, a nervous glance from Delgado finding his rival on his shoulder. The pair rode under the resort's ski lift, which was motionless and silent in high summer, like a fairground ride in an abandoned amusement park. But it signalled that the ski station summit was imminent.

As the climb bent right into the home straight, Millar made his move, ripping around the outside to skewer the Spaniard and to take that overdue third Tour stage win. Channel 4's chief commentator Phil Liggett put the victory into context, describing Millar's ride – where he had led over all four major climbs – as 'one of the great performances in post-war times in the Tour de France'. Not that Delgado would lose sleep over missing out on the stage win. The greater reward would be the minutes he was taking to further cross that divide to LeMond and Fignon. The clock had started ticking.

Back down the mountain, that inseparable PDM pair – Steven Rooks and Gert-Jan Theunisse – had broken away from the elite group, placing additional concern on the shoulders of LeMond and Fignon, the riders with most to lose. Earlier during the stage, Fignon's team-mate Pascal Simon had furiously driven the group's response to the break of Millar and Mottet. Now the Super U leader was forced to take up the running himself, putting in an impressively lengthy shift at the front of the group, dragging the tired legs of many GC rivals with him.

Unsurprisingly, Fignon dropped to the back of the group in the final kilometre, an understandable manoeuvre after such a Herculean effort. It was now up to one of the others to make their move; Andy Hampsten, in particular, appeared to be riding strongly. Fignon had other ideas, though. After a quick breather, and with the sight of the hotel his lure, he attacked down the blindside in an attempt to catch LeMond unawares, to snatch the few seconds he needed to put himself in yellow for the first time in five years. The yellow jersey streaked after him and looked like he'd done enough to stay with Fignon. But his legs couldn't maintain the pounding and he sank back into his saddle, a spent force just 500 metres from the line. While Fignon used the central white line as his guide, his equilibrium, LeMond could only dream of keeping his bike on that kind of straight and narrow. He was weaving all over the left side of the road and the Parisian was away.

Crossing the line in seventh place (Marino Lejarreta had jumped ahead to take sixth), Fignon didn't need to wait for LeMond's arrival to know he was now the leader of the pack. He didn't raise his arms in triumph, but he did puff out his chest as he came home. Based on his efforts on the climb to Superbagnères alone, the yellow jersey was deservedly his.

LeMond's front wheel rolled over the line 12 seconds later. Fignon's lead was almost as narrow as the ADR leader's had been that morning; just seven seconds. LeMond's *soigneur* Otto Jacome wrapped a snow-white towel around his rider's shoulders, like a boxing trainer consoling his fighter at the end of a tough, full-distance bout. No knockout blow. A narrow defeat on points.

'I made a mistake in trying to catch him too fast,' he told Samuel Abt, the cycling correspondent of the *New York Times*. 'I tried to bluff him by getting right back on his wheel so that he'd think he'd never be able to get away, but I blew up.'

LeMond remained philosophical about, rather than angry at, the stage result. If, before the race had reached the Pyrenees, he had been told he would ride two stages across some of the most punishing mountain passes in Europe and emerge only seven seconds down on the yellow jersey, he would have grabbed hungrily at that. Both hands and a tight grasp.

He also retained the foresight to shift the psychological burden onto the new yellow jersey during his post-stage TV interviews. 'For me, the most important thing is I'm in a very good position and the pressure's on Laurent Fignon. I think he made a very big mistake today letting Delgado go. He played the race all against me, but he has to realise that Delgado is probably the most dangerous rider now. As we approach the Alps, Delgado's getting closer to Fignon. So, for me, the race is between Delgado and Fignon, with me a...' He paused to pick his words carefully. '...close contender.'

Beyond LeMond and his entourage, Jacques Goddet, the octogenarian race director-at-large, prowled the finish line in his trademark khaki shirt and shorts. A satisfied grin played on his face. This Tour, already packed with incident, was coming to the boil nicely.

Fignon's pleasure in securing yellow was tempered by the three minutes and 26 seconds that Delgado had retrieved from him. Not only that, but the inroads made by Charly Mottet made him a very real threat too; he was now only just over a minute behind his former Super U team-mate. Fignon's extended stint driving the chase group up the Superbagnères slopes was arguably the deciding factor in whether Mottet, the virtual *maillot jaune* on the road that afternoon of course, leapfrogged him into yellow.

Not that these concerns were going to wipe the smile from Fignon's face on the podium, where he also expelled an exaggerated sigh of relief. He would be content enough that, with flat, relatively unassuming stages in the next few days as the race made its way across the south of France towards the Alps, he'd enjoy the sun on his face and the yellow jersey on his back. LeMond, Mottet and Delgado might have been circling, the scent of blood in their nostrils, but they were unlikely to make an imminent move. For the GC boys, it was now a time for recuperation and reflection after two days of phenomenal racing.

Millar, always a slightly awkward, slightly shy figure on the podium, nonetheless also wore his happiness well. A ruffle of his own hair, a single-arm salute to the crowd and a smile of contentment. A Tour with a stage win was a good Tour for the Glaswegian.

The podium smiles stopped there, though. The inscrutable Gert-Jan Theunisse had inherited Miguel Induráin's King of the Mountains jersey and received his prize with the straightest of faces. Not a flicker of pleasure or satisfaction. Nothing. The taciturn Dutchman made Millar resemble the Laughing Cavalier in comparison. The pair were now only separated by 12 points in the competition. Without the previous day's puncture, Millar could well have been getting reacquainted with the polka-dot jersey he won outright in 1984. With a stage win under his belt, it became his principal target for the rest of the Tour. 'I'll try and take it, yes,' he told *Cycling Weekly*. 'I don't want to get involved in any sprints for points on the smaller climbs over the next few days, but if he goes for them, I'll have to. If he doesn't, then I won't. I'll try and take the lead in the Alps if I can.'

For now, Millar was basking in the glow of his stage win. 'I was OK on the early climbs, but in the end Delgado had me and Mottet hanging on. He was accelerating for 500 metres at a time. If it had been 600 metres, I'd have been dropped. It was like he was one gear bigger than the rest of us. He has strength.' But Millar refused to declare that the stage win avenged his defeat in the 1985 Tour of Spain, when an apparent collusion by various Spanish teams allowed Delgado to attack unnoticed on one particular stage, in the process taking the oblivious Millar's overall lead. 'No revenge,' the Scotsman confirmed. 'I've a short memory.'

While Stephen Roche's withdrawal might have been the highest-profile departure from the Tour that day, he was far from the only rider leaving the race on this second Pyrenean stage. A full 16 riders either failed to start, retired mid-stage or were eliminated because their time was outside the cut-off limit. The Panasonic team were the big losers, with three of their sprinters being timed out. One – Jean-Paul van Poppel – had received a substantial number of pushes over the day's climbs. And this came after Panasonic leader Erik Breukink's rather calamitous stage the day before.

ADR had suffered, too. The Estonian-born Norwegian Jaanusz Kuum, the only team-mate LeMond had who was remotely close to being described as a climbing specialist, abandoned at the stage's end, leaving the American to fight his own cause in those mountain-top skirmishes. 'Greg was totally on his own in the mountains,' confirms his team-mate, the Dutchman Johan Lammerts. If he were still in contention when the race reached the

Alps at the beginning of the final week, LeMond would now need to ride even more conservatively. If so, that would provide Fignon, a man only too happy to articulate his views of his rivals, with even more ammunition.

As it was, at Superbagnères the recriminations carried on into the evening, with the post-stage war of words now seemingly a daily fixture. The intensity was tightening, especially when it came to the issue of chasing down breakaways, such as that day's Delgado/Millar/Mottet manoeuvre. 'LeMond never wanted to work to bring them back,' griped Fignon to the massed microphones of the European media. 'It's not the way the race leader should behave. I think if we had worked together, Delgado would never have opened such a gap. It's annoying for all of us.'

Fignon's annoyance at LeMond's tactics hadn't subsided by the time he wrote his autobiography 20-odd years later. 'He was incapable of attacking, as the climb to Superbagnères proved. To this day, I don't know if he managed to come alongside me once, and that's saying something. It wound me up. And when I got frustrated, when I began boiling inside, it had to come out somehow.'

Knowing he didn't have enough in himself to nullify the attack by Rooks and Theunisse, Fignon had looked across at LeMond to see if he intended to chase down the flying Dutchmen. There was no response. 'Allowing LeMond to stay on my wheel all the way to the top would have driven me mad. In the final kilometre, I did enough to get rid of him, in other words, enough for me to take the yellow jersey by seven seconds. Our hand-to-hand combat had begun.'

For LeMond, that incident on the Tourmalet, when Fignon hitched a ride from the moto, was still exasperating him. He had seen it exactly as Hampsten had; their stories matched. 'He [Fignon] was getting dropped,' LeMond would tell the author Guy Andrews. 'I turned back and he's sitting there holding on. So we get to the end of the stage and he beats me by 12 seconds. Then he's saying to the press that I'm not riding like a true leader for the yellow jersey!'

Even a good night's sleep didn't cool LeMond's blood. As told to Richard Moore, the next morning he confronted Fignon. 'I said, "Listen, you'd better shut up. I saw it. You were holding on to that motorcycle. That means you're out of the race. It's not like you're a guy in the *gruppetto* [the last group of riders on a particular stage] trying to get over a mountain. You're in the front and trying to win the Tour.'"

. While Fignon was indeed in yellow, and while Millar had taken arguably the most impressive of his three Tour stage wins, the day's real winner came with a Spanish accent. Over the course of four hours in the saddle, Pedro Delgado had retrieved more than three-quarters of the time he had conceded to Fignon after the team time trial and was now up to fourth place. His revival was irresistible. He had always been a fascinating rider to watch, jittery and instinctive, with talent to burn and a never-shrinking work ethic. As he attempted to claw back whatever seconds he could on each stage, he resembled, in the words of Induráin biographer Javier García Sánchez, 'some workaholic ant'.

'That day,' Delgado remembers, 'I started to dream that maybe I could win the Tour de France. I recovered a lot of time from Fignon and more from LeMond. I now knew I could beat them. "OK, three and a half minutes today. Maybe it's a possibility…" The main attention was on Fignon and LeMond. But it was better that all the pressure was on them so I could come along quietly. But after this day, Fignon and LeMond understood they needed to pay attention to me because I was stronger in the mountains.

'And I started taking LeMond seriously at Superbagnères. That day, he understood he could win the Tour, because his levels were not far from the specialist Fignon. He showed he could stay with us in the mountains. Fignon was aggressive. He wanted to compete. LeMond was the opposite. He was a fox. He waited and waited. He didn't move. He shifted the pressure to the rest of the riders and benefited.'

Taking three and a half minutes out of most of his main rivals for the GC was mightily impressive, even if Delgado may have been cut some slack due to the size of his time deficit at the start of the day. 'The tactics are always played out based on the situation,' LeMond confirmed. 'If Delgado is five minutes behind, you give him some time.'

Whether cut some slack or not, Millar was certainly impressed by Delgado's work-rate and speed, as he told Channel 4's Paul Sherwen: 'If he keeps going like that, we won't have to look for the winner of this year's Tour much longer.' Even a post-stage Fignon had to doff his cap in the Spaniard's direction after such a masterclass in aggressive climbing. 'I was convinced in

Luxembourg, when the Tour began, that Delgado was out of the hunt for overall victory. I must admit I was wrong.'

That early goading of Delgado about his lowly position in the GC standings was now surely a source of embarrassment for Fignon. The distance between them was narrowing by the day. He might have emerged from the first instalment of mountain stages in yellow, but the Frenchman still had LeMond right on his shoulder, with only a handful of seconds continuing to separate them. And his problem was two-fold. The speeding Delgado was increasingly visible in the rear-view mirror.

Stage 10
1. Robert Millar (Z-Peugeot/UK) 4:22:19
2. Pedro Delgado (Reynolds/Spain) same time
3. Charly Mottet (RMO/France) +19"
4. Steven Rooks (PDM/Netherlands) +3'04"
5. Gert-Jan Theunisse (PDM/Netherlands) same time

General classification
1. Laurent Fignon (Super U/France) 46:11:49
2. Greg LeMond (ADR/USA) +7"
3. Charly Mottet (RMO/France) +57"
4. Pedro Delgado (Reynolds/Spain) +2'53"
5. Andy Hampsten (7-Eleven/USA) +5'18"

TEN

DEFENCE OF THE REALM

*'He was mad about the crash. Really, really mad.
He was angry all day and all week' – Raúl Alcalá*

12 July
Stage 11, Luchon – Blagnac, 96 miles

RUDY DHAENENS HAD it in the bag. The scent of victory was in his nostrils. But, in an instant, it was all about the taste of tarmac on his tongue.

His fate was a harsh way to involuntarily surrender a certain stage win. Dhaenens had timed it so perfectly, after all. With just around a mile and a half to go in this eleventh stage – the first flat one after the high drama of the Pyrenees – the PDM rider had given everyone else the slip. Part of a six-man breakaway heading towards the Toulouse suburb of Blagnac, at the precise moment that the Fignon-led peloton bridged the gap and dissolved the break, Dhaenens attacked again. It was a textbook manoeuvre. Sharp tactical nous and immaculate timing.

With a solid posture that any time trialist would have coveted – a perfectly still upper body but legs firing like well-oiled pistons – he was eating up Blagnac's residential back streets, the layout of which suited a solo break. There was no lengthy, dead-straight finish to negotiate in full view of the marauding brigade of sprinters behind. Instead, there were plenty of bends to disappear around, to stay out of sight. And with those chasing sprinters starting to slow

121

up and play a game of bluff back down the road, only a few hundred metres remained for Dhaenens. Just a matter of seconds. He looked unstoppable.

That was until he reached the penultimate bend. The second of two closely located left-handers, the Belgian simply misjudged his speed and, in trying to adjust in order to achieve safe passage around this second bend, his back wheel slipped out from under him, sending him crashing to the ground. In one movement, he scrambled over to his bike, before slightly stumbling and having to rebalance. And that stumble did for him. By the time he was back on his feet and pulled the bike upright, the peloton swung past at high speed. There was nothing left for Dhaenens to do, except express his frustration, raising the bike a few inches off the ground before slamming it in anger back into the tarmac.

As the stage climaxed in a rare bunch sprint, Dhaenens remained at the scene of his misfortune, spinning around in bemusement, wondering if what had just happened really happened. The team cars were zooming past now, their drivers gazing across to see who the unfortunate soul was and second-guessing the fate that had befallen him. Dhaenens was too angry to dissect the crash, to consider an on-the-road autopsy. He slammed his bike back down into the tarmac again. Exasperated, incredulous.

Interviewed the following spring, he still didn't seem to have made sense of what happened that July afternoon in Blagnac. 'I took the corner too fast, maybe, or something happened with my bike, maybe, and I slipped. I still don't know.'

His then PDM team-mate Raúl Alcalá thinks he knows. While Dhaenens' final attack was cool, calm and calculated, Alcalá believes that wouldn't have been how he was feeling internally going into that final mile. 'He was mad about the crash,' says the Mexican. 'Really, really mad. He was angry all day and all week. But it was his fault because he was nervous all the time. I know riders are nervous, but he was one of the most nervous riders around.

'He was a good rider, but he was nervous, nervous, nervous. He always went full gas all the time. I told him plenty of times: 'Rudy, go calm. Relax.' Maybe if he controlled his nerves, he could have been a huge rider. Many things happened in his head…'

Alcalá's assessment of Dhaenens' potential wasn't necessarily shared by all. The *New York Times* cycling correspondent Samuel Abt described him as 'a dependable, unselfish rider of moderate talent, not a star'. This seems a little harsh, bearing in mind the Belgian's palmàres. In 1986, as the Tour reached Bordeaux, Dhaenens had struck out in a similar fashion to his attack in Blagnac. That time, however, he stayed on two wheels to take the stage victory. But his crowning glory came in 1990 when he won the world championships in Japan.

Winning the ultimate one-day title didn't seem to completely cure Dhaenens of his nervousness or insecurity, as later reported by Abt. 'Usually he looked like a small boy who asked Santa for a set of trains for Christmas and got instead underwear and a book, but his plain face could light up when he discussed the few races he had won. The world championship was the peak, of course.'

Prior to that success, Dhaenens had always believed his fate was written in the stars. 'I'm always in the top group, usually in the front, but I never win. And that's what's important in cycling races. To win, you need luck.'

And that luck would desert him in future years. In 1998, while en route to commentate on the Tour of Flanders for Belgian television, his car left the road and collided with an electricity pylon. He died the following night from head injuries. He was 36.

***

The sprinters were at least happy with the opportunity that Rudy Dhaenens' bike crash offered them. Pickings had been slim for them in the Tour until that point and to a man they were itching to duel it out on the home straight in Blagnac.

Steve Bauer had been rather anonymous in the Tour thus far, certainly in comparison to his extended ownership of the yellow jersey the previous year, not to mention his fourth place overall. But it was the Helvetia-La Suisse leader who made the first bolt for the line, presumably concerned that ADR's Eddy Planckaert, last year's green jersey winner, was not only lurking but pretty much unbeatable in a straight dash for the line.

In the end, though, it was a Dutchman – Mathieu Hermans – who snatched the victory, repaying the efforts that his Paternina team had put in during the last few miles to get him into a favourable position for the stage win. Hermans was clearly a man in form and no doubt frustrated by the lack of sprinting action so far in the race; he had taken no fewer than nine stage victories in the Vuelta over the last two years.

Another rider at the top of his game – the Italian Giovanni Fidanza, winner of the points competition in the Giro the previous month – took second, with an out-of-sorts Planckaert only able to bag third. Sean Kelly took another fifth place, having presumably held back in the final run-in as his man Dhaenens looked to have the victory all sewn up. While truly Mr Consistent whatever the terrain, the Irishman was still looking for that elusive stage win. Remarkably for a rider almost always in the mix at the finish, he'd not won a Tour stage since way back in 1982. This day he did, however, take possession of the red catch sprints jersey from Søren Lilholt. Another for the collection.

After the leg-sapping tumult of the Pyrenees, this stage had been a surprisingly lively one, especially in view of the high temperatures toasting the south of France. And the day wasn't without its casualties; there was one high-profile abandonment in particular. Fabio Parra, the Colombian initially fancied by many to at least repeat his podium finish in 1988, was one of only two riders from the Spanish Kelme team left in the race. He hadn't made his mark in the Pyrenees on the previous two days. Far from it. He had lost more than nine minutes in the mountains, his home territory.

Parra had already been dropped within 12 miles of leaving Luchon that morning and, after struggling over two comparatively tame climbs, he called time on the '89 Tour, citing tendonitis. That left just one Kelme rider, a young Colombian called José Roncancio. Whether performing an act of solidarity with his leader, or simply too embarrassed that the team would need to continue with only this rookie domestique on the road, Roncancio also abandoned. This was particularly harsh on the 23-year-old. It was to be his one and only stab at the Tour de France.

For every yin, there's a yang. And for every suffering Fabio Parra, there was a buoyant Laurent Fignon. On a day when he could justifiably have chosen to relax and recuperate within the safety of the peloton, Fignon elected to play an active part in the stage, along with his Super U team-mate Christophe Lavainne. It had been their twin motors that had driven the peloton to bring the race back together, moments before Rudy Dhaenens made his break.

As rookie domestiques fared, Bjarne Riis was in a somewhat better place than José Roncancio. He was the personal bodyguard of the yellow jersey, of the man who was now the overwhelming favourite to taste victory in Paris, to collect his third Tour title.

'Yes, there was no doubt about that,' agrees Riis. 'We all believed in him. There was a great bond between all of us. Quite a few of us had done the Giro too. We'd spent a lot of time together, building up to this. We had huge focus. We were very committed and motivated. Fignon was a guy who gave a lot of confidence to his team. He took care of us. There was a lot of respect around him because he treated his people in a good way.

'Of course, he was an introvert, but that's OK. There's a lot of pressure on a guy like that. He didn't jump around among everybody. He was very private. He was a little bit like myself, to be honest.'

However, on stage after stage, Fignon's riding style was anything but introverted. He was the dominant rider, the agenda setter. And his team were following the script. But, as hard and fast as the Super U leader rode across to Blagnac, another man was riding just as hard and fast – and he was right on his back wheel. Greg LeMond wasn't easily shaken off. Just seven seconds away.

Stage 11
1. Mathieu Hermans (Paternina/Netherlands) 3:37:47
2. Giovanni Fidanza (Chateau d'Ax/Italy) same time
3. Eddy Planckaert (ADR/Belgium) same time
4. Teun van Vliet (Panasonic/Netherlands) same time
5. Sean Kelly (PDM/Ireland) same time

General classification
1. Laurent Fignon (Super U/France) 49:49:36
2. Greg LeMond (ADR/USA) +7"
3. Charly Mottet (RMO/France) +57"
4. Pedro Delgado (Reynolds/Spain) +2'53"
5. Andy Hampsten (7-Eleven/USA) +5'18"

***

13 July
Stage 12, Toulouse – Montpellier, 150 miles

On the eve of the 200th anniversary of the storming of the Bastille, in the warm haze of late morning, Martin Kettle, a non-sport feature writer for the *Guardian*, found himself on assignment in the small town of Puylaurens, 30 miles east of Toulouse. He was on the trail of the Tour de France. But his brief wasn't to dissect tactical strategy or interrogate the riders or sniff out the latest gossip from behind the scenes.

Instead, Kettle was charged with sampling the Tour through the eyes of those on the roadside, those who arrive at their vantage points with hours and hours to spare, but who would be left behind by the speeding train of a peloton within seconds.

Filling the time and keeping the interest was the seemingly endless procession of trade vehicles offering promotional items to anyone with an outstretched hand. The first van reached the town at 9.30am; it bore the livery of *Reader's Digest* and handed out kitchen whisks. What followed were vehicles of all shapes and sizes. One had been made to resemble a cigarette lighter, another was disguised as a loaf of bread. All were touting their various wares, offering freebies to a grateful public happy to fill its boots. 'Two hundred years ago,' Kettle observed, 'the French stretched their hands for bread. Today, they strain for free plastic bags advertising the World Cycling Championship.'

The best part of two hours later, the main event was approaching, the point at which the marketing caravan would disappear and a palpable buzz would fall on Puylaurens. There would even be a small degree of competition, with a catch sprint being held in the middle of town.

Kettle painted a vivid landscape for his readers. '"Five kilometres away," a voice over the Tannoy announces and the vans hastily clear out. Police motorcyclists come through the square at speed. At 11.17, there is cheering down the hill and two emaciated riders come into the square, one in blue and one in red. Number 175 crosses the line first, snatches a drink from his cycle bottle and both ease off.

'No one in the crowd knows who they are.'

To be fair to the crowd, even cycling's most knowledgeable commentators and reporters would have been scratching their heads when trying to identify these two riders, almost certainly having to reach for the start list for assistance. GC contenders they were not. The man in blue was Dominique Arnaud, a Frenchman riding for Pedro Delgado's Reynolds team. The rider in red, number 175, was the Chateau d'Ax domestique Valerio Tebaldi, an Italian.

Their early lead grew and grew and grew, soon aided by a second Italian, the Carrera rider Giancarlo Perini. Riding through the impossibly scenic Haut Languedoc national park, their advantage rose to 29 minutes over the peloton. The unconcerned peloton, that is. None of the three were placing Laurent Fignon's jersey in jeopardy. The main field bided their time.

There was a danger to the trio's on-the-road advantage, though. It came from another protest group using the profile of the Tour to advance their cause. This time, the road was strewn with tree branches and homemade banners, the handiwork of ecologists registering their opposition to a planned waste dump. When Tebaldi, Perini and Arnaud reached the impasse, 16 miles from home, they were forced to pick a delicate path through the dumped foliage before heading back on their way towards Montpellier. Not that the demonstration was entirely peaceful and benign; the French TV host Jacques Chancel had his nose broken when tangling with protesters.

It was, though, rather fortunate for the rest of the field that the three riders had such an advantage. The margin of their lead allowed the police time to clear away both the branches and the protesters before the peloton, now escorted by half a dozen police motorbikes, surged through. (In fact, the lead car at the front of the race now carries chainsaws in order to swiftly undermine any tree-based blockade.)

The ecologists' protest was simply the latest in a series of demonstrations that had affected the Tour that decade. The increased globalisation of the event, with even more eyes watching on television from Brisbane to Bogotá, offered a very public platform on which protesters could air their grievances. The most serious of these protests came in 1982 on the team time trial near the France-Belgium border. When they reached the town of Denain after 20 or so miles, the first team on the road, the Wickes-Splendor squad, encountered the various trucks and vans of the publicity caravan blocking the road. The advance party, usually entertaining and distracting the roadside spectators ahead of the race itself, could progress no further. There was a blockade constructed by a few hundred local steelworkers, protesting at the planned closure of Denain steelworks. The plans had been announced just the day before, plans that included the loss of more than 1,100 jobs.

Police outriders turned back to warn the teams behind Wickes-Splendor on the road. Very soon, the organisers realised that, such was the scale of the protest, that day's racing would have to be abandoned. As the writer Geoffrey Nicholson reported: 'Some riders reacted with disbelief and annoyance, and a few of those already feeling the strain with evident relief'. It was the first time, in 80 years of rich Tour history, that a stage had been cancelled after it had begun.

In 1987, what might have been an even more serious protest was avoided when two members of the Basque paramilitary group Iparretarrak were arrested. Unlike the more familiar Basque separatists ETA, Iparretarrak focused their activities on the French side of the border and police believed the race to have been targeted as the Pyrenees prepared for its arrival.

In 1990, another protest was sidestepped by the race. On the third stage between Poitiers and Nantes, reports were coming in of several felled trees lying by the roadside at one particular location. A number of sheep farmers were, apparently, also in the immediate area, causing race director Jean-Marie Leblanc to halt the race around seven miles shy of the trouble spot. Maps were consulted and an impromptu diversion decided upon. The farmers, who had already held a demonstration on the first stage, had been thwarted. Legend has it that a local moped-riding teenager led the peloton through the country lanes and back onto the official route.

The Tour wasn't the only French race to be affected by protests. The most famous example of this was the fifth stage of the 1984 edition of Paris-Nice. Shipyard workers from nearby La Ciotat were blocking the route, but they didn't get a sympathetic ear from one Bernard Hinault, at that point leading a break of around 20 riders as he sought to take Robert Millar's lead in the race. When The Badger saw the demonstration spread out across the road, he wasn't exactly diligent in applying his brakes, crashing into the blockade. Then the fists started flying, Hinault wading in and striking the nearest protester before the gendarmes intervened. That evening's news on French TV opened rather pointedly: 'Ladies and gentlemen. Good evening. A lively stage in the Paris-Nice race. We were waiting for sport and got a boxing match.'

Although protests could offer a profitable photo opportunity for a Tour photographer, Graham Watson didn't welcome them. '1989 had its fair share of demonstrations, and one or two turned ugly once the protesters saw the TV cameras on them and the gendarmes drawing their coshes. Only in my youngest days did I actually take images of such events. I quickly realised the best way to deal with such people is to not take pictures, to not give them any publicity, no matter what their grievance is. Perhaps that's the purist in me.

'I suppose one of the attractions of the Tour is that it is a free show on free roads, and as such is exposed to all kinds of attention. The cyclists have a fairly laid-back approach to such strikes: on some occasions it allowed them to rest longer, or to find an excuse to pedal more slowly towards the finish.

'It's said that, at a strike in one Tour of that period, farmers blocked the roads with their tractors, forcing the race to grind to a halt during an important Alpine stage. What they didn't know was that Sean Kelly was a farmer's son who knew how to turn an engine on and then open the muck-spreader, scattering both strikers and cyclists all over the road. The strike soon dispersed and the peloton moved off.

'Basically, you can stop a bike race as long as it's not an important stage – the cyclists think it's fun. But don't block a race on an important stage or else...'

With the three leading riders in 1989 having safely negotiated the ecologists' demonstration, the small matter of who was to take the stage win could now be considered. But, little more than a mile later, there were only two contenders left. Arnaud, who had earlier punctured and been forced to catch the other two up, found his bad luck continuing. He took a bend without due care and attention, and ended up in a ditch.

It wasn't the last crash of the day. The pace of the peloton had been steadily increasing, thanks to – for a second successive day – the aggressive riding of Super U's Christophe Lavainne. Fignon had commanded him to up the speed, not because the leaders on the road represented any kind of threat overall; for all three, any GC aspirations were a distant dream. Instead, Fignon simply wanted to stretch his main rivals, those riders glued to his back wheel.

But with the pace came increased danger. In the village of Clermont-l'Hérault, 30 or so miles from the stage finish in Montpellier, a huge crash caused carnage in the peloton, with around 30 riders hitting the floor. There were some high-profile casualties among them. Gert-Jan Theunisse, who had started the race with bruised ribs after falling in the Tour of Switzerland, looked the most dramatic, his forehead streaked with red stripes of blood and which required stitching. His King of the Mountains rival Robert Millar also came down, but the pair eventually remounted and rejoined the race; Millar, though, was seen by a specialist chiropractor that evening, one who flew in from Paris to assess his neck. A couple of team leaders were affected, too. Carrera's Urs Zimmermann suffered a suspected broken wrist, while Z-Peugeot's Éric Boyer had to have a plate fitted to protect an injured hand.

Up at the front, though, one man looked worth backing. Valerio Tebaldi had previous. The winner of a stage into Reims the previous year, where he also shared a lengthy break with one other rider, he certainly knew what was needed to secure victory. Perini, conversely, had little experience of the sharp end of a stage race and was indeed pipped to the win by his tall, dark compatriot.

Arnaud, after making his acquaintance with that ditch, rode alone for the last 15 or so miles and took a comfortable third place. But the day belonged to Tebaldi, whose 21-minute win was the third biggest margin of victory over the main bunch in Tour history. Despite this, he was still almost 48 minutes adrift of Fignon and the elite riders.

Tomorrow, he would be back in the anonymity of the bunch. The nowhere man. But after several hours in front of the cameras, a few more people might just recognise Number 175 from now on.

Stage 12
1. Valerio Tebaldi (Chateau d'Ax/Italy) 5:40:54
2. Giancarlo Perini (Carrera/Italy) same time
3. Dominique Arnaud (Reynolds/France) +2'09"
4. Thomas Wegmüller (Domex/Switzerland) +21'24"
5. Jan Goessens (Domex/Belgium) +21'40"

General classification
1. Laurent Fignon (Super U/France) 55:52:12
2. Greg LeMond (ADR/USA) +7"
3. Charly Mottet (RMO/France) +57"
4. Pedro Delgado (Reynolds/Spain) +2'53"
5. Andy Hampsten (7-Eleven/USA) +5'18"

ELEVEN

NATIONAL SERVICE

'We could just see them there, hanging out in front' – Sean Kelly

14 July
Stage 13, Montpellier – Marseille, 110 miles

IT'S SOMETHING OF a myth, albeit one that seems to be both widely spread and widely held, that French riders pull out the stops whenever a Tour stage falls on Bastille Day. The common suggestion is that this is a chance to boost national pride, to unite the country, an opportunity enthusiastically grasped by home riders. The record books tell otherwise. By 1989, no Frenchman had claimed a stage win on 14 July for years. The last time had been almost a decade earlier when, in 1980, Mariano Martinez took victory at Morzine. Furthermore, since 1989, there have been only five French winners on Bastille Day. And none since 2005. In that time, British riders have claimed three victories on that supposedly red-letter date.

The fourteenth day of July 1989, however – exactly 200 years since the revolutionaries stormed the Bastille and kick-started the downfall of the French monarchy – would see a home victory. It was surely preordained, a foregone conclusion, written in the stars. But which French rider would claim it?

The stage left Montpellier at midday, when the temperatures were already steaming. The riders were in no hurry, happy to clown about when Thierry

Marie produced a trumpet and serenaded the peloton with a few blasts. The slow early miles then became even slower when yet another protest, this time in the small town of Lunel, delayed the peloton by three minutes. Imbued with the public-holiday spirit, the riders didn't seem to mind.

But, after a couple of hours and 60-odd miles of benign, relatively uncommitted riding, the race suddenly exploded in the lunchtime heat. The PDM team, against the wishes of many of their number, had been commanded by their bosses to think the unthinkable and do the undoable. They had instructed their charges to commit the cardinal sin of the peloton: to launch an attack as the field took on supplies at a feed station. A reluctant Sean Kelly led the charge, grabbing his feed bag at full tilt rather than the customary half-pace.

'This wasn't something that went down well in the peloton,' he remembers. 'We did attack, but the wind conditions weren't what we were expecting. It wasn't a side-wind; it was more of a headwind. We rode for a bit, but then realised it wasn't doing anything, so we knocked off our effort.' Kelly then received both barrels from Fignon, 'an awful bollocking' in which the bespectacled one utilised the full gamut of vernacular at his disposal. The Irishman absorbed the rant, in return offering scant justification as he knew he deserved it.

PDM's attack, though, had had a strong effect, causing a fissure in the peloton. The field was split in two, with ten riders in the top 20 of the GC stranded in the second group, among them Robert Millar. But then almost immediately came a second move, one that splintered the race even more – and it came from the unlikeliest of sources.

It's very rare that the incumbent of the yellow jersey chooses to attack on a flat, relatively straight stage. But that's exactly what Fignon, in the company of third-placed Charly Mottet, did. To the astonishment of riders, commentators and spectators, the pair flew off the front of this first group. Just what was Fignon thinking? That he could launch and sustain an attack more than 40 miles from the finish that would claim the stage victory? That he could genuinely take some significant time out of his main challengers? That he wouldn't be weakened by such an effort and thus vulnerable to a counterattack from any number of his rivals? It looked for all the world, on this searingly hot day, that the yellow jersey was committing hari-kari.

'The reason that Fignon went on the attack,' explains Kelly, 'was because he was really pissed off about us guys in PDM. We had broken the code, the rules. Fignon, when he got upset, could get very, very upset.' Did he feel that he was the big cheese of the race, the person who had the power to mete out such punishment? 'He probably did, but that was a stage where he had a claim to do that. At the end of the day, and into the following day, we weren't too popular with quite a number of the riders. I said, "Look, that was the team tactics. That was the way it was called on the morning of the stage." Team orders. That was the only excuse I could come up with.'

Mottet was surprised, and a little reluctant, to be keeping the attack going. 'I wasn't keen to carry on, but Laurent urged me to. Of course we worked together, even though we were a long way from the finish. There was some wind when we went and Laurent was keen to attack everywhere and anywhere. It was a chance to take some time off Delgado and LeMond, so worth a go. It had nothing to do with Bastille Day.'

Pedro Delgado agrees that the attack was more to do with securing the leadership of the overall race rather than a tilt at glory based on whatever the date was on the calendar. 'You can control your rival,' he explains of such a tactic. 'You don't want to stay in his pocket.'

It wasn't as if Mottet and Fignon were moving out of sight of those behind them. For sun-kissed mile after sun-kissed mile, the gap remained around 20 seconds. Infuriating for the chasers. It was like they were being taunted. And all they could do was match the pair's pace. Damage limitation.

'The French television motorbike also played his card,' claims Delgado. 'Fignon and Mottet took its slipstream. It was only a little bit, but enough to go ahead. On a bike, you can go 60 or 61kph with a tailwind. Behind a motorbike, you can maybe go 63kph. Fignon made a difference of 20 seconds, but we couldn't catch him because our speeds were very similar. Sometimes the bike was going in front of Fignon and we were very angry about it. And we were nervous because we couldn't do anything about it. Only push, push, push.

'But you need to stay calm. Maybe you'll catch him, maybe you won't. But you want to lose as little time as possible. You have to maintain your speed. If you try to catch him straightaway, you might lose your strength and then lose two or three minutes.'

Fignon and Mottet – team-mates at Super U the season before – made an excellent tandem. They relayed each other perfectly, barrelling along the flat, melting Côte d'Azur roads. Whether it was still-simmering anger or simply the heat, Fignon appeared rather red in the face, squinting through those scholarly spectacles into the sun. Mottet, on the other hand, looked a little more at ease; his cap and ever-present shades ensured he rode with comfort.

Still tantalisingly just out of reach of the chasing group, the duo had been out in front nearly 30 miles. Fignon, red-faced or not, was still ridiculously strong, completely in his element. 'That was the kind of racing he liked,' says his then team-mate Bjarne Riis. 'And it's the kind of racing I like. And it's the kind of racing the public likes. They want to see that. Fignon had good legs, he was confident and he was there. If you're a real racer, you look for opportunities. Maybe it's not planned, but it just occurs and you take it and go. I think that is what happened there. And when you do stuff like that, it's always a message.'

The message wasn't being received very warmly within the chase group. They were being powered along by fury as much as anything. 'We could just see them there,' says Kelly, 'hanging out in front. It was so difficult to close Fignon and Mottet down that it got heated in the front of the peloton.'

The main heat seemed to be within Kelly's PDM team. 'There was a bit of 'discussion' between Alcalá and Theunisse,' he confirms. 'One said to the other that he wasn't doing enough, that he wasn't putting in 100% effort. I remember I had to calm the situation down.' In the absence of a single team leader whom everyone had to obey, elder statesman Kelly was forced to play peacemaker. Alcalá was aggrieved by Theunisse's accusation that his turns on the front of the pack weren't of a sufficient intensity. He, in fact, felt that it was the Dutchman who wasn't pulling his weight. 'I didn't understand. I said to him, "You must ride like everyone."' The absence of a hierarchy within the PDM riders – a curious arrangement to many observers before the race – had led to a little local difficulty. Alcalá shakes his head. 'Many bosses and no warriors. You need warriors to be working 100 per cent. We had warriors in that team, but less than in others. Too many chiefs…'

Fignon and Mottet were eventually caught shortly after the modest climb of the Côte de Rove, following an hour of furious effort from LeMond, his first lieutenant/room-mate Johan Lammerts, Delgado, Hampsten and (at least some of) the PDM boys. There had been a shared sense of duty; they'd ridden as if on some kind of multi-team time trial. As LeMond pulled level with Fignon, there was a glance across that seemed to ask 'What the hell was that all about?'. The Frenchman would have loved every second of the break, knowing that he was stretching his bitter rival both physically and mentally.

LeMond then put an arm around Theunisse, presumably thanking him for the effort in bridging the gap to the front two. Perhaps this was a deliberate psychological counter-punch. Fignon was always a little suspicious that PDM had an unwritten pact with LeMond, a rider of theirs, of course, until just seven months previously. Seeing a fraternal arm round a PDM rider's shoulders would have firmed up those suspicions in Fignon's head, tightening the paranoia. (For the record, both the Kelly and LeMond camps pour a vatful of scorn over the notion that LeMond and PDM were in any kind of cahoots.)

This front group weren't back together for long before another attack was launched. A two-man, all-French breakaway featuring a Super U rider and an RMO rider had been replaced by a two-man, all-French breakaway featuring a Super U rider and an RMO rider. Plus ça change. The leaders had simply been replaced by their domestiques. Vincent Barteau had taken on the mantle of Fignon, while Jean-Claude Colotti took the Mottet role.

With fresh legs from sitting at the back of the chase group throughout its pursuit of their team captains, Barteau and Colotti wasted no time in establishing a decent advantage. Through the windy back streets of L'Estaque, on Marseille's northern fringes, they were off and away. After that lengthy, flat-out chase, there was little inclination within that front bunch to do so again, certainly not now all the GC contenders were back together. These two Frenchmen were largely left to it, a Bastille Day home victory now looking increasingly likely.

Barteau was very much the dominant rider of the two, with Colotti holding on as long as he might, before the Super U man went it alone on one of the climbs skirting Marseille. It was very much a display of redemption and resurrection for the man with the strawberry-blond hair. Five years previously, he had held yellow for a full 12 days in the '84 Tour, before passing it on to his team-mate and eventual winner – one Laurent Patrick Fignon.

Since then, though, Barteau had done little of note on a bike. After leaving the Renault squad, he shuffled around the pro-cycling circuit for a few years, desperately hoping for his stuttering career to find traction. Then, for the 1989 season, his former team manager Cyrille Guimard brought him back into the fold at Super U, the renamed Renault set-up. Guimard was taking a gamble, but on the roads of Marseille that afternoon, Barteau was paying him back for the faith he'd shown.

After a sharp, fast descent towards the Mediterranean and a circuit of the old port, Barteau was home and dry. A luminous, boisterous character who took up stand-up comedy in his post-racing days, he milked the adoration of the joyful Marseille crowd, blowing kisses and saluting them several hundred yards before the finish line. He knew how to enjoy it, how to soak it up, after some darker times. In a Tour that was studded with comebacks of all descriptions, Barteau's renaissance was another irresistible tale.

'Guimard was the only team manager to have any confidence in me this season,' said Barteau afterwards. 'I have proved that I can still be a good rider. My attack was not planned, it just happened. Laurent put on a good show with Mottet and, after that, I felt strong.' Barteau also found time to pay tribute to his leader's main rival, a former team-mate at both Renault and PDM. 'LeMond always believed in me and, without him, I would not still be riding.' Quite what Fignon's response to that public endorsement would have been at the team dinner that evening went unrecorded.

Colotti held on to take second, before Toshiba's Martial Gayant surged through to give France all three top places on the stage. Elsewhere, the officials were kept busy. Delgado received a ten-second penalty for taking a feed outside of the designated stations, while Sean Yates and Martin Earley were both penalised – 40 seconds and 20 seconds respectively – for drafting behind team cars. Earley's team-mate Kelly received a double punishment of ten seconds and ten points for pushing another rider. Elsewhere, Erik Breukink retired from the race 20 miles from the finish, the fifth team leader to abandon. With his sprinters already out and his captain now heading home, the disciplinarian *directeur sportif* Peter Post must have been frustrated in the extreme.

Laurent Fignon was anything but frustrated. 'I always go better when it is very warm,' explained the Parisian. 'Even if the heat is suffocating, it seems to suit me.' In these post-race interviews, he inferred that his aggressive riding was neither a show of strength to his main rivals nor an angry reaction to PDM's cheeky feed-station attack. It was genuinely all about extending his time advantage over LeMond and Delgado. 'A Tour de France can be won anywhere. Why not on a flat stage?'

The day had seen a French 1-2-3 on the Bastille Day stage, as well as their compatriot retaining his yellow jersey. The revolutionaries of 1789 would surely be smiling with satisfaction – although even they might be a tad nervous that Fignon's bemusing breakaway could sap him of strength in the coming days.

Stage 13
1. Vincent Barteau (Super U/France) 4:17:31
2. Jean-Claude Colotti (RMO/France) +45"
3. Martial Gayant (Toshiba/France) +1'16"
4. Steve Bauer (Helvetia-La Suisse/Canada) +1'21"
5. Etienne De Wilde (Histor/Belgium) +1'25"

General classification
1. Laurent Fignon (Super U/France) 60:11:11
2. Greg LeMond (ADR/USA) +7"
3. Charly Mottet (RMO/France) +57"
4. Pedro Delgado (Reynolds/Spain) +3'03"
5. Andy Hampsten (7-Eleven/USA) +5'18"

***

15 July
Stage 14, Marseille – Gap, 148 miles

You couldn't say the peloton hadn't been warned.

As he had done 11 days previously in Wasquehal, Jelle Nijdam disappointed the sprinters, who'd been hopeful of a mass run-in on an arrow-straight finish, by striking out for the line early and holding everyone at bay to take the win by a narrow two seconds.

If it felt to the non-partisan observer as though Nijdam had pickpocketed the stage win, then certainly the three riders who had been out in front for a large part of the day – and whom were caught in the final mile – must have felt distinctly frustrated. The most notable man in that front three was Luis Herrera who, with Fabio Parra having retired several days earlier, carried the weight of an expectant nation's dreams on his diminutive shoulders.

His own dreams needed attention, too. Thus far, the Colombian with the shock of jet-black hair had been unable to replicate the form that had won him the Giro mountains title little more than a month previously. He had managed 20th and 35th in Cauterets and Superbagnères respectively, simply nowhere close to where a man of his standing and pedigree should be. Herrera needed to make a move – and fast. He was 30th in the GC.

The ride to Gap might just be the one. As the race moved inland, it took in the lavender fields of Provence before cutting north into elevated ground, into the foothills of the Alps. The second half of the stage offered quite a test, sending the 155 remaining riders over a number of high-altitude climbs, including the second-category Col du Labouret. Such terrain would suit Herrera, offering a limb-loosening appetite-sharpener ahead of the main course.

After 80 miles on the road, Herrera made that move, in the company of Toshiba's Marc Madiot and Jérôme Simon of Z-Peugeot. Pilloried in the Colombian press and facing calls to have his salary slashed (especially prescient as Herrera's high salary was underwritten by the not-for-profit National Federation of Coffee Growers of Colombia), a good showing into Gap, even a possible stage win, would quieten his critics and perhaps secure his income.

The trio made their break on the Côte de Châteauredon and quickly established a decent gap. Within five miles, they were more than two minutes up on the docile peloton. Laudelino Cubino, a Spanish rider with the BH team who'd placed fourth at the recent Vuelta, tried to get across to them on the Col du Labouret, more than halving the near-six-minute lead of Herrera, Madiot and Simon.

But Cubino's solo effort was ultimately unsuccessful; on the long descent into Gap, the peloton gobbled him up without even blinking. The front three were their chief target and their sprinters were being primed. The team bosses clearly didn't think that the numbers stacked up, that the leaders could see out a 35-second advantage with three miles to go, not with 70 miles of leading the stage in their tired legs, nor with a revved-up peloton swooping down on them. Indeed, it was rather telling that Pascal Poisson, a team-mate of front-man Madiot, was second in line in the chasing group. The Toshiba hierarchy were among those who didn't have faith in the break surviving.

As the pack swallowed up the front three, Poisson flew out of the slipstream of Superconfex's Frans Maassen to stake his claim for victory. And he made a pretty persuasive case too, looking for all the world that the win was in the bag. But such thinking didn't legislate for the enormous thighs of Jelle Nijdam, who launched a counterattack. It was an intriguing run-in along the final tree-shaded avenue, a duel between two former men of the track. And despite Poisson managing to manoeuvre himself onto Nijdam's wheel, the Dutchman simply rode away from him and towards victory. All Poisson could do was raise his hands off his handlebars in frustration, although he did claim second place, just ahead of ADR's Eddy Planckaert.

The stage had crossed five significant climbs, terrain that the comparatively heavily built pursuit specialist would have been expected to suffer a little on. But he clung on and survived. 'When I looked at the profile this morning,' he admitted at the finish line, 'I didn't expect to be in the hunt for the win. If anyone had said so, I wouldn't have believed them for a moment. I had no morale. I've come out of the Pyrenees very tired. Today I had the bonk, so I ate very quickly at the end of the stage, and only began to feel good in the last few kilometres.'

Certainly Nijdam's power and strength was unquestionable. He certainly left an enduring impression on the American ex-pro Joe Parkin, who once told *Peloton* magazine about an incident involving the pair. 'Nijdam hesitated a bit too long, so I jumped in front of him, causing him to nearly fall out of the rotation. The ensuing shove was followed by a punch that was so hard I think I still have the shape of his hand imprinted on my right butt cheek.'

This would be the last chance of a stage win by an opportunistic outlier for a good few days. Accordingly, the GC contenders kept their powder dry, submerging themselves into the safety of the peloton. No headline news today. Other days, bigger battles.

LeMond, refreshed and lively, was in bullish mood after the stage, aware of how wafer-thin that seven-second deficit would be back in the mountains. He was more than hopeful of demolishing it – and putting Fignon's numbers back into the red – with a sparkling performance in the following day's individual mountain time trial. 'I expect myself to be in the top three or top four in the time trial. If I have a good day, maybe I can win. But there are three or four days in the mountains and six days to go overall, plus another time trial, so no matter what happens tomorrow, it's still not over.'

After the four non-mountain stages that had linked the Pyrenees with the Alps, the upper reaches of the GC hadn't changed since the race left Superbagnères and its spooky hotel. But the leaderboard was certain to undergo some serious revision over the course of the next few days, up on the high roads with their turns and twists and testing gradients. The Alps loomed large. Very large. Battle was about to recommence, another test of both muscle and stamina, with punches traded, albeit figuratively, even more ferociously than in the Pyrenees.

Seconds away, round two…

Stage 14
1. Jelle Nijdam (Superconfex/Netherlands) 6:27:55
2. Pascal Poisson (Toshiba/France) +2"
3. Eddy Planckaert (ADR/Belgium) same time
4. Giovanni Fidanza (Chateau d'Ax/Italy) same time
5. Sean Kelly (PDM/Ireland) same time

General classification
1. Laurent Fignon (Super U/France) 66:39:08
2. Greg LeMond (ADR/USA) +7"
3. Charly Mottet (RMO/France) +57"
4. Pedro Delgado (Reynolds/Spain) +3'03"
5. Andy Hampsten (7-Eleven/USA) +5'18"

ACT III
THE FINAL WEEK

TWELVE

L'AMERICAINE JAUNE

'The pendulum swings again' – Phil Liggett

16 July
Stage 15, Gap – Orcières-Merlette, 24 miles, individual time trial

A HOT SUNDAY in the Alps, but no time to laze about.

With the Tour officials closing the road up to the ski station at Orcières-Merlette by 7am, only the all-night crew or the early birds got their ringside seat for what would prove to be a bruising encounter. And an encounter that, after days of a largely static leaderboard, would shake up the race again. Cat among the pigeons. It was time for the potentially pivotal mountain time trial.

This annual battle against the clock at altitude had indeed proved crucial in the 1988 race, tightening Pedro Delgado's control of the GC by converting a 25-second lead over Steve Bauer into an advantage over the new second-placed rider Steven Rooks that approached three minutes. From there on in, the distance between Delgado and everyone else only kept increasing all the way to Paris. In a somewhat different situation the following year, he now needed a similarly dynamic and decisive victory to put the squeeze on both Fignon and LeMond, to reignite the game of catch-up he'd been playing since Luxembourg.

It was certainly a course to suit the Spaniard. Starting in Gap at 2,400 feet above sea level, the riders would gain a further 3,500 feet over the course of 70 or so minutes, during which time they would take in a pair of first-category climbs – the Col de Manse and up to the finish at Orcières-Merlette. Most tellingly, it would be the super-steep final five miles up to the ski station that favoured Delgado the most – and when he would most hope to propel himself further up the GC.

And he knew what was coming. With the road up the climbs closed, Delgado, escorted by his team-mate Melchor Mauri, spent the morning riding the course, studying the gradients, deducing at which point he would turn the screw that afternoon. Fignon was also out on the course that morning, in the company of Super U domestique Dominic Garde and casting baneful looks at the moto that insisted it film his preparation. Fignon, having never beaten LeMond in a Tour time trial, and with only that flimsy seven-second advantage to defend, realised that he would almost certainly be out of yellow that evening. The priority was surely to limit the time that LeMond would take from him; to ensure that any new deficit was recoverable in the Alps stages coming up. As the morning sunlight hit the bends leading up to Orcières-Merlette, Fignon had homework to do.

At the rider sign-in back down the mountain in Gap, LeMond looked relaxed. Radiant, even. A boyish smile played on his lips as he offered a shy salute to the lenses of the press. The casualness would have been a mask. Internally, he would have been focused, attentive, sharp. A man with a game plan. A man who knew how crucial the next couple of hours would be in determining whether his campaign for the yellow jersey in Paris was sustainable. He needed to regain the lead on today's stage and then – without any team-mates to aid him – stick like a limpet to Fignon's wheel for the next four mountain stages. It was a tall order, especially as there was the nagging spectre of Delgado to control, too. One eye on the Super U jersey in front, the other on the Reynolds jersey whenever it attacked from behind.

By the time that the time trial, run in reverse GC order, came down to the highest-placed 20 riders, it was Delgado's team-mate, Miguel Induráin, who put down the marker against which all other effort would be compared. Demonstrating the climbing chops he'd unexpectedly showcased back at Cauterets on the ninth stage, the man from Pamplona powered up both first-category climbs, recording a time of 1:11:25, almost a minute faster than any other rider thus far.

It was the start of Induráin's love affair with Tour time trials. In his five overall victories between 1991 and 1995, all of his stage wins came against the clock. He turned into a metronome; that day in Cauterets was one of just two non-time trial wins in the Tour. 'The stereotypical Spanish cyclist,' wrote Edward Pickering, 'is the climber, and while Induráin could ride up mountains as fast as, or even faster than, most climbers, his body type was that of the rouleur.' Pickering goes on to make the point that previous Spanish winners of the Tour – the likes of Federico Bahamontes, Luis Ocaña and Delgado – were 'unpredictable and unreliable in comparison' and that Induráin offered 'living evidence that in cycling, as in life, imperfection is what makes things interesting'.

The name 'Induráin' wasn't a byword for perfection that afternoon in Orcières-Merlette, though. His lead lasted less than six minutes. Back down the road, Steven Rooks was going like a rocket. After the seven-mile ascent of the opening climb of the Col de Manse, he had crested the mountain eight seconds up on the Reynolds rider. The format was one that Rooks clearly savoured. It was in the mountain time trial in 1988 that he made his move onto the final podium, his third place into Villard-de-Lans elevating him to second place overall, a position he retained all the way to Paris more than a week later. In the '89 equivalent, Rooks improved Induráin's leading time by a full 43 seconds.

Between the pair came the green jersey of Sean Kelly. After his phenomenally strong ride into Superbagnères five days earlier, the big man proved that day in the Pyrenees to have been no fluke, no anomaly. He recorded the day's fourth fastest time up the Col de Manse and was fifth fastest up those steep, steep last couple of miles to the finish. Kelly crossed the line 23 seconds down on Induráin, a time that would, by the stage's end, give him sixth place. He delightedly faced the press afterwards. 'I drove the course last night. I thought it would be too hard for me, but I trained halfway along the course this morning and decided I would just go as hard as I could all the way.'

One of the several hard-climbing team-mates of Kelly's, Gert-Jan Theunisse, was also especially strong on those last couple of miles, hinting at form yet to be shown. All Twiglet arms and hollow eyes, the effort that the Dutchman invested in getting up to the ski station (he was the quickest of the day up the final climb) gave him a sizeable haul of King of the Mountains points. He was accelerating away from his nearest rival, Robert Millar, in that competition. The Scot's superb form in the Pyrenees was, as in other years, not being replicated in the Alps and he finished nearly four minutes down on Rooks. Clearly duelling with other riders, rather than pacing himself against the clock, got the best out of him. It would now need something special to grab the polka-dot jersey off Theunisse's back.

Back down the mountain, another noted climber couldn't get to grips with the day's demands. Andy Hampsten had identified this stage as one that he could very much win, a stage almost handmade for him. But on the road, he looked uncomfortable, too passive. Where Rooks and Kelly had grasped the climbs by the scruff of the neck, Hampsten appeared hesitant and unsure, further proof that he was far from a reckless, push-at-all-costs rider whose style invited misfortune. On this afternoon, he was a combination of conservatism and physical discomfort. He was struggling for rhythm. In the saddle. Out of the saddle. In the saddle. Out again.

'I experimented with some wheels that I shouldn't have,' Hampsten recalls, by way of an explanation. He had put a rear disc wheel on his bike, an enhancement that the likes of Rooks, Kelly and LeMond had chosen to leave in their respective team cars. 'That was silly. It was a beautiful mountain time trial, but I blew it. I wanted to win, I took a risk and I did not have the time trial I was hoping to.

'But I'm not blaming the wheels. I certainly wasn't fit enough. The wheels, which were wobbling and came loose, weren't helping but it wasn't just that. I wasn't physically capable of taking advantage of that gift of a mountain time trial. My weakness in time trials was the negative thoughts that came in. Instead of thinking about crushing people, I would worry about not doing well.'

Whatever Hampsten was lacking in his mental make-up that day, his compatriot LeMond had in abundance. He hurtled down the ramp of the start house, a ball of energy impatient to get out onto the course. Meanwhile, Fignon sat near the rear steps. Head bowed and resting on his hands, he expelled long, slow, deliberate breaths. His nerves were almost visible.

If Fignon's body language emboldened LeMond, the raw speed of his other rival may have concerned him. Delgado was setting the fastest splits at each of the early time checks. At the first, he was 14 seconds up on LeMond. While the stage was way too short to make a race-changing incursion into the leading two's respective positions, there was a chance that Delgado could eclipse Charly Mottet and break into the top three overall. Seeing how the Frenchman was suffering, this was certainly true. There was an ever-shortening distance between the pair on the road, with Delgado the rider who looked the smoothest, fastest and most in the groove.

At the second time check, Delgado was 20 seconds up on LeMond, who in turn was 22 seconds up on Fignon. Since his win in 1984, Fignon hadn't successively negotiated both the Pyrenees and the Alps in the same Tour without, at least on one day, conceding a sizeable amount of time to his rivals. While he wouldn't lose the Tour today, whatever the time margin he would forfeit to both Delgado and LeMond in the time trial would dictate that there were sterner tests to come, ones that history suggested he wouldn't surmount. Fignon's implosion was believed by most to be inevitable. When, not if. This was why observers were increasingly seeing the final showdown of this absorbing race to be between the USA and Spain.

However, despite Delgado's fluid-looking riding, there was to be a surprise by the time he arrived at the finish. Rather than setting the day's fastest time, he came home in fourth position, having lost ground on that final sharp incline. But the issue wasn't fatigue. 'On that day,' he now explains, 'I started to have a problem with a callus. I felt it more than I felt my legs. I lost my focus and I lost my time. I had a horrible pain. When I crossed the finish line, I was so unhappy. I went straight to the mechanics' bus and said 'Give me a knife'. I cut a big hole in my shoe so it wouldn't rub the callous. I was very stressed. It would have been impossible to pedal after that if I hadn't cut my shoe. I lost 50 seconds [to Rooks] on that time trial. I was furious. I should have cut my shoe days before. I rode for four days with it giving me pain. But on this Tour, I didn't know what my mind was thinking. I could have just fixed that problem on the first day it appeared.'

Delgado came in six seconds slower than his team-mate Induráin, but the pair were outgunned by another Spaniard. Marino Lejarreta, the leader of the unfancied Paternina team, had been quietly making his way up the GC and now, taking second place on the stage, found himself replacing Andy Hampsten in the top five overall. It would be the best stage finish in the '89 Tour for the experienced Basque rider, an unsung and under-rated presence in the race's upper echelons. While the big names at the big teams dominated the headlines and the gossip, Lejarreta climbed both the mountains and the leaderboard with guile and stealth. His elevation into the top five was a salute to a deeply committed rider, one who over his career rode in 27 Grand Tours, finishing all but three of them. In addition to winning the 1982 Vuelta – after Ángel Arroyo was disqualified 48 hours after the race for failing a drugs test – Lejarreta was also the first man to ride all three Grand Tours in a single season four times over. This was a man who deserved the odd ray of limelight.

Mottet, who had stayed within a minute of Fignon and LeMond since the Pyrenees, started to run out of gas. He lost more than a minute and a half to Delgado who, while not usurping the local man's third place after the time trial, had closed the gap to just 31 seconds. It was simply a matter of time before the big three inhabited the podium places.

What position on the GC Fignon would occupy in Orcières-Merlette was rarely in doubt. Back at the very first time check, LeMond – using his aerobars again, even if he later announced that 'the bars weren't a factor today' – already had the yellow jersey on the road, his split time being 13 seconds faster than Fignon's. Wearing a teardrop helmet (while Fignon merely opted for a headband), LeMond rode away from the Parisian and stayed within touch of Delgado. Although the American also struggled on those last few miles – his shoulders rocking, his racing line a little wonky – he finished just nine seconds down on the man from Segovia to take fifth place.

By the time Fignon inched his way over the line nearly four minutes later, LeMond was back on top, this time by a margin that was eight times the advantage he previously held – albeit still only 40 seconds. Fignon looked defeated, though, the yellow jersey unzipped to his midriff. Ready for easy removal. Ready for surrender.

Delgado suggested the Frenchman wouldn't be wearing it again. 'I can still win the Tour,' he resolutely told a press conference the following day. 'At first it was between me and Fignon, but now it is between me and LeMond. I think whoever is in the yellow jersey at Alpe d'Huez will win the Tour.'

LeMond was his usual mix of excitement and caution in his post-stage interviews. 'I don't feel there's probably any rider riding better than me in the Tour de France,' he told Channel 4's Paul Sherwen. 'Now it's going to come down to the team factor. I know a lot of riders, especially the PDM team, who'll be racing against me. It will be difficult to fend them off. It's going to be difficult for me to chase every break that goes on. I just hope there will be other riders concerned about the overall and not just letting breaks get away.' After a day of aggressive time trialling, LeMond would be back riding defensively to try to see out the remaining miles of the Alps without incident or misfortune. It might be a tall order. The American was back in yellow, sure, but the race lead remained a matter of seconds rather than minutes.

In the words of Sherwen's colleague Phil Liggett, 'the pendulum swings again'.

Stage 15
1. Steven Rooks (PDM/Netherlands) 1:10:42
2. Marino Lejarreta (Paternina/Spain) +24"
3. Miguel Induráin (Reynolds/Spain) +43"
4. Pedro Delgado (Reynolds/Spain) +48"
5. Greg LeMond (ADR/USA) +57"

General classification
1. Greg LeMond (ADR/USA) 67:50:54
2. Laurent Fignon (Super U/France) +40"
3. Charly Mottet (RMO/France) +2'17"
4. Pedro Delgado (Reynolds/Spain) +2'48"
5. Marino Lejarreta (Paternina/Spain) +5'11"

***

18 July
Stage 16, Gap – Briançon, 109 miles

Greg LeMond took pleasure in a job well done on the mountain time trial by spending the subsequent rest day taking in the panoramic views of Orcières-Merlette with his wife Kathy and their two young sons. Such devotion to domestic life was rare in the peloton. Most riders happily immersed themselves in the race for every waking moment, three weeks of shutting out whatever life they had away from cycling. A short, tired call from a pay phone in a hotel lobby each evening would be the absolute best that their wives and girlfriends could expect. LeMond was different. He actively sought Kathy's presence; he felt he rode better whenever she was in close proximity. And she was happy to comply.

'For me, it wasn't the glamour,' Kathy reasons. 'It was work. I never wanted to put an extra burden on Greg. What does he need? How can I make it better? What he was doing was so hard and so demanding. I wasn't going to bring any problems I've got to him. I would never have wanted to increase his burden. He didn't have space for that.'

Kathy turned out to be something of a pioneer when it came to infiltrating the inner sanctum of men's road-race cycling. And she didn't necessarily do it discreetly, flying under the radar, a largely invisible presence. Barely seen, barely heard.

Instead, Kathy became a fixture at the finish line of nearly every stage in the '89 race, in turn becoming an obvious point of interest for the cameras of the world's media. American ones, especially. 'In all those previous years, I could barely get to the finish area. I never had a pass. I never had anything. It was just me talking my way past the gendarmes. It was a struggle.

'But in '89, on the plane transfer after he won the time trial in Rennes, Greg spoke to Jean-Marie Leblanc. "You know what? If I win this thing and my wife hasn't been able to be with me during this, I'm not getting up on the podium. I could never have done this on my own and you need to take care of her."

'That changed everything for women at the Tour. The next day, I got a car pass and a neck badge as a guest. That was great for me. I could get to the finish area. I could get to Greg's hotel more easily. I had a pass to get on the closed roads so I didn't have two hours of fighting through traffic jams any more. Most of the time I'd go to the start and always to the finish. Then I'd stay with him through his massage. Greg's different. A lot of riders really didn't want their families there. It adds stress. But, for some reason, Greg really liked having me there.'

While the LeMonds were playing happy families, Laurent Fignon was spending his rest day supplying controversial copy to the French press corps. While he admitted that his chances of winning in Paris were dwindling following the mountain time trial, he explained how he was nonetheless still in a position to stop LeMond winning. Relations between the two former team-mates, frosty throughout the race so far, plummeted to well below zero.

Not that LeMond would have let Fignon's barbs penetrate, let alone get under, his skin. Fignon frequently deployed psychology in an attempt to unsettle particular riders, but many found his methods unsophisticated and easy to brush off. Among those was Andy Hampsten.

'He really liked psychological warfare. I remember once at the Dauphiné Libéré, I was in a breakaway in an early stage with Fignon, Urs Zimmermann and one or two others. I bonked. I blew up. I ran out of energy and I was really depressed about it. Later in the race, there was a proper mountain stage that I really wanted to do well in. Fignon came up to me that day and spoke to me in English, which he hadn't done much before, if at all.

"Oh Andy, you look *terrible*."

"No, I feel really good. I blew up the other day but that was jetlag catching up."

"No, no. I can tell. You look terrible."

"Larry, give it up. It's a mountain day. We have five more hours of racing and we have three climbs. Let's just race. I'm not your main threat. I know what you're doing and you're making yourself look like an idiot. So, you've been my pal all year and now, just because it's a mountain stage…"

'I completely called him on it. He started attacking, but I gave Zimmermann a look and we both dropped him. Everyone knew he'd try to psych them out on a mountain day. But he was an amateur at his professor psych-out thing.' Despite the spectacles and his baccalauréat exam certificate that gave him the nickname of The Professor (at 18, he had enrolled on, but not completed, a university diploma in structural and material science), Fignon couldn't out-think Hampsten, himself the son of college professors. Real professors.

If, in the cold light of that July day in Gap in '89, Fignon was concerned about his outburst over LeMond, he wasn't showing it. Tanned and with an easy smile, he also seemed unperturbed about a strike by members of the press who, in protesting about his anti-social behaviour towards them, refused to take his picture for the next four days.

The gravity of the day was certainly not playing on his face. Delgado had called this stage 'the semi-final', referencing the charge up Alpe d'Huez 24 hours later to be the stage that would settle the race once and for all. And a challenging day faced them – a day almost exclusively spent heading uphill from comparatively low-level Gap. Two legendary climbs awaited them – the Col de Vars and the Col d'Izoard.

The Izoard occupies several pages in the history books of the Tour, thousands of riders having passed over it since its debut in the race in 1922. The route from the south to its near-8,000-feet summit passes through the Casse Déserte, an otherworldly landscape that's geologically closer to the barren moonscape of Mont Ventoux than to the grassy pastures of much of the Alps. It's very rocky with little sign of life. Bernard Thévenet has called it 'wild and empty' – and he should know. For it was on the Izoard's slopes on Bastille Day in 1975 that the Frenchman defeated Eddy Merckx and opened a lead that proved impregnable on the road to Paris. Not only did the mountain effectively give Thévenet the first of his two Tour victories, it also ended Merckx's era of invincibility.

Back in 1989, the action started early on the stage. Very early. Barely three miles out of Gap, a group of 16 riders had gone on the attack, clearly itching to get back to racing after the rest day. None were in danger of remotely affecting the GC – the closest to the yellow jersey was Z-Peugeot's Bruno Cornillet who was 18 minutes down on LeMond – and all bar two riders would gradually be brought back into the fold by the elite group that had formed behind them. One of these was Johan Lammerts, LeMond's ADR room-mate and most reliable helper, who was able to provide unexpected assistance to his team leader as the gap closed.

The tactics of ADR weren't too sophisticated by this point. Their depleted ranks, never the strongest when at full strength anyhow, meant they had little power or control to exert. The situation must have been frustrating to a *directeur sportif* with the brains and ability of José De Cauwer ('tactically someone who was very smart,' says Lammerts), whose advice to a yellow jersey-wearing LeMond would have barely extended beyond suggesting he sit tight and quell any attacks. There was little more he could do. But ADR did call on the guile of its senior riders, as Lammerts explains. 'Riders who are experienced know what to do. They don't need to be informed every minute about what needs to be done. We adapted to situations.' And, as his former team-mate Andy Hampsten is quick to praise, LeMond boasted 'incredible tactical sense. He smelled things happening. He knew which buddies to go and ask what was really going on in their little team. He was really, really sharp. He's just the great wheel-follower? Don't count on it.'

LeMond's sharpness meant he knew what he had to do over the day's monstrous climbs: be alert to each and every attack, and react accordingly. These might be relentless and from many different quarters. It would be a tough day, both mentally and physically. At first, though, he didn't need to worry about the attentions of Fignon or Mottet. Both men slipped back on the upper slopes of the Col de Vars, possible admissions that their respective challenges for overall glory had gone as far as they could.

Without Fignon's wheel to track, LeMond stuck to Delgado. With every Alpine mile, he was now looking like the only threat to American glory in Paris. Or so it seemed. On the ten-mile descent of the Col de Vars, Fignon characteristically threw caution to the wind to put in an extraordinary recovery, rejoining LeMond's group in the valley before the Izoard. Mottet too, seemingly burned out an hour or so before, also took his place in this bunch.

Delgado, running out of tarmac on which to make meaningful inroads on the yellow jersey, launched an attack on the slopes of the Izoard – a typical manoeuvre from him and one which usually bore dividends, one where he'd normally expect to ride away from the bunch. This time, however, he was immediately checked by LeMond and Theunisse who, along with a rejuvenated Mottet, formed a four-man split over the summit. Fignon had been dropped again.

Having successfully nullified Delgado's aggression, LeMond was forced to do likewise with an almighty attacking descent from Mottet, one that *Cycling Weekly* correspondent Keith Bingham, observing the Frenchman skimming through the bends, described as being 'more at home on the ski slopes'. Behind them, Fignon was also, again, making the best use of gravity, compensating for his deficiencies on the climbs by delivering a masterclass in balls-out descending. The speed as the race headed down towards Briançon wasn't without its dangers. On one bend, Steven Rooks – with the gravel underneath his wheels loosened by the melting tar – slid to within a tyre's width of disappearing down the steep mountainside.

LeMond then attacked further down the mountain, taking with him Mottet and Martial Gayant, whom the pair had mopped up from an earlier attack. Delgado – much happier going uphill than down – held back. It looked for all the world that LeMond had not only stymied the threats of his two main challengers, but had also widened his lead on them. But then, on the long, straight drag up into Briançon, the Spaniard recovered and finished with the same time as LeMond. Their battle had been a draw, but LeMond was undoubtedly the happier rider. One day fewer to survive, one day closer to glory.

LeMond was also the beneficiary of Fignon being unable to stay with the pace. A further 13 seconds were gained from the Super U man, pushing the lead to 53 seconds. It would be the widest margin between the pair in the entire three weeks of the race.

All of these attacks and counterattacks detracted from the performances of the two riders who finished ahead of the elite group. Bruno Cornillet had stayed out all day after that very early breakaway and took second on the stage, his highest placing in all the ten Tours of his career. Two and a half minutes up the road, though, was another survivor of that early break. Riding in the scarlet jersey denoting his status as the Swiss national champion, Pascal Richard had been at the head of the stage for all but those first three miles and thoroughly deserved his victory. Having only lasted three days in his debut Tour the previous year, the 1988 cyclo-cross world champion was showing the potential he could bring to road-racing.

But Richard's impressive solo success was outgunned by what was occurring higher up the GC. Mottet had had a particularly eventful day, looking like he was slipping down the leaderboard before reviving and putting in a series of punishing attacks on the Izoard. But if he harboured any ambitions of finishing in yellow in Paris, the world number one knew this was an outside bet. 'After the time trial,' he says, 'I knew it would be too difficult for me to win the Tour, but I gave it a go on the Izoard.' If he couldn't take the overall victory, Mottet was clearly at least going to dig deep to protect his podium place from Delgado.

The day had been one of LeMond's more proactive in the mountains and his sustained renaissance, after the near-death experience of the hunting accident, continued to surprise the seasoned, heard-it-all-before press room. 'It was simply unbelievable,' says François Thomazeau, the Reuters correspondent. 'It was probably more astonishing than Lance Armstrong's recovery from cancer, because Greg's team was terrible and because he seemed a much more fragile person than Armstrong was. He was very, very lean, and extremely fidgety, always complaining of little pains and bugs. He was like a racehorse.'

Fidgety would describe him well. And he was fidgety for good reason. 'I'm worried about everybody,' he told Channel 4. 'I'm afraid of everybody and I'm going to watch everybody. But I'm mainly going to watch Delgado from now.'

The growing consensus was that Laurent Fignon was now an irrelevance when it came to the destiny of the yellow jersey. But, as he sought sleep in his Briançon bed that night, other ideas were forming in the Frenchman's brain.

Stage 16
1. Pascal Richard (Helvetia-La Suisse/Switzerland) 4:46:45
2. Bruno Cornillet (Z-Peugeot/France) +2'34"
3. Charly Mottet (RMO/France) +4'50"
4. Greg LeMond (ADR/USA) +4'51"
5. Martial Gayant (Toshiba/France) same time

General classification
1. Greg LeMond (ADR/USA) 72:42:30
2. Laurent Fignon (Super U/France) +53"
3. Charly Mottet (RMO/France) +2'16"
4. Pedro Delgado (Reynolds/Spain) +2'48"
5. Steven Rooks (PDM/Netherlands) +6'05"

THIRTEEN

SETTING THE FIRES OF HELL ABLAZE

'Our lungs were hanging out and we watched each other, almost at a standstill, gasping like a pair of crazy young puppies' – Laurent Fignon

19 July
Stage 17, Briançon – Alpe d'Huez, 101 miles

YOU DIDN'T NEED to speak a word of French to understand the front page of *L'Equipe* that morning. As the riders silently took their breakfasts in the hotel dining rooms of Briançon, a gruelling day of three towering ascents ahead of them, the paper's headline writer stoked up the pressure, emphasising how much the race was now as much about mind games as it was about physical prowess. The headline cut to the quick: 'POKER DANS ALPE'.

Certainly Stage 17, with its monster climbs of the Col du Galibier, the Col de la Croix de Fer and the totemic Alpe d'Huez rising up into the cloudless blue sky, was likely to be the day that the main protagonists showed their respective hands. With his lead increasing, was LeMond in possession of all the aces? Did Delgado have something up his sleeve? And, with his power and influence visibly on the wane, was Fignon holding nothing more than a busted flush?

The murmur of the press room was that the latter opinion held firm. Channel 4 commentator Phil Liggett certainly appeared to subscribe to this school of thought. His pre-stage opening monologue – filmed that morning and shown as part of the station's highlights show later that evening – hinted that Fignon was undeniably losing his status as a contender. As he stood on one of the hairpins that defined that day's last few kilometres up Alpe d'Huez, Liggett delivered his piece to camera, announcing that 'today we're expecting a marvellous fight between Pedro Delgado and Greg LeMond'. He was wringing his hands in anticipation. 'This is where we feel the Tour de France will be decided. Will it be LeMond in yellow tonight or Delgado?'

At the same time that the riders were fuelling themselves up at the breakfast table and chewing over the conjecture in the morning papers, the slopes leading up to the day's finish were already heaving. Such is the draw of Alpe d'Huez. By 7am, several hundred thousand spectators were on the mountain, many of whom had been there for days, like the hardiest bargain-hunters sleeping rough ahead of the Christmas sales. Territory had been marked, vantage points claimed. Whether perched on an unforgiving boulder or reclined on the roof of a campervan, these fans faced many hours under the baking Alpine sun until the high drama unfolded before them. Those not protecting their perch could be found with paint pot in hand, applying the name of their favourite rider to the tarmac. The paintwork was drying almost instantly in the day's rapidly increasing temperatures. On these particular slopes, even the most anonymous *domestique* received a tribute in thick strokes of white emulsion, their name immortalised forever – or at least until the next time the road got resurfaced.

Often the steepest climb of the three-week race, Alpe d'Huez is special to rider and fan alike. Viewed from the air, the road up to the peak clings to a section of mountainside where no road should rightfully exist. If it were on the Italian side of the Alps, it would invariably be likened to a long strand of limp linguini dropped onto the landscape in a random pattern of loops and zigzags. The gradients are severe enough that 21 sharply ascending hairpin bends are required to provide safe passage to its summit.

The Alpe's legend isn't based on it being the most inhospitable of the race's mountains. Usually bathed in tan-friendly sunshine, it doesn't offer the bleakness of Mont Ventoux's lunar landscape, nor the rain-lashed conditions often served up by a Pyrenean peak like the Aubisque. And, being a summit finish, those 21 hairpins are only tackled uphill, so a perilous descent is avoided – unlike during the winter months when scores of hire cars cautiously make their icy way down from the ski station, their drivers' feet never off the brakes, anxious to avoid both the loss of their deposit and the prospect of a spectacular death.

Nor is it Alpe d'Huez's altitude or length that tests the riders. On this particular day, it was only the third highest peak of the stage, its 6,100 feet outstripped by both the Galibier and the Croix de Fer. And, set against those two much longer climbs, it's a comparative sprint at less than nine miles. No, Alpe d'Huez is admired and feared in such equal measure simply because – after a day of such severe uphill struggles – the steepest peak has been kept until last.

The Tour's maiden journey up Alpe d'Huez's unforgiving slopes was in 1952 when the peloton found a relatively primitive ski resort at its summit. And they'd arrived there bouncing and banging their way up a pothole-studded road that was in urgent need of the attentions of a well-drilled tarmac gang. That year, Fausto Coppi, fourth in the general classification, grabbed both the victory and the yellow jersey, a position he would retain all the way to Paris. The Alpe had proved crucial in determining the final outcome of the race, a tradition it would firmly uphold for decades afterwards.

Although none had previously taken a stage victory here, LeMond, Fignon and Delgado knew Alpe d'Huez well. They weren't intimidated by its twists and turns, its hairpins and heights. And they knew their history, well aware of how game-changing a surge up its slopes could be to the destination of the overall title. Fignon had first-hand experience of this – twice. Six years previously in 1983, his fifth place on the stage saw him wrestle the yellow jersey from compatriot Pascal Simon; it remained on his back for the remaining six days, all the way up to Paris. History repeated itself 12 months later when, having taken second behind Luis Herrera (the first Colombian and the first amateur to win a Tour stage), the Parisian swapped the tricolour jersey of the French national champion for the *maillot jaune*. Again, no one else got close enough to touch the hem of this particular garment before journey's end on the Champs-Élysées.

That year, 1984, Fignon's then Renault-Elf team-mate LeMond – riding his first Tour and wearing the rainbow jersey he'd won the previous September at the world championships in Switzerland – showed his mettle on Alpe d'Huez's zigzagging gradients. Having just finished a course of antibiotics for a bronchial infection, LeMond took an impressive sixth, a final surge ending with the scalp of Hinault in the last kilometre. By the time the Tour returned to the mountain two years later, LeMond and Hinault were teammates on Bernard Tapie's La Vie Claire squad, but had been engaged in a duel with each other across the Pyrenees and into the Alps. This was despite the older man's agreement to assist his young colleague in the pursuit of his first Tour title as recompense for LeMond's selfless loyalty the previous year as Hinault took his fifth overall victory.

The tension between the pair seemed to have dissolved when they linked hands yards from the finish of Alpe d'Huez, Hinault taking the stage win only when LeMond broke from the embrace to gently nudge him over the line first. This sense of fraternity was fleeting. In a post-stage interview – and to LeMond's astonishment – Hinault gave no assurances that he wouldn't still attack the American during the remainder of the race.

The Alpe had represented a significant turning point in the 1988 Tour too, ensuring the mountain held a cherished spot in Delgado's heart. His third place, 17 seconds behind stage winner Steven Rooks, meant he had taken the yellow jersey from Steve Bauer and held onto it for the remaining ten days all the way to the capital.

Despite what Phil Liggett's monologue suggested, Fignon's legacy on the Alpe might well count for something. It promised to be a fascinating day of racing, with the identity of the stage winner being of less concern than the identity of the man who would lead the race into the last few days. The three took their places at the table. The pack was being shuffled. The cards would soon be dealt.

***

Between the 11th and 14th centuries, the area around Alpe d'Huez was a hotspot for silver mining, drawing many different nationalities to the region. Fast-forward half a millennium and, every July that the mountain is included on the Tour's itinerary, many different nationalities are again drawn here. In 1989, while the citizens of France, Germany, Italy and Switzerland were undeniably on the slopes in large numbers, the nation most represented on Alpe d'Huez that year – as in any other – was the Netherlands.

Whether it's football or cycling, Dutch crowds are no shrinking wallflowers when it comes to showing their enthusiasm for their favoured sport. The exuberant, Dutch-led festivities on Alpe d'Huez have been likened to those at the Glastonbury Festival: both are gatherings that attract massive crowds in a way that more purist fans might look down upon. A more suitable analogy for American onlookers might be tailgating, those pre-match, beer and barbecue gatherings in the car parks of sports arenas that seem to be of equal importance to its participants as the subsequent on-field action.

The venerable cycling journalist William Fotheringham has written brilliantly about the visceral scene on the Alpe, a mountain inhabited, for this one day almost every summer, by a different breed, these 'mountain people' who seem to have suspended the usual rules of everyday life. 'There is so much noise that they don't hear the cars and vans approaching,' wrote Fotheringham. 'They walk in front of them, play chicken with them, keep painting things on the road until they are squashed, and ride their bikes downhill onto the cars' bonnets.' At the same time, Fotheringham celebrates the open-access nature of the race. 'In no sport in the world can the fans get so close to their heroes, look them in the eye, give them water, push them if the judges aren't looking...'

As someone whose livelihood depends on him being in the burning core of the action, the photographer Graham Watson admits he's often felt vulnerable on the slopes of the Alpe, in this 'vertical forest of people', as Andy Hampsten described it. 'Both now and then,' says Watson, 'it is an ugly scene that leans towards frightening, and one not easily matched with such a genteel sport as cycling. Because of the crowds, Alpe d'Huez is not a great place to work on a moto. The driver has to be extra vigilant and the photographer has to think of his wellbeing should he consider getting off among those masses for a cornering shot or a scenic masterpiece.'

Hampsten would agree that there was 'definitely an element of danger' about the mountain when it was loaded with so many people. 'They've got so much alcohol in their bodies that you can smell the odour of them sweating it out,' he told cycling historian Peter Cossins. 'They're out of their minds – so drunk that it turns into a bit of a guessing game.'

That orange is the dominant colour on these particular slopes is down to the fact that, over the years, Alpe d'Huez has frequently been a happy hunting ground for Dutch riders. Prior to the 1989 race, the mountain had been included on the Tour's itinerary a dozen times. On seven of those occasions, it was a Dutch rider – those men of the legendarily pannenkoek-flat lowlands – who was first to the line. On the Tour's second stage finish on its slopes, 24 long years after the Tour caravan had first rattled its way to the summit, it would be that son of Rijpwetering, Joop Zoetemelk, who pipped another Benelux rider, Belgium's Lucien Van Impe, to the stage win. The following year, Zoetemelk's compatriot Hennie Kuiper claimed victory in the mountain-top town.

This blossoming romance between the Alpe and the race's Dutch riders became a full-blown affair 12 months later in 1978 when Kuiper repeated the trick, finishing eight seconds ahead of eventual winner Bernard Hinault. Three years, three wins. Never mind the future; the present was very much orange. The attraction was clearly mutual. The mountain seemed to like the way the Dutch riders weren't intimidated by its gradients, while the Dutch riders – spurred on by vast numbers of spectators from the Netherlands squatting on these narrow verges – were enjoying the morale boosts offered by tens of thousands of their compatriots.

Between Zoetemelk's virgin victory in 1976 and Steven Rooks's triumph in 1988, only Hinault in 1986, aided by that fraternal nudge forward from LeMond just before the line, had scored home success here. It may be a French peak, but – for one long hot day almost every summer – it had become that incongruous contradiction: a Dutch mountain.

On that Wednesday afternoon in 1989, Gert-Jan Theunisse upheld the tradition, another man of the flatlands conquering arguably the cruellest peak in the race. After his second place behind Rooks on the Alpe the previous year, he was intent on going one better. And he set his stall out early, first to reach the summit of the Galibier, the stage's opening stiff climb and, at 8,660 feet, the highest point on that year's Tour. His efforts were rewarded with maximum King of the Mountains points, stretching his superiority over Robert Millar still further.

By the time he arrived on the lower slopes of the Croix de Fer, the second of that day's HC climbs, Theunisse had company. He'd been joined by the Italian rider Franco Vona, from the Chateaux d'Ax team, and Laurent Biondi, the Frenchman who was restoring some pride for that demoralised Fagor squad.

They weren't with him for long. Theunisse calmly shed both Vona and Biondi on the climb and rolled over the rocky summit alone. Nothing could distract him. Those dark eyes were pinned forward, fixed on an eminently possible stage win now that there was almost a minute and a half of clear daylight between him and a chasing pack that contained Millar, LeMond, Delgado and Marino Lejarreta. Theunisse's team-mates, Rooks and Raúl Alcalá, sat at the back of this bunch, keeping a close eye on those trying to reel in their man further up the road.

After a sharp, no-fear descent, Theunisse hammered along 12 kilometres of flat road that traced the valley floor. By the time he reached Bourg d'Oisans, the small town that signals that the ascent of Alpe d'Huez is nigh, his advantage over the yellow jersey group was in excess of four minutes. As he'd started the day 7'14" down on LeMond, the maillot jaune wasn't under serious threat, but Delgado's fourth place certainly was. The Dutchman, his shoulder-length Viking locks increasingly slick with sweat, was flying. He was a photographer's dream. 'He looked terrific in his polka-dot jersey, long hair and scary eyes,' remembers Graham Watson, 'but it was difficult to be with him in front and also get back to the main fight a few minutes behind.'

Powering his way towards the first of those 21 hairpins, Theunisse would have had a clear view of the names painted onto the tarmac winding its way up towards the peak. Whenever he looked down at the road, he saw his name before him – white paint, block capitals. Or, at least, thanks to the ever-encroaching crowds that turned the road up the Alpe into a long, narrow channel, he'd only see the 'UNI' from the middle of his name. But he knew.

Whether Theunisse was taking any gratification from the work of that morning's brush-toting grand masters was uncertain. With hands locked onto the handlebars and backside never rising from the saddle, there was a complete absence of expression on his face. If that day's stage was indeed a card game, not only was the Dutchman going to clean the table, he was also wearing his best poker face throughout. No indication of pleasure or pain – no smile of satisfaction, no open-mouthed grimace. Even when he crossed the line, after more than five long hours in the saddle and with the near-certainty that the polka-dot jersey was now his and his alone, there was no emotional reaction. The expression would be the same on the podium a few minutes later. His arms might have been full of flowers and an outsized winner's cheque for 10,000 francs, but his face was empty, impassive, unreadable.

And that's the way he appeared not just to outsiders, but also to team-mates. 'Theunisse was a serious guy,' confirms Raúl Alcalá. 'A strange guy. We were almost all good companions on the team, so one guy being more of a stranger doesn't matter. He never ate with us – he'd eat by himself in his room. He was on his own all the time. He was never open. I didn't understand him.' Sean Kelly says it more succinctly. 'He was a special one.'

Theunisse's inscrutability wasn't a mask for nerves ahead of the post-stage drugs test, an obligatory process for the stage winner, plus five other riders. You might be excused for thinking it was after his positive test for testosterone – and ten-minute time penalty – 12 months previously. When, in 1991, the entire PDM squad quit the Tour citing 'food poisoning', the whispers – hinting that, as only the outfit's riders were affected, they were actually showing the symptoms of iffy blood transfusions – were more than audible. Some have suggested that, rather than the more prosaic Philips Dupont Magnetics, the team's name should stand for 'Pills, Drugs & Medicines'.

Although he – as with every other tested rider in the '89 Tour – was found to be clean, the career of the enigmatic Theunisse didn't trace an entirely happy arc. His was a racing life pockmarked by positive tests. And, aside from keeping the drug-testers busy, he also suffered from – possibly not unrelated – heart problems, resulting in the fitting of a pacemaker at the age of 50. Prior to that, a collision with a car while out training had left him with a severe spinal cord injury and unable to walk for six months.

The finish line of Alpe d'Huez on that July afternoon undeniably marked the zenith of his road-racing career. Not only was it his first and only stage win in the Tour, but it also all but secured his immortality in the race's annals as a King of the Mountains winner. This was as good as it would get for Gert-Jan Theunisse. Yet you'd never know it from his body language. 'On the last climb,' this man of few words noted afterwards, 'I couldn't see anything anymore. It was like a black tunnel.'

On any other day, in any other year, Theunisse's supreme effort would be lauded as a highlight of recent Tour history, a 30-mile solo grind that represents one of the greatest performances to culminate on this particular peak. But on this scorchingly hot day in the French Alps, the Dutchman's efforts would be cast into long shadow by events a few minutes back down the mountain.

***

Prior to reaching Bourg-d'Oisans, the three main contenders for the general classification had been playing a cagey game, calmly marking each other over the Galibier and the Croix de Fer. But then, while all eyes were peeled in anticipation for Delgado to make his move on the final climb and reduce that still significant time deficit, Fignon blinked first, choosing to execute a plan hatched that morning by himself and Cyrille Guimard. 'We both knew we wouldn't have many more chances to turn the race around,' he later wrote. 'So I came up with a plan: wait until the start of the climb to Alpe d'Huez and put in the most vicious attack I could at the very first hairpin. That meant really attacking, as if the finish line was only 100 metres away ... Once I got to the Alpe, I could set the fires of hell ablaze.'

At the first hairpin, 'Virage 21' (the switchbacks count down to the summit), Fignon went, but LeMond instantly tracked him. Fignon repeated the move; LeMond, who the Frenchman had passively aggressively dubbed 'the great follower', came back onto his wheel again. They were a pair of bantamweight boxers, trying to get out of each other's reach, matching punches but tiring with each round, with each attack. Or they could be seen as a pair of yachtsmen, duelling it out like racing dinghies in the bay, darting and weaving, masters of the blind spot.

Whatever the analogy, the skirmish was taking its physical toll. 'My legs were on fire,' Fignon recalled, 'and I went again, full bore, finding strength from I don't know where. But a few minutes later, he was back at my side. It was a draw. And we were both unable to take another breath or put any weight on the wheels.'

With the fatigued LeMond doggedly sticking to the wheel of the equally drained Fignon – and with Delgado strangely resistant to putting in the expected attack aimed at tightening the general classification still further – it looked as if the time differences that had separated the trio at the start of the stage would largely remain the same at its end. But such an analysis didn't factor in the intervention of one man slightly behind them, a man not riding a bike. Cyrille Guimard.

As LeMond's *directeur sportif* at Renault, Guimard knew the American's riding style intimately and thus could quickly identify when his former apprentice's tank was running empty; the sagging of the shoulders was a conspicuous meter reading of LeMond's reserves. And here, five years on from Guimard handing LeMond his first Tour start – and four miles from the Alpe d'Huez summit – the Super U manager recognised those exact signs. If his man Fignon was to take possession of the yellow jersey again, these next few minutes were the point at which it could happen. And the boss needed to tell his rider that.

On the packed road up to the ski station, where riders, motorbikes and team cars squashed and squeezed their way through a tunnel of fanatical spectators, Guimard was working hard to get his Fiat Croma up to Fignon. In his way, though, was the Fiat Croma of his counterpart at ADR, José De Cauwer. 'They both knew my mannerisms on the bike,' LeMond later explained. 'They could both see my shoulders bouncing, which for Guimard was a sure sign I was cracking. He was desperately trying to get up to Fignon in the car, but José wouldn't let him through. They were hitting bumpers, bits of car were dropping off.' The battle for yellow was temporarily mirrored by the battle for road space between the respective team cars.

'The commissaire was on the radio,' De Cauwer told *Cycling Weekly*, 'telling me "You have to move to the side". There were huge crowds and I knew there were not many opportunities to come past, so I kept it like this for two or three kilometres, playing stupid, moving a bit so there wasn't room.'

Len Pettyjohn was alongside De Cauwer in LeMond's car. 'There was no way anybody could get up there. You can't move up on Alpe d'Huez. Even at the very bottom, there's too many people. They're smashing your mirror in all the way. I was sitting in the front seat next to José, pushing people out of the way. You just have to get straight on your rider's wheel to stop the people from jumping in on top of you.'

Guimard eventually managed to squeeze past De Cauwer and pull alongside Fignon, screaming instructions at his man. 'Attack! He's dying!' Fignon responded that, like LeMond, he too was spent. Into the next kilometre, this four-man yellow jersey pack – Delgado was still with them, aided by his team-mate Abelardo Rondón – began to slow the pace, allowing Fignon to recharge. Then, as they reached the bright yellow 4km banner that briskly fluttered above their heads, Fignon went. A bolt from a gun, those blazing fires of hell.

Within seconds he'd caught Robert Millar, who had valiantly – and in vain – tried to loosen Theunisse's grip on the polka-dot jersey, and was flying up the mountain. The response, when it belatedly came, was from Delgado, not LeMond. Guimard had read it right: the Californian was gone, the thighs weak, the lungs empty. With no chance of damage limitation, LeMond's body language was darkening with despair. He was powerless, resigned and, also dropped by Rondón, alone.

Up at the finish line, on a small monitor, Kathy LeMond was watching her husband unravel a couple of miles back down the mountain. 'I remember freaking out that I could tell that Greg was not great. He was starting to bob a little bit. And when he starts to bob, it's like "Oh God, he's struggling". There was so much anxiety watching him. You just hope so much that he can just hold on, hold on, hold on…'

Delgado, in pursuit of Fignon, caught his prey a mile and a half from the line. With Theunisse already home and dry, the pair duked it out on the wide, much flatter finishing straight, the Spaniard popping out of Fignon's slipstream to take second place and climb above Charly Mottet into third position overall. Fignon didn't mind. He was looking at the war, rather than the battle. His eye was on the bigger prize, a prize that Delgado now pretty much conceded he wouldn't retain.

'For me,' says Delgado, 'that was the day. I might not win the stage, but I could recover two or three minutes. I wanted to break away on the Galibier or the Croix de la Fer before Alpe d'Huez, but I don't know…

'I think I started to feel tired with the race. As we say in Spanish, I started to 'pay the bill' for everything else that had happened to me in the race. I needed more strength at that moment. I was starting to feel weak near the end of this long race. We arrived more or less together. After that, I said "This Tour de France is not for me".'

Although he would win at Alpe d'Huez three years later, Andy Hampsten's race was over well before this point in '89 and, suffering from a bout of food poisoning, couldn't remotely entertain thoughts of winning the stage. What made his pain even worse was that no less an *éminence grise* than Eddy Merckx was riding in the team car directly behind him. 'I was embarrassed he chose our car,' Hampsten told *Rouleur*. 'He wanted to see me win the stage and he saw me barely struggle across the line in agony.'

His team-mate, Sean Yates, was in no better shape. A frozen lasagne was to blame. 'I felt like crap from the start,' he told William Fotheringham, 'did a mental descent down the Galibier, got back on the Croix de Fer. I was drinking water and puking up, drinking and puking. It was the kind of position where you can get eliminated – I was nervous. "Got to get there, got to get there." I collapsed when I got to the top at Alpe d'Huez. I was in agony, I was history.'

Someone feeling in better spirits was the Super U rookie, Bjarne Riis, who'd completed his first ascent of the Alpe. 'Just to ride that mountain is fantastic in itself,' he smiles. 'But there's a huge difference between going flat out for the *classement* and just trying to finish the stage. I had to deliver Fignon to the bottom of the climb and then he had to take care of himself. I needed to get to the top as easily as possible, because the next day I'd have a job to do again. There are tons of people there screaming at you. Whether you're at the front or at the back, it doesn't matter. They're screaming at you. And then, of course, you come up the mountain hearing that Fignon is attacking and dropping LeMond. And that gives you an extra boost.'

Although Fignon was clearly annoyed he had again missed out on a stage victory atop the Alpe (a particular glory that would forever elude him), the cheers from the French contingent in the grandstand hinted that he nonetheless may well have greater cause for celebration. Needing to take 54 seconds out of LeMond to return to yellow, all eyes and camera lenses were trained further down the road.

LeMond, having seemingly completely blown, was recovering well as the road levelled out in that final mile. He was charging now, his pellet-encrusted body ignoring any pain as he climbed out of the saddle to churn the big gears. Taking the final left-hander onto the finishing straight, he was effectively now riding his favoured discipline, the time trial: he was racing against the ticking of the clock, trying to keep any deficit remotely manageable. Every muscle worked to keep him in touch, to keep those dreams of the top spot on the Paris podium alive. Exhausted, LeMond crossed the line a minute and 19 seconds behind Fignon, who had wiped out that morning's chunky deficit to claim a 26-second advantage overall. 'Give Fignon huge credit,' says Len Pettyjohn. 'He put the hammer down when he had the chance.'

But while LeMond had again relinquished yellow, this epic race was far from over. 'It's not the worst thing in the world,' he reasoned at the finish line, the sparkle returning. 'It would have still been hard to keep the jersey. I've been very isolated and it's taken a lot of effort out of me. People don't see me leading the whole peloton, but when you have to control the race and follow attacks, the mental pressure is exhausting.' A smile still played on his lips though. 'I'd have preferred to have only lost it by five or ten seconds, but that's the way it goes.'

It could certainly have been worse for the American. In those last three miles, Fignon had taken around 26 seconds a mile out of him. If the Parisian had heeded Guimard's advice at four miles from home, his lead in the general classification would arguably have been unassailable. Indeed, had Guimard been able to manoeuvre his car alongside his team leader quicker, there was a strong likelihood that the titanic battle between Fignon and LeMond would have ended there and then.

On this point, there's an obvious irony that played into LeMond's hands. Renowned for his embrace of new technology and equipment at each and every time trial, it was the absence of one particular piece of technology during this particular marathon stage that served him well, as he has since acknowledged. 'I look back now and think that I'd have been in trouble if we'd had intercom radios.'

He could well be right. Had race radios been used in the '89 Tour (they weren't phased in until the '90s, a move led by team-sponsoring telecoms giant Motorola), the cycling nation may well have been denied that beautifully poised, infinitely intriguing spectacle. Bjarne Riis is a little more dismissive. 'With or without radios, it doesn't matter. It's still up to the riders to make decisions. They still have to think and do things. They are not machines.'

Indeed, this most thrilling of races, one shaped more by the riders' own thoughts and deeds than by the stricture of team orders, was heading towards the climax that it fully deserved. After nearly 80 hours in the saddle, Fignon and LeMond remained divided by a matter of seconds, not minutes.

There were still a few more hands to be dealt. The game of poker continued. Aces high.

Stage 17
1. Gert-Jan Theunisse (PDM/Netherlands) 5:10:39
2. Pedro Delgado (Reynolds/Spain) +1'09"
3. Laurent Fignon (Super U/France) +1'09"
4. Abelardo Rondón (Reynolds/Colombia) +2'08"
5. Greg LeMond (ADR/USA) +2'28"

General classification
1. Laurent Fignon (Super U/France) 77:55:11
2. Greg LeMond (ADR/USA) +26"
3. Pedro Delgado (Reynolds/Spain) +1'55"
4. Gert-Jan Theunisse (PDM/Netherlands) +5'12"
5. Charly Mottet (RMO/France) +5'22"

FOURTEEN

WIDENING MARGINS

'I was sure I had won the Tour' – Laurent Fignon

20 July
Stage 18, Bourg d'Oisans – Villard-de-Lans, 56 miles

'WE ARE ADVERSARIES. We'll never be great friends, but we'll talk to each other now and again. There is no animosity.'

Laurent Fignon's words about his relationship with Greg LeMond – delivered to Channel 4's Paul Sherwen in the evening glow of the terrace of Fignon's Alpe d'Huez hotel – suggested something of a charm offensive after the ugly nature of his public pronouncements over the previous days. Was this an attempt to heal the growing rift between the two top riders? Or was it designed to project a more conciliatory, less combative public image, in the process appearing more media-friendly?

If it was the latter, it didn't last long. The next morning, as he descended the steps of the Hotel La Belle Aurore and climbed into the back of his team car to drive down the mountain to the day's start in Bourg d'Oisans, Fignon appeared in less outgoing mood. On shutting the car door, and despite the decidedly clement temperatures, he immediately wound the window right up – a barrier of silence between the painfully private man and the prowling, prying press corps.

By contrast, in the back of his own team car, Greg LeMond's guard appeared to be down – as was his window. The conversation was perfectly audible. Chewing his thumb, he asked some – possibly rhetorical – questions of José De Cauwer and his Coors Light boss Len Pettyjohn in the front. Uncertainty was hanging in the air. And LeMond's nerves weren't eased when the car headed back down the mountain, revisiting the scene of his pain the previous afternoon.

This wouldn't be a day for either man to simply sit tight. That tactic suited neither. The final-day time trial was playing on both their minds. Fignon had to expand his lead to a defendable, safe amount; LeMond had to make sure that whatever his adversary's lead was come the morning of the Paris stage, it had to give him something to realistically attack on the streets of the French capital. Twenty-six seconds was satisfactory as a carrot, but a target of several seconds fewer would be even better. Matching, or eclipsing, Fignon's time into Villard-de-Lans was crucial.

The main contenders would be keeping their powder dry for later in the stage, so a break over the Côte de Laffrey – one led by Fagor's Laurent Biondi and including two stage winners in Robert Millar and Pascal Richard – was kept on a long leash. This breakaway had dissolved by the time the race arrived at the foot of the Côte de Saint-Nizier. By then, the main contenders weren't exactly jockeying for position so much as being swept along by the pace-setting PDM juggernaut. The team's target, alongside trying to break the occupants of the top three GC places, was to reel in Luis Herrera, a remnant of the previous break who had stayed out front. But just as the group was about to absorb the Colombian, one of their number launched a devastating attack. It was an unlikely attacker. It was the yellow jersey. He was off and away.

'My legs had suddenly begun to feel like they used to when I was younger,' Fignon later wrote. 'Rooks and Theunisse and the PDM team were setting a searing pace, with no idea that I was about to be the beneficiary. I caught everyone napping and although LeMond and Delgado worked together, they couldn't keep up. It was an example of my favourite tactic: use a situation in the race to take my opponents by surprise.'

Fignon allowed himself a long, lingering look back down the mountain. It was a satisfying sight. The rest were floundering and he was riding like a true Tour statesman. This was a classic show of strength from Fignon, a measure that he could justifiably be mentioned in the same breath as the greats. It was the way that someone like Eddy Merckx would have ridden if he were leading the race. The Cannibal wouldn't have been content to sit on wheels and defend his position. He would have added a sheen of flair to any victory by riding to extend his lead. Not showboating; simply stressing his own dominance.

Three men reacted to Fignon's attack – Delgado, LeMond and Theunisse. The first four on the road were the first four in the GC. The Spaniard was doing the majority of the chasing, the other two happy to be given an escorted ride back towards Fignon. After an extended period of high-tempo riding, though, Delgado swung out to the left-hand side, having had enough of unilaterally pulling LeMond and Theunisse along. At that moment, LeMond reached down to his shoes as if attending to an errant pedal clip, presumably hopeful that Theunisse would then take up the running in the pursuit of a podium place on the Champs-Élysées. But Theunisse refused to take the bait. He knew the other two riders needed to make contact with Fignon more than he did. The three of them then all sat up and exchanged glances. A game of bluff where no game of bluff should be. These were riders who all needed to improve their current standings, who needed to retrieve time either on each other or on Fignon's yellow jersey.

Instead, while each showed their reluctance to take the mission on, Fignon was actually increasing his advantage. Delgado blinked first, aware that he was the one with the biggest deficit to overhaul should he believe that the ultimate glory was still possible. Off he flew again, an acceleration fuelled by anger and frustration. Suddenly, having just protested about how fatigued they were, LeMond and Theunisse found their legs and were right on Delgado's tail as ever.

For all intents and purposes, that could have been the moment that the overall victor was decided. It wouldn't have been a concession as such, but a display of brinksmanship that could have handed Fignon an unassailable lead. It still might have done. All the workload was placed at Delgado's door, rather than the effort being shared three ways. Phil Liggett was certainly a believer in the moral responsibility the other two should have shouldered.

'It was the moment that LeMond should have paid up and taken his share of the pace-making,' argued the veteran broadcaster.

Fignon wasn't about to complain. He was too busy tackling the steep slopes of the Côte de Saint-Nizier, climbing at an extraordinary 19mph. His performance bore all the hallmarks of a deserving champion, one who had taken the race on at various junctures. He rolled over the summit 15 seconds up on the three behind; Theunisse mysteriously found his legs 200 yards from the banner and led Delgado and LeMond over, in the process bagging, of course, all available King of the Mountains points.

Down in the valley on the other side, Raúl Alcalá led Sean Kelly and other riders up to the LeMond group. If Fignon was at all nervous about the gathering storm that was this enlarged bunch, his riposte was his superb descending. So imperious were his top-speed skills that the gap between him and the others soon lengthened to 45 seconds. He was flying along for everything he could get, for every second he could plunder and add to LeMond's deficit.

As he embarked on the three-mile climb to Villard-de-Lans, Fignon's lead had flared out to 52 seconds which, added to his overnight lead of 26 seconds, meant he had accumulated a virtual lead over LeMond of well in excess of a minute. Yes, there were still two stages before the Paris time trial, but if he reached the capital with this kind of advantage ahead of a measly 15-mile run-out against the clock, the title was certain to be his.

As it was, that lead of 52 seconds would be halved by the finish line, a combination of three things: Fignon tackling a headwind without the protection of others; his body beginning to tire after superhuman efforts on successive days; and the belated momentum of the chase group.

As he approached the finish, Fignon didn't care. He was half a mile ahead and was still going to add a significant chunk of time to his lead. For a man not unconditionally loved by the French public, the reception as he negotiated the final left-hand bend was markedly uninhibited. He seemed to have finally won their hearts – or, at least, the hearts of those assembled here at Villard-de-Lans. A French Tour victory, on the 200th anniversary of the Revolution, appeared to be the necessary currency for new-found popularity.

Crossing the line, Fignon – almost always the little black cloud to LeMond's ray of sunshine – was joy unconfined. He excitedly raised his arms and flashed wide-palm waves to the crowd. It seemed that this was judgement day, the stage on which the destiny of this zigging, zagging, topsy-turvy race was finally decreed. 'He knows that today he's won the Tour de France,' declared Phil Liggett in his commentary box. 'I'm sure of that.' No one in Villard-de-Lans, or watching on television, was inclined to disagree. It did seem like the most rational conclusion to make, the last time-check putting his overall advantage at comfortably more than a minute.

Certainly, according to Bjarne Riis's autobiography, that was the unequivocal feeling within the Super U camp. 'The Frenchman was all smiles at the dinner table that evening,' the Dane wrote. 'He'd got through the mountains well, despite the competition from LeMond, and was now in a very good position to win the Tour de France. "I should win if I can keep riding like I am now," he announced confidently.'

His team-mates, perhaps misguidedly, started to let their minds wander towards matters financial. 'At the hotel, the others on the team had started to work out what Fignon winning the Tour would mean for us in terms of prize money. The win would net him 1.5 million kroner (£123,500), which would be shared out between the riders and team staff.' They dared to dream, when perhaps they would have been better advised to keep their counsel.

There was no such euphoria in the ADR camp. As he received his post-stage massage from his *soigneur* Otto Jacome, LeMond spoke to ABC. It was the most sombre, most sober interview he would give in the entire three weeks of the race. Where his eyes normally flashed with excitement, that evening they were flecked with sorrow as he contemplated the Tour's final day denoucment. 'If it was a 50km time trial,' he reasoned, 'there would be some good hope. It's still not over, but it's less likely today. I've done my best but Fignon yesterday and today has been extremely strong.'

There would have been even less hope without the collective effort of the chase group on that final climb. And it was an effort that would have reduced, if not burst, Fignon's bubble that night. A margin of 50 seconds should still have been sufficient going into the 15-mile final-day time trial, but it would be unnatural if some nagging doubts, however small, didn't remain. One thing in particular was tormenting the race leader, as Sean Kelly explains.

'I remember Fignon saying to me many times, during the Tour and after, "You guys at PDM were riding for Greg LeMond." When Fignon went on the attack, it was Rooks and Theunisse who did the chasing. I said, "No, there was no agreement." Years later, when we had both retired and were working for Eurosport, he said, "Now you can tell me the truth. Were you really working with Greg in that Tour?" "I can tell you the truth. And, as I told you before, there was never any agreement between us."

'It was just that Rooks and Theunisse were strong in the mountains and that Greg worked his tactics very well. He just followed them and they did a lot of the chasing work. Look at the footage of some of the mountain stages. You can see that it was Theunisse and Rooks, and maybe some of the other guys in the team like Alcalá, who were doing the pace-setting on the climbs. I remember on a number of occasions Fignon did attack because he was the better one in the mountains, but he never got any great advantage from all of the attacks. PDM were the ones securing the pace and doing the chasing, and Greg worked it very well. But you can see why Fignon was asking the question.'

Kathy LeMond's perspective of that stage is in stark contrast to that of Fignon. The complete opposite, in fact. 'That was a weird day. There was collusion on that day with PDM *against* Greg. And, oh my God, was Greg furious. Nobody would work with him.' She's referring to the reluctance of Theunisse to do his share on the front of the three-man group as they made their way along the floor of the valley with around 15 miles left. As *Cycling Weekly*'s Keith Bingham opined, 'If only Theunisse had worked with them they may have got Fignon back.' But by this point, the Dutchman knew a podium place was almost certainly beyond him and so chose to move to the front of the trio only when they approached a summit, allowing him to gather as many King of the Mountains points as were available and at least cement his possession of that jersey.

The fear of collusion – highly unlikely after LeMond had left PDM with such a sour taste in his mouth – indicated how brittle Fignon might have been, despite that reassuring lead he had. Andy Hampsten again indicates how the Frenchman was the weaker one psychologically. 'He was trying to fill five pages in *L'Equipe* with "I have it in the bag" and "This time I've got the American". When he was trading blows with LeMond and gaining 20 seconds, he gave enormous significance to it. He wanted to be the master of the game and Greg knew that. As we Americans say, if you're going to swing your stick, you need a really big stick. Don't take a little penknife out and start swinging that in a gunfight. With Greg knowing him so well psychologically, he loved those back-and-forth battles. It was fun for him.'

For all Fignon's comments to the contrary ('I was sure I had won the Tour'), there were still several variables that could decide the final result. And, behind the mask, he knew this. One hundred and seventy-two miles still remained. One hundred and seventy-two miles where something untoward might well occur. A crash. A puncture. An illness. Perhaps even the emergence of a boil in a delicate place.

Stage 18
1. Laurent Fignon (Super U/France) 2:31:28
2. Steven Rooks (PDM/Netherlands) +24"
3. Gert-Jan Theunisse (PDM/Netherlands) same time
4. Marino Lejarreta (Paternina/Spain) same time
5. Sean Kelly (PDM/Ireland) same time

General classification
1. Laurent Fignon (Super U/France) 80:26:39
2. Greg LeMond (ADR/USA) +50"
3. Pedro Delgado (Reynolds/Spain) +2'28"
4. Gert-Jan Theunisse (PDM/Netherlands) +5'36"
5. Charly Mottet (RMO/France) +7'29"

FIFTEEN

NO SURRENDER

'They escaped disaster by the skin of their teeth – and loved the moment too!'
– Graham Watson

21 July
Stage 19, Villard-de-Lans – Aix-les-Bains, 78 miles

GOODBYE TO THE Alps. Goodbye to the mountains.

This final Alpine stage offered a fierce contest, no doubt. It certainly didn't have the air of a backslapping parade. But the majority of these three-and-a-half hours became a salute to – and a celebration of – the most tenacious, most consistent climbers who had jockeyed and jousted each other over the previous three weeks.

With four not-insignificant climbs ahead of them, the stage was dominated from an early point by the top four in the GC – Fignon, LeMond, Delgado and Theunisse – plus seventh-placed Marino Lejarreta, a man directing a covetous stare towards Charly Mottet's fifth position. This quintet had already made their move by the time the gradients of the second climb, the first-category Col de Porte, began to tighten. They were more than a minute on the chase group that contained all of the usual suspects (including the three other PDM strongmen – Kelly, Rooks and Alcalá) as they crested the summit. Well, all the usual suspects bar Mottet. He was a further minute back and struggling. Possibly a stage too far. The popular thinking – that a three-week Grand Tour was too much for him to sustain at the top of his game – was proving true.

The same five tore up the Col du Cucheron, each rider with a different motivation. Fignon wasn't one to defend, to sit at the back of this small bunch to observe and react. He was happy to lead them up the slopes of this second-category climb, perhaps sniffing after a few more seconds to take his advantage over the psychological barrier of a full minute. Delgado was now largely resigned to that third spot, so the priority for him was to shadow fourth-placed Theunisse, and possibly also grab a stage win on the flat roads of Aix-les-Bains. Theunisse, while in no danger of not winning the polka-dot jersey, nonetheless jerked into action whenever anyone launched an attack near any of the day's summits. He still wanted as many points in the King of the Mountains competition as possible. Not that the easy accumulation of these points ever provoked a smile from him. The grumpiest king since Henry VIII.

If this lead group did survive the day, Lejarreta would be the rider with most to gain. Starting the day a minute and two seconds off fifth place, the Basque rider's aim was to leapfrog Mottet and Rooks to take the highest Tour placing in his lengthy career. At the rate these five were riding, this looked like a foregone conclusion. And then there was LeMond, spending a large part of the day sitting on the back of the bunch, the other four constantly in his eyeline. Was he going to settle for second or would he attack in order to pare that 50-second deficit down to a more manageable amount for Paris?

Whatever their motivation, everyone was watching everyone else. And when Fignon pulled to the side of the road after dragging the others up on another stamina-sapping charge, his open invitation for someone else to make the pace fell on deaf ears. They simply all snaked behind him as he weaved back and forth across the road in a game of Follow My Leader.

As on the Col de Porte, Delgado was first over the Col du Cucheron, denying Theunisse the maximum points both times. The phlegmatic Dutchman didn't seem to be too aggrieved about this: the polka-dot jersey wasn't coming off his back. Delgado led the rest over the summit of the Col du Granier too, but not before a little spicy action on the climb of the race's last major mountain. With less than a mile of incline remaining, LeMond put in an attack which Fignon was sharp to, quickly neutralising it. LeMond went again. Fignon answered again.

The descent down the Granier's northern slopes was steep and dangerous, but that didn't stop LeMond – a man clearly not content with second place overall – from taking some big gambles as they roared down towards Chambéry, the location of the following month's world championships. He was in search of anything he could get that would improve his chances of causing a shock in Paris, even if it were only a handful of seconds. Fignon, probably an even better descender, wouldn't let him get a thing, though.

But it wasn't the descent, with vertical drops just a foot or two away, that caused the five grief. It was a good old-fashioned roundabout. Coming into Chambéry too fast to successfully negotiate the roundabout, Lejarreta ploughed straight ahead into a spectator barrier. The others all followed. All except Delgado, that is, who managed to avoid the fence and stay upright, but sportingly elected not to take advantage of his opponents' misfortunes by disappearing towards the horizon. The episode symbolised the respect and sense of fraternity within the upper echelons. The photographer Graham Watson noticed it too. 'Once they'd realigned themselves, TV showed all three podium finishers with beaming smiles on their faces. They escaped disaster by the skin of their teeth – and loved the moment too!'

On the flat roads between Chambéry and Aix-les-Bains, racing along the east bank of the Lac du Bourget, the pace was high, pretty much everyone taking their turn on the front. If it wasn't for the array of different jerseys, spectators would swear they were watching a well-drilled team time trial.

As expected, once within sniffing distance of the finish, LeMond proved himself to be the man with the most electrifying sprint and took the stage victory to his clear delight. Fignon extended an arm of congratulation, happy to concede LeMond the stage win. Those 50 seconds remained unharmed.

'I wanted to win today,' LeMond told Channel 4. 'That was a big deal for me. I knew if I took Fignon's wheel, I would win.' Delgado agrees that the stage win felt inevitable. 'He waited to win the stage. He was a specialist at that. Maybe, if I was in his body, I would do the same.' The hard-working Lejarreta got his just reward too, gaining enough of an advantage over Mottet and Rooks to move up into fifth. '

While the final five fighting out the sprint finish in Aix-les-Bains had arguably been the most consistent performers in the mountains, their success set others' shortcomings into sharp relief. Aside from the underachievement of Andy Hampsten, the most conspicuous disappointment in both the Alps and the Pyrenees was the comparative no-show of the Colombians. Fabio Parra, a podium finisher 12 months before, stepped off his bike just after the race left the Pyrenees, while – despite launching the odd, spasmodic attack – Luis 'Lucho' Herrera never threatened the upper reaches of the GC. The Colombian cycling revolution, this wave of exciting riders who emerged in the early '80s, now looked to be on the wane, at least where the Tour de France was concerned.

Delgado, a man with a pair of very capable Colombians in his Reynolds team in '89, offers his opinion on why the country's impact wasn't felt for longer. 'The Colombian riders rode like they did back in Colombia. I took part in the Tour de Colombia once and everyone flew off from the start. They were competing without tactics. The tactic was attack, breakaway, escape. But to win the Tour, you have to be more controlled. At that time, the Colombians were very, very good climbers, but they didn't have the discipline to win the race.' Phil Liggett identified a parallel situation in the commentary box during the '80s. 'The Colombian media came in full force,' he told *Bicycling* magazine. 'They would be commentating in a voice fit for a finishing sprint when the race had just left the start town.'

Aside from tactical differences, cultural separation also dogged riders' progress in the sport's heartland. 'The hardest thing for Colombian riders was being in Europe for a month,' says Delgado. 'They missed their family and their country. Back then, it was very typical for a Colombian rider like Lucho Herrera to want to go home after the first stage. Fabio Parra, though, understood that he needed to live outside Colombia for a month or two to be a professional cyclist.' Not that, of course, such an approach did Parra too many favours in 1989, joining the rest of his team in abandoning the race several days before the race reached the Alps.

Raúl Alcalá, the highest-placed Latin American rider in '89, agrees that distance from home was a major factor for the Café de Colombia team. 'It costs a lot to bring the team over for a few races, so it was best for them to keep the whole team together for as long as possible in Europe. Sometimes, the Colombians were tired from racing all the time in Europe. They preferred to go back and forth to Colombia. That was perfect for them. They got homesick all the time. They called home to Mama, to Papa to say they're OK.'

Herrera was the best-placed Colombian in the '89 Tour, but his 19th place was undeniably a disappointment, more than 36 minutes down on the yellow jersey in Paris. In fact, he finished just one GC position and one minute ahead of his team-mate, Alberto Camargo, the young, largely undistinguished domestique. Furthermore, Camargo's eighth place into Villard-de-Lans on Stage 18 was higher than any of Herrera's finishes in the entire three weeks.

Colombia's most decorated cyclists would each only finish the Tour on one more occasion; Herrera came home 31st in 1991, while Parra finished 13th the previous year, before racking up two further abandonments. But the biggest pin deflating the country's cycling bubble wasn't the form of its top riders. On 3 July 1989, just as the Tour was belting around the Spa-Francorchamps Grand Prix circuit, the International Coffee Pact collapsed. Under the agreement, the coffee industry, a fundamental pillar of the Colombian economy, enjoyed protected status for its prices. With this safeguard suddenly removed, the price of coffee dramatically fell by 60% within 24 hours. The first casualty for the National Association of Coffee Growers of Colombia was obvious; the sponsorship of a professional cycling team was now no longer an imaginative marketing tool but an unsustainable luxury. Accordingly, 1989 would be the last time the Café de Colombia team would light up the Tour de France.

In the years that followed, European teams would employ Colombian riders more and more as domestiques. Some might say that the move away from starring roles for the country's cycling talent was already in place. After all, the Colombians who had most impact in the '89 Tour were Delgado's two loyal lieutenants, William Palacio and Abelardo Rondón, who nursed their leader from the *lanterne rouge* to the podium. Until the arrival of their compatriot Santiago Botero, who won the King of the Mountains jersey in 2000, Colombian eyes drifted away from the Tour de France, and cycling in general, attracted by national sporting success elsewhere, most conspicuously, in football and Formula 1.

As Colombian attention declined, interest in the Tour from the US was at an all-time high. While a handful of American newspapers already sent a correspondent every year to report on the whole race – and ABC gave it airtime with highlights packages – editors across the nation didn't want to miss out on what LeMond, Fignon and the rest were serving up. Not only was this epic sporting contest offering more twists and turns than the maziest Alpine pass, but LeMond's back story offered the classic overcoming-the-odds tale that proved irresistible to non-sports fans too. Accordingly, the American presence in the press ranks substantially swelled in that final week, many journalists taking crash courses in this alien, exotic sport.

And LeMond was intent on making sure the drama wouldn't end until the last pedal stroke of the entire three weeks. He was fired the same question over and over. Did Fignon have too much advantage going into the last two days? 'No, no no! Fifty seconds is a very good advantage but, I tell you, he's going to have some sleepless nights.

'He won't beat me by 50 seconds.'

Stage 19
1. Greg LeMond (ADR/USA) 3:17:53
2. Laurent Fignon (Super U/France) same time
3. Pedro Delgado (Reynolds/Spain) same time
4. Gert-Jan Theunisse (PDM/Netherlands) same time
5. Marino Lejarreta (Paternina/Spain) +4"

General classification
1. Laurent Fignon (Super U/France) 83:44:32
2. Greg LeMond (ADR/USA) +50"
3. Pedro Delgado (Reynolds/Spain) +2'28"
4. Gert-Jan Theunisse (PDM/Netherlands) +5'36"
5. Marino Lejarreta (Paternina/Spain) +8'35"

***

22 July
Stage 20, Aix-les-Bains – L'Isle d'Abeau, 79 miles

'This was a vacation. A long-awaited vacation.'

You couldn't blame LeMond – or anyone else in the peloton, for that matter – for taking their foot off the gas. Up until now, it had been one of the most extraordinary Tours ever, full of daring and drama, intrigue and incident. There hadn't been so much as a single stage that could be described as mediocre. But it was perfectly acceptable if this, the race's penultimate stage, fell into that category. Everyone needed to take a breath before Paris, after all.

The tenor of the day was set early on when Fignon temporarily exchanged the *maillot jaune* for Teun van Vliet's Panasonic jersey. And his playful mood continued, launching a semi-serious attack on this benign peloton, a wholly unnecessary move for the leader of the pack, unless he thought that he could pick up a few more seconds to plump up that 50-second time cushion.

Deprived of the usual final-day mass sprint on the Champs-Élysées, the finish into L'Isle d'Abeau represented Sean Kelly's last hope of a stage win in the '89 race. Phil Anderson clearly fancied tasting victory, too. After one such win in the Giro the previous month, the Australian TVM leader wanted to repeat the feat and was anxious – once the attacks starting coming thick and fast on this otherwise most passive of stages – to be part of each and every breakaway. In the end, he went himself, timing his solo break just as the peloton were closing on Histor's Wilfried Peeters, an earlier escapee.

Anderson was soon swallowed up by the peloton as the teams of the big sprinters prepared to lead out their speedsters for a rare mass sprint – only the third of the entire three weeks. It appeared that Jelle Nijdam, in search of a hat-trick of victories, had the stage nailed when he struck for home 300 yards out. But he had possibly attacked a little too soon and hadn't legislated for a pair of fast-arriving sprinters in good form. While Nijdam successfully held off the challenge of Kelly, who had to be content with third, the Dutchman was pipped to the line, by the thinnest of margins, by the Italian Giovanni Fidanza. After five top-ten finishes in the race (including second behind Mathieu Hermans in Blagnac, following Rudy Dhaenens' late crash), the win was certainly deserved for the rookie Chateau d'Ax man.

But that wasn't it for the day. The riders then crossed to nearby Lyon to board a specially chartered, high-speed TGV train that would take them up to Paris, ahead of the following day's time trial. It would prove to be a rather interesting journey.

'The train ride before the final stage is my favourite part of the Tour,' laughs Andy Hampsten. 'The maximal kick in the sac for every bike rider was getting on the TGV and being served meat patties that were burnt on the outside and frozen on the inside, and rice that was cooked three months ago. But we knew this. We were smart. We had our own cook and he made us a beautiful pasta salad and chicken breasts. We were having a big picnic. Greg, with his inability to sit down – and with hardly any team-mates left to talk to by this point – was roaming up and down the train. "Hey Greg! Come and sit down." I wasn't a threat to him on GC and we were all friends, so we sat him down and fed him.

"Greg, we think you can win this race."

"Oh no. I *know* I can win this race."

'The main riders were in the first carriage,' explains Delgado, 'including LeMond, Fignon and me. Cyrille Guimard was there too. He was opening champagne bottles and toasting me – "Thanks for being such a very good adversary." I said, "OK, but the Tour de France is not finished yet. Tomorrow is 25 kilometres. Maybe LeMond can recover some time. Maybe, 40 seconds. And maybe you'll have a puncture or something like that."'

Delgado shakes his head with disbelief – disbelief he's been holding for the last three decades. 'I didn't understand it. Incredible. Just stay focused for one more day.' He sighs. 'That champagne would end up tasting bitter.' If Delgado had been the one with the 50-second lead, would he have been confident of defending it in the time trial? 'Oh no, no, no. No champagne. There might have been 50 seconds, but the race isn't over until the finish line.' This was a dictum that Guimard instilled in LeMond back in the Renault days of the early '80s. Perhaps he should have heeded his own advice.

Hampsten tells a similar story about the presumptuousness of the yellow jersey on the transfer up to Paris. 'On the train, Fignon came to LeMond, in front of some journalists, and congratulated him on his second place. It was all this "after that terrible injury", "it's been an honour battling you", "we're going back to my hometown and I'm going to be triumphant in Paris". As they're shaking hands with photographers and journalists all around, Greg looks him in the eye. He knew his playbook. He got it. But it wasn't that Larry was trying to do some double or triple psychology. He really thought he was going to hold that 50-second lead. But Greg realised he had completely let his guard down. He was thinking "I'm just going to do a time trial. That gun's going to go and I'm going to go so fast."'

Journalist François Thomazeau sees it differently, believing that the race leader was far from cocksure. 'Not only was Fignon not overconfident, he was full of doubts. I'm sure he started the race with so much fear of losing that he did lose. And he was really injured. You could tell the pressure and doubts on the evening before when the riders took the train back to Paris. I was on that TGV and Guimard was refusing access to the Super U compartment. He was in an extremely bad mood and smelling of whisky, which was never a good sign. You could feel the tension.

'As I couldn't work, I found myself sitting next to Greg. He had been left on his own; not a single journalist on the train was interested in talking to him. While Fignon's camp was unavailable, LeMond was in great spirits, so thrilled and happy to have made it back to the Tour de France and finishing second. That was the great irony. You had a guy who thought he had lost the Tour and was cheerful as can be, while the guy who was about to win it was tense and refusing to talk! Greg told me his whole story in great detail and you know what? I was so convinced Fignon would win the Tour that I didn't take notes or record our chat. My worst professional mistake...'

By the time the train arrived at Gare de Lyon in Paris, Fignon was in a black temper. The hordes of photographers and cameramen waiting on the station platform weren't conducive to an improvement in his demeanour. 'We had hardly begun to move along the platform before someone bunged the usual camera under my nose and began throwing aggressive questions at me,' he wrote in his autobiography. 'Worn out by the stressful ambience, I spat at a camera crew who were in the way. Just my luck: they were from a Spanish channel against whom I had no grievance at all. Afterwards, as soon as any news story about my arrival at the station was run, the images were played again and again. It wasn't the best publicity.'

A separate report suggests that the Frenchman issued one cameraman with a not-so-polite invitation: 'You want a punch in the mouth?' Fignon himself admitted he gave the man from Channel 5 a shove. 'I didn't even think about what I was doing.'

Less than 24 hours later, though, a surprise right hook was coming Fignon's way. A metaphorical punch, sure, but one that packed enough power to hurt forever.

Stage 20
1. Giovanni Fidanza (Chateau d'Ax/Italy) 3:26:16
2. Jelle Nijdam (Superconfex/Netherlands) same time
3. Sean Kelly (PDM/Ireland) same time
4. Mathieu Hermans (Paternina/Netherlands) same time
5. Carlo Bomans (Domex/Belgium) same time

General classification
1. Laurent Fignon (Super U/France) 87:10:48
2. Greg LeMond (ADR/USA) +50"
3. Pedro Delgado (Reynolds/Spain) +2'28"
4. Gert-Jan Theunisse (PDM/Netherlands) +5'30"
5. Marino Lejarreta (Paternina/Spain) 8'35"

ACT IV
EIGHT SECONDS

SIXTEEN

CAPITAL GAINS

*'Some Spanish journalists thought that I went slowly so that I wouldn't be the
first rider to ride the race quicker than the winner' – Pedro Delgado*

23 July
Stage 21, individual time trial, Versailles – Paris, 15 miles

AS THE MAN who held the record for the fastest individual performance
in the 86-year history of the Tour de France, Sean Yates would have gazed
along the route from the Palace of Versailles to the Champs-Élysées and
fancied his chances. Slightly downhill and with a discernible tailwind in the
air, the hope of glory in the final stage of this epic race was an irresistible
prospect. If he were successful, it would represent the very pinnacle of his
career, a moment unlikely to ever be equalled.

That Sunday afternoon represented 7-Eleven's last tilt at some success
at the end of a disappointing, misfiring Tour. 'We hadn't won a stage and
Andy Hampsten had slipped out of contention bigtime. So what was left?
It got to the last stage and no one had won anything. Jim Ochowicz said,
"I'll give you $20,000 if you win the last time trial." Maybe he thought the
money would make the difference between winning and not winning. I
told him I'd try as hard as I could, whether I was getting $20,000 or not,
because that's what I did. I never rode for money. I liked the way I lived and
I liked to ride my bike. It wasn't that I was saving up for my third Ferrari or

anything. Twenty thousand dollars wasn't suddenly going to make me go 2kph faster.'

Despite 7-Eleven's trademark relaxed environment, Ochowicz's wager indicated a man under pressure. 7-Eleven as a company was in serious financial trouble and potential new sponsors needed to be approached. A stage win would certainly help these discussions after the disappointment of Hampsten's Tour. Success in the Giro was one thing (Hampsten won in '88 and was third in '89), but American sponsors wanted success in France, in the sport's blue riband event. The one being broadcast to the nation on ABC.

'Andy was a good athlete,' says Yates, 'but he was never a guy – or certainly didn't portray himself as a guy – who said, "I'm going to fucking win this thing. I will deliver. Boys, you've got to be fucking on it." You're either like that or you're not. And that just wasn't his character.'

Although he rode satisfactorily in some of the Alpine stages, Hampsten wasn't ever a contender for a stage win. 'I saw all the battles going on. There were eight or ten of us around LeMond and Fignon, but it was largely the two of them fighting it out. It was ping, bam, boom.' And it would be the other American who made the headlines back home. 'I spent my career trying to win the Tour de France and the dirty secret is that it never happened!'

Nonetheless, Hampsten was looking forward to that afternoon's innovative final stage. 'It's fine being sucked along on a free ride down the Champs-Elysées,' he told Samuel Abt, 'but arriving alone and not having to share the cheers is a wonderful reward for everybody.' He came in 28th on the day and 22nd overall. Team-mate Yates fared better, finishing fifth, mirroring his position on the Rennes time trial. But he never got his hands on those '20,000 pieces of inspiration'.

The other British rider, Glasgow's Robert Millar, enjoyed a bittersweet Tour. His brilliant ride to Superbagnères, leading the way over all the day's big climbs, was arguably the most impressive Tour victory of his career and, although he slipped a position on the GC on the time trial into Paris, his tenth position was his second-highest overall finish. But in the Alps he couldn't stay in touch with Gert-Jan Theunisse in the pursuit of his other ambition, the polka-dot jersey. He finished third in that competition, the pair separated by Pedro Delgado.

Theunisse's jersey was one of four that the PDM team brought away from the race. Sean Kelly was in possession of two of them – the green points jersey and the red catch sprints jersey – while the previous year's King of the Mountains, Steven Rooks, had to be content with winning the combined competition, rewarding the rider showing the most consistency across all the other categories. PDM's haul was bountiful; four jerseys, four stage wins and four riders in the top ten overall, plus they held off Delgado's Reynolds squad to take the team competition too.

'The management were happy with the riders and the results,' says Kelly, 'but they were looking at LeMond who had just been with them. "What did we do here? Did we get it wrong? Should we have held on to him?" They didn't say it directly, but that was something they were thinking about. I could read it. And it's normal that the general manager and the *directeur sportif* would think in that way.' The team's PR man, Harry Jansen, was more transparent and direct. Speaking of the multiple jerseys their riders had bagged, Jansen admitted 'we would give them all up for the yellow jersey'.

The Dutch press, though, weren't too impressed with the haul. Four riders in the top ten, yet none in podium places, let alone winning the race. 'They thought Theunisse could have been higher, but the tactic was never for the rest of us to support one guy. We all rode our own race.'

Kelly, whose 47th position on the final time trial meant he swapped places with Millar in the GC, had enjoyed one of his best Tours. A stage win remained elusive, and there was no early capture of the yellow jersey that he'd hoped for, but his extremely impressive climbing ensured that the winning of his fourth green jersey was little more than a formality. And it all came well into his thirties.

Certainly the move from KAS had suited him; the removal of all those Spanish stage races from his schedule had meant he was in fine fettle for the Tour itself. 'I felt much fresher than in previous years, thanks to the programme in the early part of the season. I felt I had more energy. Over the years, fatigue was a problem. Usually, when I got into the second week of the Tour, I would feel it.'

Kelly wasn't the only PDM new boy to have an impressive Tour. Martin Earley had taken that victory in Pau, as had Raúl Alcalá at Spa-

Francorchamps. Despite finishing eighth overall, Alcalá ran out of juice in the final week – or, at least, he didn't have enough juice left to make a meaningful impression in the Alps. 'I tried to keep my form as long as possible. For me, the Alps were more difficult than the Pyrenees. When the Alps come first on a Tour, riding Alpe d'Huez is a great feeling. But if the Pyrenees come first, I'd get in trouble in the Alps because I'd get more tired. I always got this feeling from around Stage 13 or 14 onwards. I was there, very near the front at the finishes in 1989, but I didn't have enough power to win the stages. On the last seven or eight kilometres of a stage, I was going at the same tempo. I see guys go, but I can't go with them. I was like an automatic car. You put your foot on the gas, but you go the same speed.'

Two climbers who fared better than Alcalá in the high mountains were Charly Mottet and Marino Lejarreta, two diminutive men who finished within a minute of each other. Their respective Tours, though, were rather different. Mottet securely held third place for a week between Superbagnères and Alpe d'Huez, before fatigue appeared to set in and he faded. By contrast, the longer the race went on, the higher Lejarreta rose, finally taking possession of Mottet's fifth place on the final day in the mountains.

Lejarreta's compatriot, Pedro Delgado, had – as Laurent Fignon had rudely pointed out to him on the race's early stages – discovered that the deficit he had to eradicate was too great, especially with Fignon and LeMond being at the height of their powers. As he lined up for the time trial, he was in a quandary.

'The day before, I was two minutes and 28 seconds behind. I started two minutes and 42 seconds late in Luxembourg. Someone said, "Hey Pedro, maybe you will be the first rider in Tour de France history to ride the race in less time than the person who won it." At the end, I was more than three minutes down on the classification. I rode the time trial without motivation. First and second places were too distant to recover and, behind me, nobody had put my third position in danger. So I just completed it. Nothing more. But some Spanish journalists thought that I went slowly so that I wouldn't be the first rider to ride the race quicker than the winner.'

'The fightback by Delgado even now gets overlooked by the bigger fight,' says Graham Watson. 'Looking back, it was amazing how hard Delgado raced because of his early losses. He'd normally have lost many minutes in the long time trial on Stage 5, but instead hit back and used that performance to reach even dizzier heights later on. We will never know if he'd have won that Tour with a safer and normal Prologue, but in all likelihood he would have – and this Tour would never have ended so famously.'

Certainly, Delgado's irresistible surge up the GC, from the indignity of being the race's first *lanterne rouge* after the Prologue, owed plenty to the strength of his team, specifically the dedication of his faithful helpers Induráin, Palacio, Rondón and Gorospe. Indeed, Reynolds were the only team in the whole race to have a full complement of riders taking to the time trial start line at Versailles. All nine members were reporting for duty.

(Delgado might have been the '89 Tour's first *lanterne rouge*, but its final one, the Paternina sprinter Mathieu Hermans, endured a double indignity. Not only did he become, after his victory in Blagnac, the first stage winner to finish in last position, but this wasn't the first time he'd ended up bottom of the barrel. He was merely repeating his feat of 1987.)

Delgado had been desperate to win the '89 Tour in order to disprove the doubters, to blow away the clouds of suspicion that had followed him around since the probenecid affair the previous summer. After the Prologue debacle, his furious charge up the GC (which incredibly didn't include a stage win) was, of course, an attempt to get remotely close to that ambition.

There were no positive tests in the '89 race, no whispers of chemical enhancement tainting the battle for yellow. Six riders were tested every day: the stage winner, the runner-up, the yellow jersey, second place in GC and two riders selected at random. 'Testing wasn't as stringent as it is now,' says Sean Yates, 'but that's probably more to do with the products that are out there these days that they're searching for. '89 was before that era.'

While it would be naïve to imagine every single rider in the peloton was squeaky clean, it is fair to judge this race as one of the last classic encounters before EPO arrived and changed the game entirely. 'In the '80s and early '90s,' explains Stephen Roche, 'you'd feel a guy with natural talent could still come out and win, because whatever was on the market could increase performance by three to five per cent. So somebody who had a lot of class could beat a guy who was taking something. In the late '90s and early 2000s, some of the products on the market at that particular time added 30-40 per cent increase in performance. So no matter how much class they had, it was impossible for someone who was trying to be clean to beat somebody who had taken something.'

As EPO put its icy paw on the shoulder of the pro cycling ranks, a rider of class like Delgado found himself off the pace, average at best. 'One year I'm in the first group. The next year, I'm in the last group, like a very bad rider. I did the same as I did every year, so what happened…?'

Back in the late '80s, Greg LeMond gave the journalist Samuel Abt an overview of drug intake within the peloton. 'Of course, a small minority of cyclists do use drugs. There are more than 700 professionals in Europe. A lot of them are broke and they're all human. There are few people who, knowing that if they take something they may do better, are capable of refusing it. But the tests are pretty strict, so I honestly believe there is very little drug use in the major events. In smaller races where there are no drug tests, it can be a different matter. Not everybody in those races is riding on water … It's mainly the second-raters who do it.'

With no one testing positive, and no clouds of suspicion hanging over the result, as there had been the previous year, nothing could detract from the drama, from the sheer sporting intrigue, of the final day in '89. With 136 riders having now rolled down the start ramp at Versailles, to be welcomed onto the Champs-Élysées without, as Andy Hampsten explained, having to share the cheers, only two riders remained.

What was left was a duel, a shoot-out, a boxing match. Cycling's fight of the century.

Fignon vs LeMond.

***

'There's a lot to be said about feeling good and not having pressure,' says Len Pettyjohn. 'When you're in the jersey, the collar is very tight.'

As he had for three weeks, the Coors Light team manager, embedded with the ADR team throughout the race, had a front-row seat on that final morning. He could gauge how calm and collected Greg LeMond was and, from across the hotel breakfast room, how Laurent Fignon was tying himself up in knots.

'That morning we were laughing and having a good time. Greg was very relaxed as he had nothing to lose at that point. He had been out practising on his time trial bike, but there was a problem because the bars were slipping and the mechanic was sitting there cutting up a Coke can to try to put spacers in between the bars. We looked over and there was Fignon, in the back of the parking lot, with time trial bars on his bike. He had them out and was practising. He was looking over at Greg and you could see he was really nervous. So we went in to have breakfast and we were all laughing. We watched the Super U team walk in and Fignon looked over again. Greg waved and smiled. Fignon's face was white. He was feeling the pressure. You could see the fear.'

The doubts would amplify with each hour that the time trial grew closer. With such a lead on a short stage on the familiar streets of his hometown, how could Fignon fail? Logic was on his side. But there were ways that the presence of technology could precipitate a defeat. Firstly, Fignon could simply be beaten by the physical advantages that the technology gave LeMond, by the appliance of science. Secondly, whether LeMond actually received a boost from his equipment or not, the fear that he might could be enough to tie Fignon in knots too.

It wasn't as if Cyrille Guimard was a technophobe. Far from it. Over the previous decade, the Super U boss had been in the vanguard of innovation, especially any new thinking that involved aerodynamics. He was the man who introduced Fignon and Bernard Hinault to sloped-framed bikes, as well as becoming an evangelist for the use of disc wheels. But, for some reason, he shied away from the aerobars, despite seeing how they had helped LeMond cut through the wind and the rain on the Rennes time trial. When pushed, he would mumble an excuse, saying how they had actually tested them but found they adversely affected Fignon's ability to breathe. LeMond was delighted to hear this admission. 'Thank God people are sceptical...'

'Winning by ourselves without artificial aids was something we valued,' Fignon later wrote. 'And we had an inviolable principle in the biggest races; we would only use new equipment if it had been tested properly before the event. We had to make absolutely certain it was reliable, particularly for the Tour de France where we only ever rode trusty, solid kit that we knew how to use.'

Fignon's definition of 'artificial aids' clearly didn't include disc wheels. He plumped for two discs for the final time trial, both decked out in the national colours of France to match his tricolour handlebar tape. Such showiness was consistent with the supposed inevitability of the result. Stephen Roche notes how 'on the Champs-Élysées that morning, there were blue, white and red T-shirts with "Fignon: Winner of the Tour" on them'.

Aside from their presumptuousness ('They were so sure they'd won that they put on a show'), Roche sees Super U's decision to use both these disc wheels as fundamentally flawed. 'That was a huge, huge mistake. That day, coming in from Versailles, all the side streets would have produced side-winds. If it had been a dead straight road with a headwind, it would have been beneficial. But when you had changes in direction and the wind coming in from the left and the right, when it came to taking your hand off the bars to change gear, you wouldn't do so as you'd be afraid of the wind taking your front wheel. It would be very uncomfortable. If they'd calculated everything precisely, they wouldn't have taken a risk on a full disc at the front. But because they were so far ahead, they did take the risk.' So while it wasn't that Super U weren't embracing technology to secure Fignon's place on the podium, it was that they appeared to be embracing the *wrong* technology.

LeMond, on the other hand, had done his calculations and was insistent that his bike be set up just how he wanted it. 'I wanted Greg to ride with the front disc,' admits Len Pettyjohn, 'but he refused. That was his call. At that time, the nature of wheel aerodynamics was such that you really could get pushed across the road with double-discs. It was dangerous. Greg said, "You know what? I want to go as fast as I can go and I don't want a distraction. I don't want anything to bother me. So don't put that front wheel on."'

LeMond was also insistent that he wasn't to be told any of his split times out on the course. That would take the psychology, the thinking, out of his performance, freeing him up for the purely flat-out physical assault. Fignon, however, even if he didn't want to, would get a sense of how he was riding in comparison with LeMond. Another contribution to add to the ever-growing pile of psychological burdens.

'When you start losing time,' says Pettyjohn, 'it creates panic. That's just the reality of bike racing. Then you start to push a little harder and you go over the limit. Your heart-rate spikes and then you have to slow down. If you go fast, slow, fast, slow, guess what? You go slow. And getting a message in your ear that you're losing time when you feel like shit is not a good thing. Everything would be a distraction for Fignon that day.'

Aside from the psychology, Fignon also had a physical issue, one he believed 'no one suspected a thing [about] because we had imposed a media blackout'. He had developed an excruciatingly painful saddle sore, just below one of his buttocks, right at the point where his shorts touched his saddle. He hadn't slept well because of it for two nights, and no matter how much embrocation the team doctor administered, the pain wouldn't subside.

But, despite the psychological and physical pressures heaped up on Fignon, he knew – like almost everyone else – that he was still the overwhelming favourite to be standing atop the podium that afternoon. Yes, LeMond would probably take the stage win, but erasing that time deficit was surely beyond him. 'I could not lose. I could not see how it could happen. It was not feasible.' Almost everyone else felt that way too. His team-mate Bjarne Riis believed that 50 seconds would be an ample buffer. 'Yeah, absolutely. We were pretty confident.' While a Super U insider would be expected to be calmly optimistic, the impartial photographer Graham Watson agrees with the universal appraisal of the situation. 'It would have been a drunk or rare bird that stood up before the stage and announced LeMond would beat Fignon.'

There was one person in Paris who doubted destiny – Gregory James LeMond. His resolve, hinted at in those nightly post-stage TV interviews, had grown and grown with each day. LeMond had done the maths and he had convinced himself. He was a believer. And that morning, as Kathy explains, he converted someone else to the faith.

'My dad was the nicest, most optimistic guy you could ever meet. That morning, when everyone was sitting around the Hilton in Paris, he said he was going to go for a walk. What he really did was take a cab and go to see Greg at the Sofitel. Greg had just come back from his morning warm-up and said, "I feel really good, Dave. I think I can do it." Dad comes back to the Hilton and tells me he thinks Greg's going to do it.

'"Oh my God, Dad. Stop it. That's impossible."

'"No, no. I went and saw him."

'"What?! I don't even talk to Greg on the morning of a time trial. He's always keyed up."

'"No, we had a good talk."

'My dad was so sure that Greg was going to win that he took Geoffrey, our five-year-old, and stood by the podium with him so he could see his dad win this thing. My dad believed so much in Greg and I was the naysayer! I was like, "Let's not be so greedy. Do you know how lucky we are?" We would have been very happy with second.'

As the shadows lengthened in the late-afternoon sunshine, the last two riders circled each other in the warm-up area, two boxers waiting for the other to land the first punch. LeMond certainly didn't look like someone who might be happy with second place. Instead, with Oakley shades, teardrop helmet and those aerobars, he appeared inscrutable. Invincible, even. Fignon, on the other hand – professorial spectacles, ponytail flapping lightly in the breeze, regular handlebars – looked vulnerable. Beatable, possibly. These last three weeks had been a battle royal between riders, between styles, between philosophies. It was about to be decided once and for all.

Thirty minutes and the champion would be anointed.

SEVENTEEN

THIRTY MINUTES FROM IMMORTALITY

'Eight seconds for 3,500 kilometres is not much, but that is the law of sport'
– Cyrille Guimard

THE LAST TWO gladiators prepare for battle.

4.12pm

Greg LeMond lifts his cherry-red Bottecchia bike up the metal steps of the time trial start house for the fourth and final time in the 1989 Tour de France. All three other occasions have been vital in getting him to this particular juncture, in keeping him just about within touching distance of Laurent Fignon, but this is the one that will matter. If he gets it right, this is the time trial that the world will remember forever.

He allows himself a quick glance up the boulevard that stretches into the distance before him. Just a glance, though. His eyes, encased in those Oakleys, look back down to his thighs. Spending the next 15 miles almost exclusively in the tuck position, this will be his view for the next half-hour. Or notably less, if things go to plan.

The fingers of the official's right hand count down the last few seconds before departure and off he roars.

4.14pm

Fignon takes his place in the start house, electing not to wear a helmet or sunglasses. He's not wearing the headband he wore for the mountain time trial either. The hair isn't even all pulled back out of his eyes; what remains of his floppy fringe hangs and sprouts in different directions. He looks far from invincible. The pursed lips and occasional nervous glance confirm this.

4.15pm
LeMond is on the charge at an impressive lick, upholding his one tactic: to go as fast as he can for as long as he can, not unlike a 400m runner asked to run the 10,000 metres at their normal one-lap pace. Having already passed through the Porchefontaine neighbourhood, he flies under the railway viaduct in the suburb of Viroflay.

4.16pm
LeMond bears left onto the Avenue Roger Salengro. The Sunday afternoon crowds are thick here, raising their hands to shield squinting eyes from the sun.

Their hearts skip a beat when his bike momentarily, and inexplicably, wobbles. He's immediately back on the straight and narrow, though. It will be the only time in the whole run that LeMond looks remotely human. The *Guardian*'s correspondent refers to him, in his crouched position, as 'a praying mantis in search of the Fignon fly'.

4.18pm
Fignon now reaches the Avenue Roger Salengro, but the news is of concern. Despite having only been on the road for four minutes, he is already seven seconds down on LeMond. The psychological pressure just got upped by a notch or two.

LeMond motors on, past red-brick schools and tiny *tabacs* and mechanics' garages and tatty petrol stations. This is not the Paris of the tourist brochure. That will come. For now, the Tour visits the Paris of ordinary Parisians.

4.20pm
Fignon looks up to his left, momentarily distracted. Perhaps he hears a radio with the commentary turned up loud. Or maybe it was a shout from

a first-floor balcony, a fan offering an informal time check. Guimard brings his car closer for reassurance.

A mile or so up the road, LeMond bears right to follow the south bank of the Seine towards the centre of the capital. Out of the suburbs and into the city.

4.24pm
Near the offices of *L'Equipe*, LeMond crosses the Seine on the Pont d'Issy les Moulineaux, before sharply swinging right to follow the north bank of the river. He has eight more miles left to ride of this titanic race and, even though he himself is deliberately oblivious to it, the time split at this point excites the world. After seven miles, LeMond is comfortably outpacing everyone else who has passed here today. His time is 20 seconds faster than the next quickest, the Swiss rider Erich Maechler from the Carrera team. Even if he were getting the time checks, who and what has come before would be of no concern to the American and his team. Everything, absolutely everything, is about how his time compares to Fignon's.

4.26pm
Fignon reaches the Pont d'Issy les Moulineaux. There's a pause before his split is announced. And while his time is better than that of the current leader – his team-mate Thierry Marie – he nonetheless trails LeMond by 21 seconds and has yet to reach the halfway mark. Touch and go, touch and go.

Cyrille Guimard, in a possibly fate-tempting yellow shirt and with his elbow hanging out of the window, pulls the team car up to within shouting distance of Fignon. The news is delivered. Will it make him instinctively push harder or will some hastily applied mental arithmetic suggest he'll be just about safe if he maintains his current speed?

The hazy appearance of the Eiffel Tower in the distance signals the race is approaching the end game.

4.28pm
LeMond passes under the Pont de Bir-Hakeim and is now level with the Eiffel Tower on the other bank of the river. José De Cauwer keeps his distance

in the team car trailing him, obeying his rider's orders. No information, no distractions.

At the finish line, Kathy LeMond – in her shades and polka-dot dress – sits nervously. Before her, two-year-old Scott is oblivious to the tension, sleeping through the time trial in his pushchair. As she watches events unfold on a TV screen, that last split time has given Kathy hope. She turns to her mother. 'Oh my God. I think he might be able to do this.'

4.31pm
LeMond has now barrelled through the series of tunnels alongside the Seine, including the Pont d'Alma tunnel, scene of – eight years later – Princess Diana and Dodi Fayed's fatal car crash. Back down the road, on the other side of the tunnels, Fignon has reached the Pont de Bir-Hakeim. The latest time split? The pair are now divided by 29 seconds.

4.32pm
Sixth-placed Charly Mottet completes his time trial and completes his race. Once he finds out how the duel behind is shaping up, and with LeMond imminently to arrive on the Champs-Élysées, he elects to hang around the finish area. A young lad asks for an autograph. He gets some advice from his hero, too. 'Watch this. It will be historic.'

4.35pm
Fignon has now cut away from the river and is on the Rue de Rivoli, passing under the banner indicating that just four kilometres of this year's Tour remain. He'll soon be across the Place de la Concorde and into the lion's den of the Champs-Élysées. LeMond is already more than halfway up the iconic boulevard, hugging the left-hand kerb to give him the most shelter.

4.37pm
LeMond takes the turn in front of the Arc de Triomphe, his arms coming off the aerobars for the first time since Versailles so that he can safely negotiate the hairpin. Once speed has been regained, it's back into the tuck position that's served him so well until now and a flat-out push downhill to the line. It's the last effort after more than 2,000 miles and 87+ hours in the saddle.

He's a blur to the packed pavements, and the packed pavements are a blur to him.

4.38pm
All the vehicles trailing LeMond, save for a couple of official cars, are diverted away from the finish down a side road, meaning José De Cauwer is unable to watch the moment his team leader completes his Tour of duty. Race radio will have to suffice for now.

Beyond the finish line, LeMond's beefy *soigneur*, Otto Jacome, hears the latest split. '48? Ooooh! Oh my God! Jesus Christ…' This may just well be the crowning glory of the Mexican's long association with LeMond, the man whose presence, says Kathy, 'was like therapy for Greg. He had someone he could trust after the backstabbing of the '86 Tour – to know his food was safe and his bike was right.'

4.39pm
LeMond crosses the line in a time of 26 minutes and 57 seconds – an astounding average speed of 34mph. It is the fastest stage in 86 years of the Tour de France. Sean Yates's record has been smashed. Kathy hugs father-in-law Bob before her husband whooshes by, freewheeling through the finish area. In all the hubbub, he doesn't hear her cries: 'Greggggggg!'. Jacome rushes to greet his rider, attending to his immediate needs like that boxing trainer, instant praise in the ear of his fighter at the end of a bout. Then the pair are lost, swallowed by a media scrum. It is now a waiting game. Fignon must finish in less than 27 minutes and 47 seconds to take the title for the third time.

4.40pm
Fignon is struggling for momentum on the gentle rise towards the Arc de Triomphe, coming out of the saddle in a desperate search for rhythm – or, with that boil a constant thorn, in a desperate search for a pain-free riding style. He is nowhere near as fluid as LeMond was. To the naked eye, he looks like he's continuing to lose time. When he reaches the hairpin, this is confirmed. The kerbside crowd winces and a nation grows fearful. Fignon is now 53 seconds behind, making LeMond champion as things stand. It's

no longer defence and preservation. He now needs to actually *gain* a few seconds on his rival before the finish line, less than two minutes away. If he doesn't, the race will have slipped through his fingers.

In the finish area, LeMond, his ears cocooned in a chunky pair of Radio France headphones to eavesdrop on the station's commentary, doesn't dare to dream. In fact, he's still in the dark, unable to hear anything because of all the noise around him.

4.41pm

The huge flotilla following Fignon down the Champs-Élysées – including around 20 motorbikes and, with the Frenchman being the last rider, the broom wagon – is waved off the course. Guimard disappears down the same side road as almost everyone else, leaving Fignon to face the last agonising minute alone, a vulnerable figure on this wide boulevard, a tiny boat in a giant ocean.

4.42pm

A side-wind slightly blows Fignon off course, but it's inconsequential. It's already over. The target time has gone. The unforgiving official clock – as Delgado found all those weeks back in Luxembourg – waits for no cyclist, regardless of the hue of his jersey. The margin of defeat is eight seconds. Eight. Seconds.

Fignon dramatically collapses to the ground, in front of a cordon of gendarmes protecting the finish area. Darkness descends on his world. The colours fly away. Then the tears come, great sobbing tears of despair. The glasses off, the guard down.

A few yards away, Kathy LeMond's anxiety hasn't abated. She searches for clarification from all around her. 'Did he win or not?' She spins around and Greg is trotting towards her, clip-clopping across the road in his cleats. His embrace and passionate kisses answer her question. She is married to the Tour de France champion once again.

***

Paris was stunned. Europe was stunned. The world was stunned.

Something very epic had just occurred. The words of Daniel Mangeas, the announcer on the Champs-Élysées who had embarked on an impromptu countdown over the PA system, had ensured the drama was high for all those gathered in the capital. 'When Fignon was approaching the line,' Mangeas told *Cycling Weekly*, 'my colleague shouted at me that he had ten seconds left to save the Tour. I just started counting down like that. Ten, nine, eight, seven... I got to zero and that was it. Greg had won the Tour and, above all at that moment, I wanted Fignon not to have heard me counting down.'

Already back in his hotel room, Johan Lammerts had showered and lay on the bed. He couldn't believe the performance that his room-mate had just put in. 'It was so exciting, seeing Greg pedal with so much power.' The French TV commentator, though, focused less on LeMond's achievements and more on the self-destruction of the hometown boy: 'Laurent Fignon a perdu le Tour de France'. His voice was a mixture of the sorrowful compatriot and the story-hunter journalist.

On the Reynolds bus, an undressing Pedro Delgado had been shaken by the roar from the finish line. 'I heard an explosion. "What happened?" "Fignon lost." "What?!" "Yes, by eight seconds." Incredible.'

In the sponsors' pavilion just a stone's throw from the action, the Super U entourage had been in a cheery mood for much of the day. As Fignon rolled out from Versailles, his team-mate Bjarne Riis was basking in the glow of having finished his first Tour. That was before the time splits began filtering through, after which the pavilion grew increasingly quiet. 'All the riders were standing there,' Riis recalls, 'watching the last couple of minutes. "Oh no, no, no!" We were thinking about the prize money we were losing that we'd been working for the whole race. But it wasn't just the money. We felt so sorry for him. We had been so supportive but everything had fallen apart.' The only sound breaking the shocked silence in the pavilion were the sobs of the wives and girlfriends gathered for the intended celebrations. Thierry Marie, who had finished second on the stage, couldn't be comforted. 'If only I could have swapped my time trial with Fignon's...'

All had witnessed arguably the greatest comeback in sporting history. In comparison, even an occasion of the magnitude of the Rumble in the Jungle – where the 32-year-old Muhammad Ali regained the world heavyweight title having been stripped of it (and his boxing licence) seven years previously – had been cast into the shadows. This was now the biggest sports story of them all. The Tour de France had been won by a man who had cheated death, who had pellets still lodged in his body, who had been on the verge of quitting the sport the previous month, who had largely ridden solo because of the weakness of his team, and who had produced the fastest time trial in the race's history, overturning a seemingly impossible time margin.

In the Channel 4 studio in London, pundit and two-time Olympic medallist Mick Bennett gave a from-the-heart appraisal of what he'd just seen: 'The most exciting piece of television I think perhaps since JR got shot.' The full drama of the occasion had been experienced by British viewers through the excitement and expertise of commentators Phil Liggett and Paul Sherwen.

'Oh, bloody hell,' says Sherwen. 'Phil and I will always talk about that being one of the greatest moments. We work as a team. I went to university and did a science degree. My background is mathematics. To this day, I'm always trying to work out the permutations. Back then, when I was working things out and passing information on to Phil, he trusted me incredibly – "This is what's happening, this is the gap, it's going this way, it's going that way, blah blah blah". Eventually, though, on the finish line, it wasn't me who called it. Phil called it to perfection.' In bringing the '89 Tour to British viewers, they operated like a pair of election night broadcasters, Liggett calling the results and Sherwen offering the data-driven predictions. In place of a swingometer, though, was just some paper and a pen. And perhaps a pocket calculator.

An election only has one winner. The rest have to lose. And none lost as heavily as Fignon. The author Edward Pickering made an excellent attempt at inhabiting the Parisian's head as he fulfilled his obligation to attend the podium presentation. 'Imagine the confused sense of self-consciousness he must have felt with every movement, the stabbing jolt of adrenalin in his chest, the jelly weakness of his legs, the knowledge that if he could just do the day over again, there's no way he'd lose the yellow jersey.'

'Being on the podium with Fignon was terrible,' says Delgado. 'He had the Tour in his hands. I felt bad for him. For his sporting character, he was more deserving to be the winner. He was more aggressive, more athletic. I would have preferred to have lost to him, not LeMond.' There were brave smiles on the podium – from Fignon himself and from the other two directed at him. But neither LeMond nor Delgado would have wanted to be standing in his shoes, caught in the collective gaze of a disappointed nation.

History was being made at the presentation. It was the first time that three previous winners stood together on the podium; they were also the respective winners of that season's three Grand Tours to boot. Plus, with LeMond's father-in-law handing over five-year-old Geoffrey to his dad (who promptly placed him on the top step of the podium), 1989 was the first time that the champion's offspring joined in the celebrations, a practice revived in recent times by both Bradley Wiggins and Chris Froome. 'They hadn't seen each other in so long,' says Kathy. 'It was really sweet that my dad did that.'

The inquests had begun the moment Fignon collapsed in a heap on the tarmac from exhaustion and would be conducted long into the night. Had he been over-confident or eaten up with nerves and worry? Should he be chastised for not adopting aerobars or commended for his neo-purist stance? Or was he, despite riding his own fastest time trial ever, simply defeated by a remarkable, seemingly superhuman effort? The protagonists lined up to offer their diagnosis.

'Fignon should have won,' Marino Lejarreta told *Cycling Weekly*, 'and I think if he'd really considered LeMond a threat, he would have gone all out in the first half of the race and wiped him out. Fignon paid a high price for underestimating him.'

José De Cauwer's assessment was shot through with the insight of a *directeur sportif.* 'Fignon is a proud man. He wanted to win the Tour in a certain style, by clenching his fist and shouting "I will win the Tour this way". But he didn't make the smartest decisions.'

'He definitely regretted not using aerobars,' concludes Bjarne Riis, 'no doubt about that. The only reason he didn't was because he was unsure of their potential and didn't have enough time to test them out. He was probably a little stubborn, too. But at that point it was too late.'

Sean Yates puts it down to technology. 'Physically, they were neck-and-neck. It was purely down to the aerodynamics. Ultimately the blame should be upon Guimard, although you can't really blame him when the knowledge was not out there. Even my best friend – who's got honours degrees in mathematics and physics and this, that and the other – could not see the advantage of tribars. This is a guy with degrees from Oxford. I'm a guy who's never taken an exam in his life and to me it's a no-brainer! When you study a downhill skier, they keep compact for a reason. It's to make them go a lot faster. But back in those days, no one really had a grasp of how important aerodynamics were – having tribars or wearing a helmet. Or not having a ponytail…'

The inventor of those aerobars, Boone Lennon, modestly attributed it to LeMond's superb fitness, which improved day after day on the Tour. 'He probably could have done what he did anyway is the feeling I have. The handlebars were perhaps a replacement for a weak team. He didn't have a team to help him through all the road stages, to do all the chasing down and the counterattacks and so on. The handlebars helped him out in the time trial as a replacement for that.'

Paul Sherwen believes Fignon's wellbeing to have been crucial. 'It was totally and utterly illogical that Greg won. But did we know the physical situation with Fignon? Did we know he was injured? Did we know he was as badly off as he was? And that's where you still keep the suspense in the sport.'

And Fignon had kept the suspense, with no one outside his team knowing how serious his saddle sore was. That evening, in the aftermath of the time trial, he admitted he'd not slept well for two nights because of the pain. But then came an even more staggering disclosure. 'If the race had gone on until Monday, I believe I would have abandoned.' Ex-rider Sherwen knows how much such discomfort can affect performance. 'If Fignon didn't have the saddle boil that he had, it would have been a lot closer. And if the time trial had been 20 kilometres, he'd have won. That's why the Tour de France organisation was so lucky with the design of the route.'

The anticlimax that might have been offered by an inconsequential final-day time trial had been averted. Instead, three weeks of fierce, guts-out, heart-on-the-sleeve racing was blessed by the high-drama denouement it truly deserved. That last final-day time trial in 1968, the one that had produced the narrowest margin of victory in the race's history, hadn't just been equalled, it had been eclipsed. 'Fortune favoured them,' agrees Yates. 'They couldn't have written the script any better. Well, I suppose the French guy could have won it by two seconds…'

Despite having left his Tour director role more than a year earlier, Jean-Francois Naquet-Radiguet could bask in the satisfaction that the final day he'd decreed had been rewarded with the brilliant finish. The greatest ever. 'Of course,' he told Daniel Friebe, 'you could say Laurent Fignon lost the Tour because of me. I thought he was going to hunt me down and kill me! But that was the race. You either want sport, competition, a race, or you can have a procession. I thought we wanted sport.'

In his autobiography, Fignon describes, very vividly, what the minutes after the time trial felt like. 'I walk like a boxer who's concussed, in an improbable world of furious noise. The steps I take are robotic and aren't directed at anything. I've no idea where I am going and who is making me go there. I feel arms supporting me, helping me to stand up. People make noise around me. Some shout. Some look haggard, groggy, wiped out. Others are celebrating.'

Punch-drunk and perplexed, Fignon's reaction was, quite understandably, the polar opposite of LeMond's. 'I was afraid I would lose by just one second,' the American gushed in the chaotic aftermath. 'I could hear the speaker counting down the seconds. It was terrible. But today has been the greatest moment of my life.' The smile was broader than the Seine, the eyes sparkled brighter than the stars.

That night, and with just three other team-mates making it to Paris, the ADR celebrations weren't overly flamboyant. The remains of the squad, plus Kathy and parents, went for a meal and took in a show at the Moulin Rouge. By midnight, the LeMonds were back on the Champs-Élysées, reliving the previous three tumultuous weeks over late-night ice cream. Super U still had their party ('a good few litres of champagne,' says Bjarne Riis), but when the first editions of the morning papers began to appear late in the night, someone sensibly decided to keep them out of Fignon's eyeline.

There were so many points in the race where, had things happened only slightly differently, the result would have taken a much different complexion. Certainly, with a victory of such a slender margin, it would have taken very little to produce a much-altered race. What if Pedro Delgado had remembered how to tell the time? What if the ADR team hadn't performed so well in the team time trial? What if Cyrille Guimard's car could have forced its way through to Fignon earlier up Alpe d'Huez? What if PDM hadn't so enthusiastically pursued the yellow jersey into Villard-de-Lans? And what if Boone Lennon hadn't applied the science of skiing to the beautiful sport of cycling?

Ifs, buts and maybes. The language of the peloton.

'Greg won because he was able to pull off an amazing time trial on the last day,' Fignon generously reflected a few years later. 'Me? I wasn't able to go any faster. So there you have it. There's no injustice.

'It's just that I lost the Tour by eight seconds. That's all.'

Stage 21
1. Greg LeMond (ADR/USA) 26'57"
2. Thierry Marie (Super U/France) +33"
3. Laurent Fignon (Super U/France) +58"
4. Jelle Nijdam (Superconfex/Netherlands) +1'07"
5. Sean Yates (7-Eleven/GB) +1'10"

Points competition
1. Sean Kelly (PDM/Ireland) 277pts
2. Etienne De Wilder (Histor/Belgium) 194pts
3. Steven Rooks (PDM/Netherlands) 163pts

King of the Mountains competition
1. Gert-Jan Theunisse (PDM/Netherlands) 441pts
2. Pedro Delgado (Reynolds/Spain) 311 pts
3. Steven Rooks (PDM/Netherlands) 257pts

Combined competition
1. Steven Rooks (PDM/Netherlands) 15pts
2. Laurent Fignon (Super U/France) 20pts
3. Sean Kelly (PDM/Ireland) 22pts

Team competition
1. PDM (Netherlands) 263:19:48
2. Reynolds (Spain) +1'19"
3. Z-Peugeot (France) +44'22"

Overall

1. Greg LeMond (ADR/USA) 87:38:35
2. Laurent Fignon (Super U/France) +8"
3. Pedro Delgado (Reynolds/Spain) +3'34"
4. Gert-Jan Theunisse (PDM/Netherlands) +7'30"
5. Marino Lejarreta (Paternina/Spain) +9'39"
6. Charly Mottet (RMO/France) +10'06"
7. Steven Rooks (PDM/Netherlands) +11'10"
8. Raúl Alcalá (PDM/Mexico) +14'21"
9. Sean Kelly (PDM/Ireland) +18'25"
10. Robert Millar (Z-Peugeot/GB) +18'46"

EIGHTEEN

THE AFTERMATH

'Fignon never once set foot on the Champs-Élysées again'
– Kathy LeMond

THE MORNING AFTER the afternoon before.

If Greg and Kathy LeMond needed to reassure each other that the extraordinary events of the previous afternoon had indeed happened in exactly the dizzying, delirious manner they remembered, they were to only switch on a TV set or glance up at a newsstand for confirmation. In every direction they looked, there were images of LeMond's astonished face breaking into that boy-next-door smile. Not that the coverage universally focused on his record-breaking ride and near-tragic back story. Laurent Fignon's brave capitulation received equal billing. Perhaps France preferred this particular sportsman as humbled loser than cocksure winner. Sympathy for the old devil.

LeMond's impact wasn't limited to the cycling-literate quarters of old Europe. When the United States woke up later in the day, it was to the story of a new sporting hero, a tale with many tick-boxing ingredients: a blond-haired, blue-eyed protagonist, slightly flawed at the edges, whose life had known lashings of triumph and adversity. An editor's dream. And those American editors did LeMond justice; *USA Today*, the *New York Times* and the *Washington Post* all put this comparatively little-known athlete on their front pages. It didn't end there. In their year-closing issue five months later, *Sports Illustrated* would anoint LeMond as their Sportsman of the Year, beating the likes of Joe Montana and Wayne Gretzky to the honour and being rewarded with the front cover and a 14-page interview.

Not that the LeMonds were remotely ready for their lives being prised open for public consumption. After Greg raced a 37-mile exhibition race around the Normandy town of Lisieux just 24 hours after the time trial, the family sneaked away to nearby Deauville, going into hiding for a couple of days in one of the seaside resort's many hotels. 'We didn't go back home to Belgium for two days because it was like a riot in our street,' says Kathy. 'There were thousands of people there. Our neighbours were calling us and saying, "Don't come home. It's just crazy."'

Over the weeks that followed, LeMond took part in nearly a dozen criterium races. Not only were these races pleasingly lucrative to the world-conquering but still unpaid cyclist, but tradition also dictated he be allowed to race in the yellow jersey he won in Paris. Time to bask in the golden glow the jersey emitted. As a fellow competitor in several of these races, the still-grieving Fignon found this difficult to stomach. 'I gritted my teeth,' he said. 'My blood froze.'

And it wasn't just the criteriums. LeMond found his earning potential had gone through the roof, with offers from teams to lead their squads into the 1990 season flooding in. Not that the bidding war had broken out only after his coronation in Paris. Ever since he won the Rennes time trial during the first week of the Tour, teams that had previously refused to take a gamble on him – or, indeed, had refused to take his return remotely seriously – were now forming an orderly queue and expressing their desire to lure him away from ADR. In fact, one team boss – Roger Legeay from Z – had approached LeMond prior to the time trial, when the American had yet to prove himself at all.

'Roger Legeay spoke to Greg before Greg had won anything,' confirms Kathy. 'He said, "You know what? I think you can do this." He was very kind to Greg that day. And not a lot of people, not a lot of coaches, were kind to him during those couple of years. They were laughing at him.'

Once victory at Rennes was confirmed, the feeding frenzy began. Len Pettyjohn, in France as the boss of sister team Coors Light but without a portfolio of specific duties on European soil, took it upon himself to become the unofficial deal-maker. He would be the man to meet and greet, and to be wined and dined by, LeMond's many suitors. Pettyjohn's first lunch date was with one of the team directors of a French squad.

'Greg's going to be available next year. What's your interest?'

'Well, what do you think in terms of salary? We know Greg might be expensive, but we're very interested in having him on the team.'

'You have to understand his salary is six, seven hundred thousand dollars. Clearly he's worth that, which means you're going to have to pay more than that.'

'No problem, no problem. We can do seven.'

The next day, Pettyjohn found himself having lunch with another team.

'Greg's going to be available...'

'Oh yeah? How much?'

'Well, it's going to take at least seven-fifty, maybe eight.'

'We can do that. No problem.'

'The next day I had another lunch with somebody else. After about five lunches, we were at a million dollars. LeMond comes back to me. "Oh my God! Let's have more lunches!"'

Three teams in particular were under serious consideration. Joining Z in the thoughts of Pettyjohn and the LeMonds were Toshiba and 7-Eleven. The American team seemed the most obvious fit, even more so after the Tour ended and their existing leader Andy Hampsten had registered that disappointing 22nd place finish. Jim Ochowicz's team appeared to be Bob LeMond's preferred destination for his son, too; the ADR experience had singed LeMond Sr's fingers, as well as leaving bank accounts somewhat lighter than they should have been. It was left to Pettyjohn to sound a note of caution.

'Bob goes, "I don't trust the Europeans now. Look at what they did to Greg before." I said, "OK, Bob. Here's the deal. Look at this report." At that time, 7-Eleven were going public and they did a leverage buyout to sell the company. They were so much in debt. They were on the verge of bankruptcy. "So, whatever you think of the Europeans, and whatever you sign with 7-Eleven, the team is going to go away and they're going to fail." And after one more year, 7-Eleven went away. And that's when Motorola came into the picture.

'Ochowicz wasn't going after any other riders at that time, either. He was convinced Greg was signing for him. But all the time behind the scenes, he was being out-negotiated. If he knew, he'd have pissed a shit-fit.'

That Team LeMond drew back from discussions with 7-Eleven – which were quite advanced, with a contract having been drawn up – secretly pleased Hampsten. 'It wasn't a make-or-break situation. It would have been great for the team, but it wouldn't have been my first choice. It would have meant I absolutely wouldn't have been the leader. While it would have been really cool and fun to have helped Greg win the Tour, I'd rather be the captain.'

That left Z and Toshiba at the negotiation table. The latter's presence was surprising, given that they were the team that had callously served notice on LeMond distastefully soon after he was discharged from hospital after the hunting accident. The fact that they were the team offering the fattest contract – $6m over three years – might explain why they were still under consideration. Alternatively, LeMond might just have been stringing them along, a minor act of revenge after his treatment by them. 'I wanted to screw Toshiba,' he later admitted to *Procycling* magazine.

Certainly LeMond would have enjoyed one particular approach they made to Len Pettyjohn a month after the Tour ended. 'The night before the world championships in Chambéry, teams were still coming up to me – "Is it possible to still negotiate with Greg?" Teams were now desperate. I was having dinner with Alexi Grewal, who was on the American team for the world championships, when the director-general of Toshiba came over. There was no chair, so he got down on one knee and leaned against the table. "It is very important that we negotiate again with Greg."

'This was a man who, a few weeks before, would not acknowledge my presence. Now he's so desperate that he's almost begging. Alexi was shaking his head, laughing. "I told you. They're all crazy here."

In truth, Roger Legeay and Z were always the preferred choice, thanks to that chat on the rest day ahead of the Rennes time trial. 'There is something to be said for people who are with you when you're not great,' says Kathy. 'You feel more comfortable. They seem more honest. It's easy to jump on the bandwagon, but it's pretty darned nice to have someone who believed in you before.' An agreement was made on the morning of the world championships – a three-year deal worth $5.5m – although, at that point, nothing was signed.

A spanner was tossed into the works that afternoon when, in the sheeting Chambéry rain, LeMond gloriously won the world title for the second time, brilliantly outsprinting Sean Kelly and the young Russian rider Dmitri Konyshev. 'Roger Legeay came to our hotel that night,' recalls Kathy. 'He was just shaking. "I suppose you want something more now." Greg said, "No, no, no. I already told you yes. We're good."'

As well as the faith shown in him by Legeay, LeMond had been lured by the opportunity to lead a much stronger squad than the paper-thin one he inherited at ADR. At the 1990 Tour, in Robert Millar, Éric Boyer and Ronan Pensec alone, he had three riders with experience of finishing in the race's top ten. Millar, of course, would also provide LeMond with formidable assistance in the mountains, an alien concept during his season at ADR. Plus, not only could he also take his close friend and colleague Johan Lammerts with him, the contract with Z determined that the team would ride LeMond bikes. This had been a potential deal-breaker.

Not that extricating himself from his existing contract at ADR was without its complications. Despite not having paid LeMond his two blocks of wages for January and July, as well as his bonus for winning the Tour, François Lambert still believed he had a legitimate claim to LeMond's services, even though a 30-day resignation notice had been served on him for violation of the contract.

'Lambert no doubt thought that my Tour win would bring in sponsors and solve all the problems,' LeMond told *Procycling*. 'It didn't matter. I'd already decided that I was leaving. I would only have stayed if there'd been a major new backer and if Lambert had left. He embarked on this vast PR campaign, telling everyone that I was betraying the team that had saved me. He even got my own agent to sue me for ten per cent of what I went on to earn at the Z team.'

There's a fantastic story that not only illustrates Lambert's desperation to hang on to LeMond, but also his shaky grasp of matters legal. It's a tale that has a different version according to whoever's telling it. Details get changed or blurred – the when, the where, the who, the how much. But the fundamental ingredients include Lambert's 6.9-litre Mercedes; a 200kph drive through the night; an alleyway in Luxembourg; a gunnysack filled with Belgian francs; several thousand dollars' worth of speeding tickets; a kitchen table covered with cash; and a deflated team boss who's just realised the redundancy of the whole endeavour.

Essentially it's the story of how François Lambert turned up at the LeMonds' house in Belgium in the wee small hours, ready to pay them what he owed in outstanding wages. Greg and Kathy weren't home, but Bob and Bertha LeMond were house-sitting. Having presented the cash, Lambert believed he'd righted his wrongs and that his team leader now had to honour the second and final year of his contract.

However, the cash only covered the January amount. July's money, plus the Tour win bonus, remained outstanding and Lambert was now outside the time period for making the payment, allowing LeMond to walk away. The next morning, Bob LeMond called his son, asking for advice. 'Take it to a bank and wire it to America!'

The announcement of the deal with Z was made at a press conference in a hotel ballroom in Paris in mid-September. There, LeMond expressed his delight in joining such a professional and experienced team ('Z has the climbers I will need to help me win the Tour again'), while he also fended off questions as to why he hadn't done the obvious thing and signed up with 7-Eleven. 'It just didn't work out,' he defended. 'There were some things they just couldn't guarantee. We tried to work it out, but in the end Z was a better deal for me. I had to think of my career.'

Not only had LeMond been a popular Tour winner in '89 among the French population, but the decision to join his third French team, after Renault and La Vie Claire, further endeared him to the nation. 'I think the French really appreciated Greg because he learned French,' says Pettyjohn. 'He made a clear gesture, a clear attempt, in his own charming, boyish way. They really embraced him.' Having a French-sounding surname, one that suggested a rich lineage on his father's side, possibly with an ancestral chateau or two lurking in some corner of the family tree, certainly did him no harm.

Less than 12 months later, LeMond delighted Roger Legeay by securing a third Tour title. Although, at two minutes and 19 seconds, the margin of victory was somewhat more comfortable than in '89, the race was far from a foregone conclusion. LeMond didn't win a single stage and only took the yellow jersey from the emerging Italian rider Claudio Chiappucci on the penultimate day. True to form, he had taken the lead thanks to his performance on the race's last time trial.

His decision to join the well-organised Z team, with experience running throughout the entire squad, meant LeMond's extraordinary record in the Tour had been maintained. Enhanced, even. Five starts, five podium finishes, including, now, a hat-trick of victories. He had also become the first rider to win the Tour with three different teams – La Vie Claire, ADR and Z.

'Z got a great deal,' says Pettyjohn. 'They won the Tour. And most teams would be happy winning the Tour de France one time, no matter how much it cost. It's much different in Europe than it is in the United States. The sport is so big in Europe – you can get patrons who will pay, whereas in the United States, it has to make business sense. It makes emotional sense to the European guys.'

As cycling's first non-European superstar, LeMond had helped transform the Tour into a global event, in the process improving the financial stability of the professional rider. 'Everything came together for him. And, again, it was the second time that he impacted the sport in that way, that an athlete could command that kind of salary. When he first signed for Renault, that was an astronomical amount of money. That caused all kinds of headlines – and there were mostly critical headlines, because people looked at him as being so greedy. How could an athlete expect or demand or be worth that kind of money? But Greg turned the sport around.'

**

As the world gathered around LeMond on that Sunday afternoon in late July to cheer, celebrate and sing his praises, to bathe him in the sunshine of popularity, Fignon entered a period of introspection, self-analysis and mourning. 'I went home. Alone. Just sitting. Or wandering about with my eyes going nowhere.'

Staying out of the public eye was probably the best course of action. 'Monsieur Eight Seconds: just try to get your head around the weeks that followed my defeat,' he later reflected. 'Imagine the mocking remarks from the people who didn't like me. Think of all the shocking, over-the-top stuff that was said and written.'

After the Paris time trial ended, Pedro Delgado witnessed exactly what Fignon would be subjected to in the following weeks, months, even years: his fellow countrymen making no attempt to disguise their pleasure at his humiliation. 'Not all the French people loved Fignon. After that day, I took a taxi to go to the hotel. The driver said "Ah, you are Pedro Delgado! I support you. I love you."

"OK, thank you, thank you."

"I was happy for Fignon to have lost the Tour de France."

"Why? You are French."

"He's a bad guy. I don't like Fignon."

This was not an atypical response. Fignon talked about the 'morbid curiosity' when he appeared in that summer's criterium races: 'Just imagine: "there he is"; "that's him"; "the loser".' Morbid curiosity was at the paler end of the spectrum. Scorn and ridicule became the norm, the dish of the day. Every day, every single day. Fignon just had to work out strategies to cope with it without further ostracising himself from the cycling fans of his homeland. 'You never stop grieving over an event like that; the best you can manage is to contain the effect it has on your mind.'

Once that painful boil had cleared up, he was back in the saddle, fulfilling his criterium contracts before heading to Utrecht for the seven-stage Ronde van Nederland – aka the Tour of Holland. Just 11 seconds separated the first four in the general classification, but it was Fignon who took the overall victory, a single second the difference between him and team-mate Thierry Marie. The summer of fine margins continued.

From there, Fignon and Marie travelled to northern Italy to create a formidable partnership at the Baracchi Trophy, a two-up time trial. With two of the world's greatest time trialists joining forces, the result was a foregone conclusion. These wins in the Netherlands and Italy not only accelerated Fignon's mental recuperation, but also kept him out of arms' reach of his detractors back home.

At the end of August, Fignon was back in the Alps for the world championships in Chambéry. But if he went there in search of revenge over

LeMond, he was out of luck. His nemesis across the three weeks of the Tour wasn't going to roll over. If fact, he wasn't going to give Fignon an inch. On the final lap of the circuit, the Frenchman launched attack after attack. Despite being lashed by heavy rain, making visibility difficult through his spectacles, the Frenchman put in what looked like a decisive break on the sharp ascent of Côte de Montagnole, leaving the likes of LeMond and Sean Kelly in his wake as he tried to bridge the gap to the three leaders. It brought back all the memories of the Villard-de-Lans stage in the Tour, when he simply pushed down hard on the pedals and moved away from his rivals.

This time, however, LeMond had an answer, eventually appearing on Fignon's shoulder, having seemingly appeared from nowhere. He then gamely put in three more attacks on the damp, 60mph descent, but LeMond nullified each one, before taking the victory himself. Fignon's only consolation was that his sixth place – allied to the wins in the Tours of Italy and Holland, and being runner-up in the Tour de France – ensured that he became the new world number one by the end of the year.

But the pair weren't to re-engage their rivalry in the Tour the following summer, Fignon abandoning on the fifth stage with an ankle injury. By then, his team had found a new sponsor – Castorama – in whose colours he rode to sixth place overall in 1991. His final Tour was in 1993, his final day a mountain stage into Val d'Isère. 'I felt fantastic and attacked at the foot of the Galibier,' he told *Cycle Sport*. 'I felt I was climbing well. But in the blink of an eye, 30 riders had come past me, and I believed I was in good form. Thirty riders, just like that. And after that, I was riding with people I did not believe I would ever be riding with in the mountains. People who were riding on EPO. At that moment, I knew that I was dead. Too old. Finished. I rode in, tried to lose as little time as possible, and abandoned the race the next day.'

Despite still being regarded as the tragic figure who lost the '89 Tour rather than the triumphant victor of the race in both '83 and '84, Fignon remained in cycling after his retirement. For many years, he organised big races, such as Paris-Nice. By then, the maddeningly impetuous man he'd often been during his riding days had noticeably mellowed. Having been awarded the 'prix citron' by the press pack for being the rudest, most uncooperative rider on the '89 Tour (he won by an absolute landslide), a new Fignon emerged once he was permanently out of the saddle. As Edward Pickering wrote, 'the touchy, arrogant, over-sensitive double Tour winner/Tour loser seemed to have been left behind in the pages of old newspapers and magazines'.

Pedro Delgado agrees. 'A lot of people in France grew to like him later. After the Tour of 1989, his character changed totally. He was more relaxed, more friendly. For him as a person, it was better that he lost the Tour that day.'

Not that he ever exorcised the ghosts of that final-day time trial. It not only defined his public persona, but was also a permanent presence in his psyche, as Kathy LeMond reveals. 'A few years back, he and Greg golfed together. He told Greg losing by eight seconds had been the worst thing of his life. Greg felt so bad. Fignon said that almost every time he walked to his mailbox, he'd count out eight and say "Oh my God. Eight seconds. That's nothing."

'Greg said that, the day they were out golfing, two different French people came up and said to him "Hey Fignon! Eight seconds!" – like he was a loser. He had to deal with that every day, instead of "Oh my gosh, you won two Tours and you also came second". It was really a burden. But he was so, so talented. Greg said, "Can you believe he's looked at as a failure, rather than the winner that he actually is?" We had no idea.'

Verbal taunts weren't the only ongoing legacy, the only still-visible scars. In the summer of 2016, the LeMonds had lunch with Fignon's widow, who told them something astonishing. 'After 1989,' Kathy explains, 'he never once set foot on the Champs-Élysées again. And he lived in Paris. For a Parisian to not go on the Champs-Élysées? How do you avoid it?' It was the equivalent of a Manhattanite steering clear of Fifth Avenue for two whole decades, or a Londoner giving Oxford Street a permanent wide berth. For Fignon, his home city forever reminded him of that fateful Sunday in July.

His escape from this torment was even more tragic. Having been diagnosed the previous spring, Laurent Fignon succumbed to cancer of the lungs and the digestive system on the last day of August 2010. He was 50 years old. Even in death, though, the personality traits of his younger days continued to outweigh his extremely notable achievements on a bicycle. His obituary in the *New York Times* bore the unbelievable headline: 'Laurent Fignon, Gruff French Cyclist, Dies At 50'.

'My career saw the end of the last untroubled age of bike racing,' he elegantly reflected in his autobiography, published a year before his death. 'The men of that era still looked each other in the eye. We didn't tiptoe away when the time came to light the fuse: we preferred rousing anthems to gentle lullabies.

'And we didn't mind getting burned if necessary. A true cyclist sometimes has to bite the dust before he can reach the stars.'

The painful warrior famoused for fight
After a thousand victories once foil'd
Is from the book of honour razed quite
And all the rest forgot for which he toil'd

William Shakespeare, Sonnet XXV

BIBLIOGRAPHY

Samuel Abt, *Greg LeMond: The Incredible Comeback* (Stanley Paul)

Guy Andrews, *Greg LeMond: Yellow Jersey Racer* (Bloomsbury)

Klaus Bellon Gaitán, 'Nervous But Prepared', in Ellis Bacon & Lionel Birnie, *The Cycling Anthology, Volume Two* (Yellow Jersey)

Peter Cossins, 'Dutch Mountain', in Ellis Bacon & Lionel Birnie, *The Cycling Anthology, Volume Six* (Peloton Publishing)

Geoff Drake (with Jim Ochowicz), *Team 7-Eleven: How an Unlikely Band of American Cyclists Took on the World – And Won* (Velo Press)

Laurent Fignon, *We Were Young and Carefree* (Yellow Jersey)

William Fotheringham, 'Napoleon', in Ellis Bacon & Lionel Birnie, *The Cycling Anthology, Volume Two* (Yellow Jersey)

William Fotheringham, *Roule Britannia: A History of Britons in the Tour de France* (Yellow Jersey)

Daniel Friebe, 'The Cognac Salesman and the Conman', in Ellis Bacon & Lionel Birnie (eds), *The Cycling Anthology, Volume Five* (Yellow Jersey)

Javier García Sanchez, *Induráin: A Tempered Passion* (Mousehold Press)

Johnny Green, *Push Yourself Just A Little Bit More: Backstage at the Tour de France* (Orion)

Sean Kelly, *Hunger: The Autobiography* (Peloton Publishing)

Paul Kimmage, *Rough Ride: Behind the Wheel with a Pro Cyclist* (Yellow Jersey)

Richard Moore, *Étape: The Untold Stories of the Tour de France's Defining Stages* (Harper Sport)

Richard Moore, *In Search of Robert Millar* (Harper Sport)

Richard Moore, *Slaying the Badger: LeMond, Hinault and the Greatest-Ever Tour de France* (Yellow Jersey)

Richard Nelsson (ed), *The Tour De France ... To the Bitter End* (Guardian Books)

Edward Pickering. 'Superbagnères', in Ellis Bacon & Lionel Birnie (eds), *The Cycling Anthology, Volume Five* (Yellow Jersey)

Edward Pickering, *The Yellow Jersey Club: Inside the Minds of the Tour de France Winners* (Bantam)

Eric Reed, Selling *The Yellow Jersey: The Tour De France in the Global Era* (University of Chicago Press)

Matt Rendell, *Kings of the Mountains: How Colombia's Cycling Heroes Changed their Nation's History* (Aurum)

Bjarne Riis, *Riis: Stages of Light and Dark* (Vision Sports Publishing)

Stephen Roche, *Born to Ride* (Yellow Jersey)

James Witts, *The Science of the Tour de France* (Bloomsbury)

Les Woodland (ed), *The Yellow Jersey Companion to the Tour de France* (Yellow Jersey)

Sean Yates, *It's All About The Bike: My Autobiography* (Corgi)

Also, back issues of *Cycling Weekly, Procycling, Rouleur, Cycle Sport* and *L'Equipe* were vital, as was the website tourfacts.dk, an invaluable repository of statistics otherwise lost to the passing of time.

ACKNOWLEDGEMENTS

I couldn't have told this amazing story, with all its fascinating strands and diversions, without the first-hand testimony of so many who were right there in the white heat of those astonishing three weeks. It was an absolute privilege to hear the tales and opinions of many legendary names from the pro cycling ranks in the late '80s – Alcalá, Delgado, Hampsten, Kelly, LeMond, Mottet, Riis, Roche, Sherwen, Yates and so many more. Thanks guys.

For arranging interviews or offering up phone numbers or just passing on general encouragement, gratitude goes to Mike Anderson, Rob Banino, Ian Cleverly, Daniel Gray, Andy McGrath, Mercedes Martinez, Barry Meehan, Christel Roche, Ian Rooke, Keith Sinclair and Graham Watson. For his cover-designing skills, a salute goes out to Joe Eden at Tidydesigns.

For their enthusiasm, knowledge, friendship and occasional translating skills, James Witts and Keith Warmington deserve their respective places right at the head of the peloton.

For igniting each other's passion for cycling as teenagers in the late '80s – when we'd shimmy up lampposts to watch the likes of Roche, Kelly, Elliott and McLoughlin fly past at seemingly impossible speeds – a shout-out to my old pals Steve Cooper and Martin Stanton.

Thanks to Mogwai whose score for the film *Zidane* proved a suitably epic, but not intrusive, soundtrack to long writing shifts. Similarly, on the home stretch, my own blast down the Champs-Élysées against the clock, British Sea Power's euphoric *Machineries of Joy* fired me towards the finish line.

A hearty tip of the hat goes to Pete Burns at Polaris for his editorial rigour, unflagging enthusiasm and flexible concept of deadlines. Also,

THREE WEEKS, EIGHT SECONDS

much gratitude to my steady, wise and graceful agent Kevin Pocklington, Guimard to my Fignon (maybe). Chapeau to you both.

But the biggest thanks go to Jane, Finn and Ned for their patience, tolerance and understanding. The man with his head in his laptop at the other end of the kitchen table loves you very much.